P9-DNI-956

A GIRL FROM TEXAS

THE LIFE, LOVES AND BATTLES OF
RUTH CONERLY
AMERICA'S EXTRAORDINARY ARTIST

S.E. WOLF, M.D.

Antigua Odisea Publishing

A GIRL FROM TEXAS
by S.E. Wolf, M.D.

All rights reserved. No part of this book including art, photographs and illustrations may be reproduced or transmitted in any form or by any means, electronic or mechanical, including photocopying, recording or by any information storage and retrieval system, without the written permission of the author, except for a brief text quotation in a review.

Copyright © 1999 Txu 919-564 by S. E. Wolf, M.D.
Published April, 2006
ISBN 0-9770225-3-6
Library of Congress Control Number: 2005931658

Q
Antigua Odisea Publishers
E-mail: antiguaodisea@msn.com

Printed and bound in the United States of America
by Publishers' Graphics, LLC, Carol Stream, IL

Disclaimer:

Every effort has been made to make this book accurate as to facts, persons, and dates, using an occasional pseudonym for discretion. But just as Ruth never made lengthy explanations of how each brush stroke was applied, this book is not a treatise full of notes and references, but rather a fast-moving drama of a multi-faceted life.

Words for Reflection

Bill Skuce in ARTalk for The Tico Times
May 17, 1996

Women have been missing from art history. Major survey history books minimize the contributions of women to Western Art. Does it not seem strange that in a book as widely used in art history courses as H. W. Janson's, women's black and white illustrations number 19, as opposed to 1,060 by men artists, and two of women's color plates, as opposed to 175 of men's?

Neglected indeed, by art historians (all of them male) are the many women artists who over the last five centuries have produced work in a remarkable range of styles, techniques and subject matter and figured prominently in history as painters, sculptors, Legion of Honor recipients and Ford foundation Fellows.

Since antiquity there have been women artists succeeding, supporting themselves – and often their families – with private clientele and large-scale private and public commissions. Many of these women received significant critical attention for their work.

Why is it then that we hear nothing of them? If they were once reputed, what has happened to their reputations?

ACKNOWLEDGMENTS

This book could never have been written without the cooperation of so many. Firstly, I am grateful to Dr. Ilse Leitinger, whose words: "She is alive! Give her her place in history!" set the wheels in motion and to Dorothy Black of the Daughters of the Republic of Texas; to Andrew Shapiro of Metro Creative Graphics for the wealth of Conerly Christmas art; to Holly Schmidt of Marshall Field's for the Conerly WW II art; Alamo Library Directors: Cathy Herpich and Elaine Davis, Rosie Asche, daughter of Austrian painter Franz Strahalm, Dorothy Ladore, for her memories of Ruth professionally, Jane Conerly, Christian and Zelda Smith, Barbara Howard, Martha Conerly, Kay Ford, Mary Lee, Reverend Bob Tucker, Layne and Helene Carver, Denny Graves and Pierce McGrath. Little short of miraculous was David Conerly's discovery of those two 75 year-old letters.

To all who helped in the research surrounding the death of Ruth's father with its historical and medical implications: Mary Yonker, Sheila Mitchell, Albert Williams, Desiree Lyon, Dr. Geoffrey Dean, Dr. Martin Warren, Dr. Kenneth Astrin, Dr. Karl Anderson, Dr. Alvaro Gallegos, Dr. Robert Palmer, Dr. Minor Vargas, Dr. Juan Jaramillo, Ruth Ellis Layton, Edward Merritt, Marcel Haulard, Mary Ellen Lamkin and Selma Reneger, my sincere gratitude.

From first outline to final publishing, I was fortunate to have the expertise of: William Iles, Dr. Lorraine Bloomquist, Christian and Zelda Smith, Col. Gary Bacon, Roberta Haynes, Dr. Kenneth Olson, Susan Liang, Gypsy Cole, Charles Swett, Liz Carpenter, Rosella Blinn and Mary Bachman. Special gratitude to Hilda Bigalow for permission to use her poem, *I Had a Father,* Bill Skuce for his moving words on women artists, to airline captain Joe Rose, Tilda Tilton in computer research and Thiemo Caliebre for his cover design and expertise in photography, computer and graphic arts.

To the many companies, museums, institutions and persons who contributed with permission to use reproductions of Conerly art, my most sincere gratitude. I regret being unable to contact persons and companies seemingly no longer in existence or use all the wonderful art offered.

CONTENTS

PREFACE

Leafing through the portfolios of illustrations, tattered newspapers and news articles on her mother's life and career, Sharon was overwhelmed with nostalgia and awe. Since childhood, she had heard people say that Ruth Conerly was a great artist. Admittedly few could portray people, action, war, high fashion, the spirit of Christmas the way Conerly did!

More than the art though, chronicling a half a century of American history, reporters were always trying to find out what lay *at the root* of Ruth's creative genius. Was it innate talent or the result of an orderly educative process? Or might there have been some *hidden* factor? And although Ruth could be honest to a gasp, she never mentioned the tragedy that wrecked poverty and ostracism of her early life, making her rise to the top echelons of commercial art so phenomenal.

A medical doctor in Costa Rica, Ruth's daughter lived submerged in the demands of a busy medical practice. To fit signs and symptoms into a pattern that might save a life or calm unfounded fears required time and dedication.

"But your mother is alive," writer and anthropologist Ilse Leitinger insisted. "She is a part of history. Give her the place she deserves!"

How? Even having the time, how could a doctor capture the spirit of an artist? How could *anyone* put all that fight and passion in any orderly narrative form! And tell *all* the truth?

Hardly could she imagine that a series of coincidences was about to lure her across continents and back into time for that life and art and a medical mystery going back to the long-denied legend of a prince and a Quaker girl!

Chapter I

Fateful Decision

Everyone is a prisoner in a sense. Locked in by walls and uncertainties, searching for wings. But can prison bars be purely imaginary?

Specifically, Preston wondered, looking about his dreary Texas cell, could pain, the most terrible imaginable, be "all in his head" as doctors were telling him? Hallucinations?

He didn't think so. But that September of 1920, Preston Conerly realized he had run out of options. Foolish to think his mother would accept his decision to end his life. Instead she had cried out in horror, offered her home and savings and when he refused – hadn't his illness already reduced his own family to poverty? – she called the doctor and sheriff who came with two constables, all determined to protect him from himself.

"We can't lose any more time. We must intern him at the asylum in Terrell now," the doctor insisted. And when no room was immediately available, the sheriff had a solution.

"We'll keep him in jail in the meantime! He'll be safe there."

Preston argued and when they tried to take him by force, he fought. But his mother's face, an image still vividly before him, was the stronger force. Alone now in a cell, he hoped God would forgive him and his family would understand, but all this pain and useless expense on doctors had to stop. In all his youthful dreams, determined to acquit himself well in life, never did he imagine it would all end like this.

Far worse though to be locked away in an asylum where no one believed he suffered real physical pain.

It was clear now that the famed doctor he had traveled so far to consult never believed a word he said and had even convinced other doctors that Preston was a hypochondriac. In answering his wife's letter, the doctor had even convinced her that he was a victim of some lunatic obsession.

To Preston's last telegram beseeching, *"Advise the human thing to do for least suffering. Bowels are burning up. Can I be operated on?"* the doctor's laconic reply, just received, removed any vestige of hope:

> *"We are quite in accord with your physicians and relatives that most of your complaints are imaginary and we do not believe we can be of any further benefit to you."*

While driving to his mother's home in Marshall, Texas, his eldest son Ed had replied in short taciturn phrases, finally shouting he was sick and tired of hearing about this imagined sickness and ordering him out of the car. Walking those last miles was an agony. Mouth dry, intestines twisting in waves of heat, he made the decision to end this nightmare. Only the method eluded him.

Now enclosed in a jail cell, there were few options, but he had always been a resourceful person.

Taking two letters from his pocket, he read the first, to his elder son Ed.

> *Dear Ed,*
> *I have about given up hope of recovering.*
> *My liver and stomach hurt all the time leaving me with a headache. I can't sleep and bring up pure gall, the coat of which sticks to my tongue. Calomel or any medicine does me no good. The Drs. say I am too weak for another operation and they do not seem to know my trouble...*
> *I have some requests to make.*
> *Do not gamble. Try and select Christian associates and attend Church. Assist your brother and sisters to be self-supporting. Take care of everything as well as you can and be head of the family. Stick to one another and be true to your mother.*
> *If the bank closes us out, you can take what is called bankruptcy by applying to Federal court and save something. It's up to you now to make a success of the business. You can do it. When you want business advice, ask the bank or your mother. Tell your mama I*

still have a bond and some war stamps in the bank and
to put them in her mama's chest. Destroy this letter.
Love from Dad

Preston wondered why he mentioned all those symptoms
Ed did not believe in, when the main thing was that he take
care of the business, the family and be considerate of his
mother. Wasn't that enough to put on the shoulders of a
sixteen-year-old boy?

The letter to his beloved Lizzie proved far more difficult to
write. Even now gazing at it, his heart ached.

Dear Sweetheart,
You can't help but be worried with all you have on
your poor little self. Forgive me. But I do not want to go
off and be shut up to suffer. Doctors seem to advise this
to keep the patient from being a nuisance. I do not want
to be a burden and I can't keep housed up this way.

My mind would not cause this pain, bringing up pure
yellow gall. Maybe after I'm gone they'll come up with
the cause, some fancy named sickness.

Have some understanding about the mortgage and
what we owe. If half were sold that would cover more
than the debt. If sued, take bankruptcy. For those that
owe us, don't sue anyone who wants to work in the
shop. Hon, get my war bond and those stamps out of
the bank and keep them in your mama's trunk.
Love from Dad.

P.S. In the kitchen is a bottle called Pijorea – good for
your gums. Destroy this letter.

After adding that last postscript he placed the letters on a
small table nearby. Then turning up the mattress of his cot,
he pried loose a piece of wire from the mesh. For a long time
he worked, filing the wire to razor sharpness, pausing only so
that the sound would not alert someone. Finally satisfied with
the results, he said a last prayer for his immortal soul and
plunged the wire deep into the side of his neck.

II

But Fighters They Were!

Alone in her room, Ruth yearned to see her daddy suddenly walk into the room. In all her twelve years she had never imagined such a thing. Watching him suffering with that illness no doctor could diagnose, and some considered a madness, had saddened her. But never did she imagine he would lose the battle. Not her daddy, so strong and brave and full of stories of ancient heroes and gallant knights.

Unable to understand how a person so essential in her life could be suddenly gone, Ruth could not help wishing it was some terrible mistake. And on hearing the door creak open and seeing her mother Lizzie come in, she dared to hope.

Elizabeth Davis Conerly, ever straight and erect, with the posture of someone who had just taken a deep breath or was tightly corseted, was not one to crumble under adversity. Even in her robe, her red hair plaited for bed, she had the commanding aura of a schoolteacher, which in effect she had once been. After searching Ruth's tear-drenched eyes for the absolute attention that was promptly forthcoming, she said, "Our situation is perilous."

Lizzie's ability to reduce things to fundamentals had always amazed Ruth. But as her mother synthesized her own situation – widowed, impoverished, with a bankrupt business and five children to feed – Ruth marveled at her composure.

"How did it happen, Mama?" Ruth questioned.

To this, her mother gave no explanation. Instead she summarized Ruth's situation. The college education planned for her was now out of the question and the prospect of a *good* marriage – meaning with a man of suitable means and family background – was no longer an option Ruth could count on.

A pretty face attracts many beaus but a wealthy father attracts a husband.

While their immediate priority was to eat and keep the family together, exerting every effort to hold on to the business, Ruth must decide how to support herself.

"*You must be supporting yourself by age fourteen,*" Lizzie specified.

Ruth's mouth and throat went suddenly dry. For a young girl brought up in moderate affluence, the situation was as fairy-tale bizarre as Hansel and Gretel sent into the forest with breadcrumbs or Cinderella reduced to rags and cleaning chimneys.

**Ruth Conerly
Age 12
Clarksville, Texas
1920**

But Ruth harbored no doubt it was for real. And never in her life would she forget it. Hardly less intimidating was the time and the place.

To the casual eye, Clarksville, Texas in 1920 was like any small Texas town with its courthouse and statue of a Confederate soldier in the Town Square. But Clarksville, nestled in the Red River Valley, had an aristocracy engendered in the early frontier days long before places like Houston or Dallas ever existed. Located fifteen miles south of the Red River, it was a first landing step for settlers coming into Texas in the early 1830s and by 1850 could boast of the only courthouse in two hundred miles with lawyers, merchants, doctors and stores.

The Civil War brought humiliating defeat, quartered soldiers, plundering taxes and a seething hatred for Northerners and their greedy emissaries and carpetbaggers. Not until 1900 and the rush to plant long-staple cotton was Clarksville to experience a new prosperity: twenty-five millionaires in a population of 4500, families that traveled abroad, shopped in New York and sent their sons and daughters to the finest schools in the East.

Poor was bad, but poor in Clarksville in 1920 was an absolute catastrophe!

Right now Ruth was not sure she even liked Clarksville. Born in Marshall, Texas on October 27, 1908, she considered Marshall far friendlier and more beautiful, in spite of their cutting down all those trees to plant long-staple cotton. When the cutting and planting spread northward to the sandy loam of Clarksville, Ruth's father had decided to open a business there.

"Support myself by age fourteen?" Ruth questioned in a daze. "Doing what, Mama?"

"People generally do well working at what they enjoy," was the only enlightenment Lizzie offered.

Alone again, Ruth felt like a rag doll drained of its sawdust. What did she enjoy doing? Her mother had meant *work*, of course. Not reading, drawing or modeling figures in clay. Immediately the image of a doctor who cured people, like her mother's father, Dr. John Jones Davis III, came to mind. If he were alive he would have cured her daddy. Then realizing that doctoring meant college – no longer possible – she discarded the idea. Next she conjured up the image of a graceful dancer, like in the new movie shows; but this too was quickly put aside. Impossible with her foot. Infantile paralysis (polio), the doctor had called it. Barely three when it happened, she could remember very little really, except what her father said, how the doctor had told them she could not possibly live.

"But your mama was determined not to lose her little chick," he added with that smile of pride he always reserved for Lizzie. "And remembering how you loved color, how as a baby you'd coo and laugh, playing for hours with the strips of bright colored fabric she hung across your crib, your mama hurried down to the dry goods store. There she chose the brightest many-colored fabric, rushed home and started sewing you a little robe. Your mama was certain that if you would just open your eyes for a second and see that robe, you'd reach out for it. And, she was right. You *did* open your eyes and reach out for that robe... and life."

Fresh tears welled in her eyes. What wonderful stories her daddy could tell! Then forcing her attention back to the crucial matter at hand, she wondered, what *did* she enjoy doing and could presumably do best?

She could at least walk now, and even dance. She loved to dance. The limp was not too noticeable. It bothered her that one leg was thinner than the other, one foot more deeply arched. At times it could be brought sharply to her attention, like the time she was running a race at school and winning, until a voice from a cheering playmate came through loudly, "Come on, Crip! That a-way, Crip!"

At least by now she had learned not to brood over what could not be changed, or go around slugging people for mentioning it.

Staring into the darkening corners of her room, she recalled a past scene wherein someone was holding her and scolding, "If you don't hush and stop crying, this Indian is going to take you away!" The woman holding her was pointing to a sculptured figure of an Indian, and Ruth recalled becoming instantly quiet. Not out of fear, however, as was surely intended, but in awe of its beauty, wanting to touch and examine it.

Anyone so fascinated by a work of art could not be happy eking out some miserable living, peering hungrily into windows where people feasted and danced. It had nothing to do with Clarksville, where success was measured in dollars and cents, but rather responded to something innately personal, tied up with all those stories of ancestral glory, defeats and comeuppances, and how Great-grandmother Sarah and Grandmother Rebecca had danced beneath glistening chandeliers. And her daddy's great, great, great grandfather had been a king... according to family tradition.

Obviously, she'd have to chose her work well and work hard at it. And if it meant a struggle, even a fight, by golly, a fight there'd be! She could hardly sell out all those ancestors in the family relay race, bad foot or not.

The nitty-gritty of exactly what she would do, what she *could* do, faded momentarily as Ruth's imagination was stirred by images of the struggle itself.

From the far reaches of time past, an arsenal of family stories and homespun lore came surging forth – heroes, warriors and illustrious forebears beyond most children's fantasies marched grimly forward. Suddenly she was amid maps, planning the strategy of the battle to come. Beneath cannon and rockets' red-glare, a regiment of men fell into place, stern faced, swords drawn, alert to her command. On one flank came the Calhouns, Scots and fighters; on the other, Irishman Cullen Conerly, who fought in the American Revolution; and Dr. Samuel Stephens, Irish surgeon, who served under Napoleon. Unfurling their Civil War banners came grandfathers Davis and Conerly who fought for the Confederate States of America.

Well, admittedly not all fought on the winning side. But fighters they were, by golly!

BUT FIGHTERS THEY WERE!

Dr. John Jones Davis III
1838-1885

Buxton Ryves Conerly
1847-1913

III

A Tangled Legacy

In 1920, storytelling was a sacred tradition and children listened raptly at the knee of a parent or grandparent, begging them to repeat favorite tales. Family stories, passed down for generations, were considered an integral part of a child's identity and pride. Thus it was with Ruth – so much that little can be understood about her without a glimpse at this tangled legacy of family lore.

For general order, Ruth divided her stories into her mama's side and her daddy's side. The first, coming mainly from her mother Lizzie and her grandmother Rebecca, went back to 1746 when Catherine Calhoun was *not* carried off by the Indians but died fighting, defending her farm and four children from the Cherokees. By 1811, the time when Great grandmother Sarah Calhoun was born, life had become more gracious with less fear of arrows and tomahawks.

Sarah grew up on the Calhoun plantation near Abbyville, South Carolina in a home adjacent to that of her cousin, John Caldwell Calhoun.

Senator, Secretary of State, Secretary of War and twice Vice President of the United States, under John Quincy Adams and Andrew Jackson, John C's debates with Daniel Webster in the Senate defending the agricultural South from the powerful industrial North won him the title of "Champion of the South and States' Rights."

Among the many stories Great grandmother Sarah passed on was how in 1826, when she was fifteen, John C. and his wife Floride brought her the latest fashion from Washington – a bustle. On seeing the strange contraption of entwined wire – designed to increase the size of a lady's derrière – Sarah's maid Dinah thought it a rat trap, causing John C. to give a tongue-in-cheek speech defining its *proper* use.

When Sarah married Colonel William Sims of Carrolton, Georgia, whose saddle and bridle factory later supplied the Confederate cavalry, carriages came from miles around. A festive occasion at the Calhoun plantation was not to be missed. Sarah's daughter, Rebecca, would later describe the balls and cotillions at Abbyville and how as a child she would look down between the banister rails to where skirts floated and happy voices exclaimed. Like other belles of the period, Rebecca painted, except that her paintings were placed in fine frames in front rooms.

Rebecca was in the gardens of the Calhoun plantation, painting when Dr. John Jones Davis III rode there from Georgia to propose. A graduate of the University of Atlanta with a Doctorate in Medicine and Doctorate of Divinity, Dr. Davis was a cousin of Jefferson Davis, their newly elected President of the Confederate States. Not long after their wedding the Civil War broke out. Dr. Davis immediately enlisted as a private.

"Dr. Davis wanted to fight for the South," Grandmother Rebecca explained, "but he was soon requisitioned to serve as assistant surgeon to staff officers of General Robert E. Lee."

At the knee of Grandmother Rebecca, Ruth learned how Dr. Davis – for that was how Rebecca always referred to her husband – labored long hours to save shattered limbs instead of hastily amputating.

"One evening though, while attending the wounded on the battlefield," Rebecca said, "Dr. Davis found my own beloved brother Louis. Dear Louis knew he was dying and that Atlanta was lost and our sister Mary was there alone. Louis told Dr. Davis how terrified Mary had been by the sound of the cannon and guns closing in and how he had promised to go back for her. Kneeling there, Dr. Davis forgot his own danger and was captured by Yankee soldiers. Imprisoned in the worst of conditions, he surely would have died, *were it not for the fact that he was a Mason.*"

This secret order, Rebecca explained, promoted brotherly love and assistance among its members, eclipsing all North-South politics and loyalties. With that explanation, Rebecca would tell how two Northern Masons disguised as Ladies of Charity had gone into the prison, *and three Ladies came out!*

The story of Dr. Davis's escape from a Northern prison always made Ruth clap her hands and beg Rebecca to tell how Dr. Davis made his way back to his regiment. Especially, she loved the part about how the men, on seeing him coming in, shouted out along the lines, "Davis is back! Davis is back!"

But then Rebecca's expression would grow somber as she told how at the end of the war Georgia was a land laid waste by Sherman's march across the South. Those soldiers that returned found little more than charred remains and a chimney where their home had once stood. Everywhere there were occupational forces and carpetbaggers bent on stealing the land of widows and orphans. After the war, Dr. Davis traveled the Palmetto Trail as a Methodist minister with the North Georgia Conference. But on receiving a letter from a school-friend who had gone to Texas, he loaded family and possessions in wagons and aboard his phaeton leading the caravan, set out for Texas.

Born in Texas, Ruth's mother Lizzie could clearly remember how her father, Dr. Davis, would walk down the church aisle, remove his black cape with a flourish and as a hush fell over his parish, take a sip of water.

Dr. Davis built a fine home, a pharmacy, and a dry goods store in Atlanta, Texas. He was proud when a man rode there from Georgia, saying he had come all the way to shake the hand of the man who had saved his arm during the Civil War, when another doctor was about to cut it off. But one day in 1885, Dr. Davis went out to hunt. He laid his shotgun against a fence post and was climbing through when the gun fell and went off. Lizzie would never forget hearing that deadly shot.

According to custom, Rebecca's son inherited all, taking good care of the family, but when he too died, his widow remarried and moved to Europe, leaving Rebecca, Lizzie and her sisters destitute. A resourceful person, Lizzie promptly got a job teaching. She was home for the summer when a young man drove his carriage to Atlanta, Texas to investigate a rumor.

Preston Conerly had heard that a remarkable beauty lived there. And on seeing Lizzie in her high-necked blouse and tiny waist, her flaming red curls piled high, Preston knew the rumor was true. Here was the proud look idealized by artist Charles Gibson of the well-bred American girl that men only hoped to find in flesh and blood.

"And I fell in love! As sudden and fulminating as a thunderbolt!" Preston declared.

How Ruth loved her daddy's stories! The only problem was the stories from her father's side were complicated.

Romantic, but complicated...

**Elizabeth Davis
1878-1975**

**Thomas Preston Conerly
1878-1920**

In fact, had her great uncle Luke Ward Conerly – lawyer, historian and writer – not recorded it all in his book, "Source Records of Pike County, Mississippi 1789-1910," Ruth doubted she would have gotten it all straight.

Uncle Luke's book told all about the families of Pike County, Mississippi from the first settlers in rustic homes, evolving into graceful plantations lining the Bogue Chitto River, places whose names twisted around the tongue like soft cane molasses: the Tangipahoa, the Topisaw, Silver Creek, Magees Creek and the Bahala. Uncle Luke described how young men with red-topped boots and girls with coquettish smiles danced the fandango figures: "Virginia reels," "Heel and toe," "Fisher's hornpipe" and "Pigeon wing." How fiddles, banjos and guitars were joined by pianos, violins and flutes, and how in 1860, the fife, the drum and quills sounded as young men under the Confederate flag and Quitman's Guard banner marched off to the Civil War.

And few came back.

In his book, Uncle Luke traced the Conerly family back to 1751 when John Connerly (then spelled with a double "n") obtained a land grant in North Carolina from King George II. John's son, Cullen Conerly, served with the North Carolina Militia in the American Revolution fighting King George III, had ten children with wife Leticia "Telishe" Ward. In 1822, Cullin's son, Owen Conerly, Sr. migrated to Mississippi where his son, Owen Conerly Jr., married Ann Louise Stephens, great-granddaughter of King George III.

That Owen Conerly Jr. would marry the great granddaughter of the king his grandfather had fought against puzzled Ruth. But the Conerlys always seemed just as proud of King George as Cullen Conerly who had fought against him.

On page 53, Luke Ward Conerly described their descent from King George III:

On the 27th of May, 1759 George, while Prince of Wales, married a Quaker girl, Hannah Lightfoot. They had a son Buxton Lawn, who married Mary Dawson...

According to the story, Buxton Lawn had come to New York in the early 1800s, followed by wife Mary, but somehow they missed each other and Buxton returned to England while

Mary and her three daughters – Mary, Eliza and Ann – made their way to New Orleans where son Robert had prospered forming the Southern Bank. Daughter Eliza married William B. Ligon, whose schooners plied the waters from New Orleans to Covington, Pensacola and Texas, later helping with the Texas revolution. And Buxton's daughter Ann, from whom Ruth descended, married Dr. Samuel James Stephens.

Luke Ward described his grandfather Dr. Stephens as "a native of Ireland, an eminent physician and surgeon, attaché of the staff of Napoleon Bonaparte, who came to Louisiana after the fall of his illustrious chief."

And again, the Conerlys seemed every bit as proud of Dr. Stephens, who had fought with Napoleon against the British, as British King George III, making Ruth conclude that in love and war peculiar things happened. More significant for Ruth, Ann Lawn and Dr. Stephens produced Ann Louise Stephens, mother of Luke Ward and Ruth's grandfather Buxton.

In his book, Uncle Luke described his mother Ann Louise as "well educated, a woman of fine mental qualities, a great reader, historian and conversationalist who read and spoke French and English fluently. A prolific writer, she contributed to various newspapers."

When her sons Luke and Buxton went off to the Civil War, Ann Louise sent supplies to the Confederate army, smuggled cotton to foreign markets and wrote articles on behalf of the Confederate cause for English and French newspapers. So effective, in fact, was her writing that agents were sent to incite the slaves to rise up and kill her.

But instead, the slaves sent warning to Luke and Buxton who got leave, came home, killed the agents, then returned to their lines.

Complicated as it all was, Ruth now had her father's descent pretty well sorted out. In short, George, while Prince of Wales, married Hannah Lightfoot. Their son Buxton Lawn married Mary Dawson and their daughter Ann Lawn married Dr. Stephens and their daughter Ann Louise Stephens married Owen Conerly Jr. whose son, Grandfather Buxton Conerly, married Grandmother Myra Jane Collins, who told Ruth, "none of that twaddle is going to put any food on your table!"

And if Ruth was still impressed with this rather awesome ancestry, she soon learned that no one in Texas knew anything about George III. Or cared. Once her schoolteacher said King George III was that crazy old tyrant who ruled England when America won its independence. After that, Ruth stopped mentioning the matter. Far more deserving of admiration in Texas, she found, was that her grandpa Buxton Conerly had fought in the Battle of Fort Gregg, the last battle of the Civil War. His account of that battle was an oft-quoted classic reprinted in magazines and books on Civil War history. This was real prestige!

GENEALOGY OF RUTH CONERLY

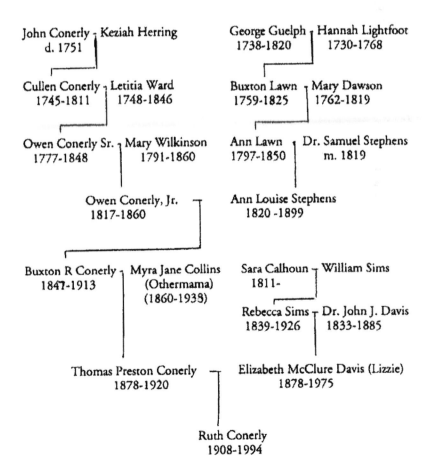

John Conerly ⌐ Keziah Herring
d. 1751

Cullen Conerly ⌐ Letitia Ward
1745-1811 | 1748-1846

Owen Conerly Sr. ⌐ Mary Wilkinson
1777-1848 | 1791-1860

Owen Conerly, Jr.
1817-1860

Buxton R Conerly ⌐ Myra Jane Collins
1847-1913 | (Othermama)
(1860-1938)

Thomas Preston Conerly ⌐ Elizabeth McClure Davis (Lizzie)
1878-1920 | 1878-1975

George Guelph ⌐ Hannah Lightfoot
1738-1820 | 1730-1768

Buxton Lawn ⌐ Mary Dawson
1759-1825 | 1762-1819

Ann Lawn ⌐ Dr. Samuel Stephens
1797-1850 | m. 1819

Ann Louise Stephens
1820-1899

Sara Calhoun ⌐ William Sims
1811-

Rebecca Sims ⌐ Dr. John J. Davis
1839-1926 | 1833-1885

Ruth Conerly
1908-1994

By now Ruth could even tell the story of the Battle of Fort Gregg with a creditable amount of military strategy and gory detail, leaving out her grandmother's inevitable ad lib, "Your grandpa Buck probably hid behind a tree!"

Grandmother Myra Jane, alias Mrs. Buxton Conerly, alias "Othermama," (never grandmother!) had a deft touch for sticking a hatpin in any high-sounding flatulence. "Wish in one hand and poop in the other and you'll see which gets full first." Othermama's sidelong comments, like her stories, could be gasp-provoking, never to be repeated, of course, under the threat of death.

A beauty in her younger years, still buxomly attractive, Othermama lived in Marshall, Texas in a stately white-columned home facing the post office.

Mrs. Buxton Conerly, nee Myra Jane Collins
"Othermama"
(1860-1939)

She was only fifteen when her father insisted she marry the twenty-eight-year-old Buxton Conerly.

"An old man twice my age!" she denounced indignantly and then told Ruth how she spent her wedding night under the bed while Buxton pleaded, "Now Myra Jane, what will people think your sleeping under the bed like that?"

And Othermama's reply from under the bed was irrefutable: "How is anyone going to know, lest you tell them as much!"

"But you finally did come out from under the bed, didn't you, Othermama?" Ruth once questioned.

"Yes, I finally came out," Othermama admitted.

"And you did learn to love Grandpa Buxton just a little bit, didn't you?" Because it always seemed so sad that Grandpa Buck, such a fine hero in the Civil War who had killed so many Yankees, could be hog-tied by a slip of a girl.

"Oh, I suppose so. A woman can't live with a man all those years and not learn to care for him a mite."

"And you never fell in love with anyone else? Really madly in love?" Ruth once asked. Because it seemed sad that someone as beautiful as Othermama could live without romance. And to Ruth's astonishment, Othermama told her of a secret love, swearing her to silence "Cross your heart and hope to die!"

It was an Othermama story Ruth would vividly recall in a moment of her life.

Ruth was barely five when her Grandpa Buxton died "from that fool smoking of his," Othermama elucidated. Finding herself in economic straits, Othermama had converted her home into a boarding house where people of means and celebrities such as the legendary actor Douglas Fairbanks found comfortable lodging. One summer, while on his customary tour of theatre performances, Fairbanks showed up with a different wife, not nearly so charming, which piqued Othermama. But such personages lent luster to her position in the community, a matter of great importance.

Never, of course, did anything take precedence over her son, her beloved Pressie. Compared to him, all splendor paled. Othermama loved pointing out that both her children, Preston and Mabel, had inherited her blue eyes. And all her grandchildren too – "except Ruth with those brown eyes, red hair and freckles like her mother Lizzie."

Othermama could never understand how her Pressie married Lizzie. "I swear I'll never forget the day Pressie drove up in his carriage with Lizzie with all those freckles and that red hair!" It was also beyond Othermama's comprehension how Lizzie could have all those children, one after another that way! "Poor Pressie barely shakes out his pants and hangs them on the bedpost and Lizzie's pregnant again," she would declare. First came David Edward (Ed) in 1903, followed by beautiful, blue-eyed Christine. In 1908, Ruth was born, followed by Preston Jr. (Mutt), a pair close in age and loyalty. A fifth child, baptized Myra Jane after Othermama in hopes of appeasing her wrath, only succeeded in making Othermama certain that Lizzie's red hair and freckles were at the root of such an indecent fertility. Along with all those Lydia Pinkham pills.

But if Othermama considered her beloved Pressie beyond any wrongdoing, Ruth was in total agreement, idolizing her father above all things. Even now in her present root, hog or die calamitous predicament, she could not believe he would have left her alone intentionally. In every situation he had always been there with a funny story, ready to listen and advise her on what course to take.

And suddenly the thought came. What if tucked away in her memories of him lay a clue as to what she should do? Grasping tenaciously onto this idea like a piece of sturdy flotsam adrift in a stormy ocean, she let her thoughts drift back, seeking her father's presence.

Preston Conerly
Age 42

IV

A Father Who Read To Her

Ruth could almost see him now, a dynamic man with kindly blue eyes, always ready to tell some wondrous tale of ancient heroes or modern inventors. This new twentieth century, he claimed, was proving a veritable renaissance of science and art. Who could tell what unimaginable things were yet to come!

For Preston, a book with fine paintings and illustrations was as important as food on the table. Once while reading to Ruth, Preston was amazed when his three-year-old daughter whispered several lines before he had read them. Exploring this phenomenon, he discovered she could not actually read but was reciting verbatim lines previously read to her – a feat he considered far more remarkable, suggestive of an extraordinary *visual* memory. Even so, he enjoyed bragging to friends that his three-year-old daughter could read and was not above accepting a "sporting wager" on it. Then feigning to choose a book at random, he would place it before the obliging Ruth who would happily perform.

Lizzie considered this dishonest, hardly exemplary for a child. But Preston laughed good-naturedly, much the same as he did whenever Lizzie complained that he was spending too much on useless "bric-a-brac." He understood Lizzie's frugality, how her mother was left homeless. But how could Lizzie not love things like that Oriental rug he had just bought, or the piano for Christine? How Ruth wept in frustration when Christine forbade her to touch it and knocked her off the stool on finding her there.

Ruth could not remember exactly when she started her drawing, but one day, satisfied with the results, she showed it to her father.

"My goodness," he exclaimed. "I believe I detect artistic talent here!"

From then on, finding enough paper for her sketches became a thing of constant concern for Ruth, and the delivery boy from Allen's Butcher Shop soon learned that the Conerly order must be dispatched in extra sheets of butcher paper for the little red-headed girl waiting.

Obtaining clay for modeling her figures was a simpler matter. Clay was abundant in East Texas. Othermama said Ruth must have inherited her talent for modeling from her grandpa Buxton, who liked to sculpt figures in limestone. "And I swear Buck could make a figure look every bit like the person he intended!"

One day, observing Ruth's interest in the paintings of Treasure Island, Preston said that just as there were great writers like Robert Louis Stevenson, there were artists like N.C. Wyeth who stirred people's imagination with their paintings, making them want to buy books. And Ruth wondered if she might be able to do such wondrous paintings of adventures and battles.

On hearing someone remark that her father had fought in the Spanish-American War, Ruth could not imagine him ever killing anyone. She would soon learn otherwise though, that her daddy was indeed capable of killing, when his family was in danger. The events of that night were still vividly engraved on her mind years later when she wrote:

"We were living at Kingsville, Texas where Daddy was an auditor on the Texas and Pacific Railroad. I was about seven and had been playing with a little friend, the banker's son, all afternoon. That evening his father called Mother to see if I could go to the movies with them, but Mother said no. There'd been a lot of trouble along the border lately and she'd rather I came on home.

That night as my friend and his father were coming out of the theater a group of Pancho Villa's bandits rode into town and shot the father. As they kept on shooting, Daddy organized the men in an outside ring of houses with some of the women loading their guns. The other women and we children were put in a house in the center. People said Daddy was a crack shot and kept the bandits from breaking through. A few days later, Colonel Pershing came down with the army and we were sent to Houston.

In Houston my father got the idea of opening a business in Clarksville, Texas. I remember his talking to Mother about a plan he had. 'Cars are the coming vehicle,' he said. 'The days of the horse and buggy are over!'

Clarksville, he said, had twenty-five millionaires and was a crossroad, famous for its long-staple cotton then selling at terrific prices. The only place growing that quality of cotton was Egypt, and Germany was sinking ships. He was sure that people would soon be buying cars and trucks. Mother was afraid for him to use our savings in the venture, but Daddy went to Akron, Ohio, learned tube and tire vulcanizing and how to manage a garage."

Preston Conerly had barely established The Conerly Vulcanizing Company and The Conerly Garage in Clarksville in 1916, when President Wilson declared war on Germany. And long-staple cotton, urgently needed for uniforms and bandages, began selling at ever-higher prices. As vehicles went into mass production, Preston's vulcanizing business in the heart of cotton country became a highly profitable enterprise. Even eight-year-old Ruth made her first money in sculpture and contributed to the war effort. She modeled a clay bust of the Kaiser, charging a penny a potshot at the county fair.

By the end of the war, The Conerly Garage was a thriving enterprise. Preston had every reason to be proud of his foresight and confident of the future. But one evening, he became violently ill with such pain in his abdomen that Lizzie called the doctor. Seeing Preston writhing in pain, the doctor decided to operate. But the surgery revealed nothing – no appendicitis, no gall stones, no hernia or cancer. And after a harrowing convalescence, new symptoms appeared: headache, pains in the legs and chest, insomnia, difficulty in swallowing. Totally puzzled, the doctor called in a colleague. But he too shook his head, equally perplexed.

Desperate, Preston traveled north to the most prestigious hospital of the time. There a renowned physician examined him and suggested that Preston might be "overly nervous." But told him to report any further development.

Over the next six months, Preston sent dozens of letters all the while consulting an ever-expanding circle of doctors. With expenses spiraling, Preston began to think he might have some unknown illness and feared for his family should he die. Just when things seemingly could get no worse, the doctor made a frightful diagnosis.

Lizzie had a tumor.

Several months earlier, on failing to get her period, Lizzie consulted the doctor who diagnosed *early menopause*, most likely brought on by so much stress with Preston's illness, caring for four children and trying to keep a business running. But when Lizzie's abdomen began to swell, the doctor changed his mind. It could only be a tumor. They must operate immediately.

On opening Lizzie up, the doctor quickly sutured her closed. Two days later the *tumor* was born. Weighing only two and a half pounds, so tiny an infant could not possibly survive, the doctor said, but Grandmother Rebecca felt there might be a chance. Recalling Dr. Davis's advice with early babies, she said the secret lay in keeping the baby *warm*. So at night when all were exhausted, tiny Janey was tucked in a shoebox and put behind the iron stove, where embers were still warm.

With Lizzie languishing pale and weak and bills piling higher, Preston's unconditional love outweighed all practical concerns. He bought Lizzie a gold thimble edged in tiny diamonds, which Lizzie in tears flung against the wall. It was the only time Ruth could remember seeing her mother lose her composure. Soon after, Ruth and her brother Preston Jr. (Mutt) were sent to visit their Aunt Mattie. With him Mutt took his new air rifle, a gift from his father. In Texas, where a boy's development was marked more by his rifle gauge than actual years, this first step of manhood represented a serious father-son bonding with lessons in its care and dangers.

Arriving at Aunt Mattie's home, Mutt felt uncomfortable when Mattie's son, Reese, considerably larger, eyed his air rifle with covetous eyes. As Reese looked down on Mutt's scrawny frame with a smile of exaggerated evil, Mutt clutched his gun closer.

Ruth had no immediate misgivings until her teacher came to call on Aunt Mattie. The teacher said Ruth's arrival at school made it impossible to keep order. Ruth's red curls perturbed the boys.

At that point Aunt Mattie's daughter Anna, always first to raise her hand in class, confirmed the accusation: "Ruth tosses her head on purpose that way whenever there's any boys around, just to attract their attention!"

Aunt Mattie looked over her spectacles at Ruth, shook her head and *tsked*. The next morning she braided Ruth's hair tightly to the point of scalping while Ruth yelped and protested that braids made her look ugly, not understanding the point at all.

The next day, Reese pleaded sick with a face of such affliction that Aunt Mattie insisted he stay home from school. Mutt knew he was faking it and feared for his air rifle. The school bell had barely rung that afternoon when Mutt was out the door, racing home. Finding his air rifle full of smut and lacking ammunition, Mutt harbored no doubt who the culprit was. Seething with rage, he confronted Reese, warning that if Reese ever so much as touched his gun again, he was "gunna beat the living tar out of him."

Reese laughed derisively at such bold posturing and the very next day the gun suffered a worse defilement. Forgetting the difference in size, Mutt did the promised thing. He beat the living tar out of Reese, who ran crying to his mother. Seeing her son's blackened eye, Aunt Mattie chased Mutt with a switch and Ruth too when she tried to break the switch. The atmosphere was still tense the next day as Aunt Mattie prepared dainty pastries for a group of ladies due for afternoon tea.

"Mind you," she warned shaking a finger, "I want no problem from anyone. You children hear me?"

That afternoon, Ruth smiled as she extended a tray with the sugar bowl to one of Mattie's friends and the lady turned to Mattie inquiring, "And these children, Mattie? What are they doing here?"

"Aww, their Ma had another baby, their Dad's lost his mind, and they have to stay with us!" Reese clarified contemptuously.

Ruth's smile withered. Her cheeks burned. In spite of every effort to abide by the rule – c*hildren should be seen and not heard* – the words could not be contained.

"Well, it's a far sight better to have a mind to lose, than be like Reese, who never had a brain in his head to begin with!"

You could have cut the silence with a knife. One guest studied the ceiling while another became concerned with a fold in her skirt. A third sputtered her sip of tea. Aunt Mattie's guests had barely left when she bellowed, "Where's that Ruth!" and went after a switch. When Ruth outran her and Mutt broke the switch, Mattie called their father.

"Preston," she snapped. "You come after these children right now. I can't do a thing with them. And that Ruth..." she gasped, incapable of finding words for anything so felonious, finally proclaiming her greatest maxim of condemnations – "That girl will come to no good end, you just mark my word!"

On picking them up, Preston agreed with Mattie.

"Absolutely, absolutely!" he said shaking his head as though incapable of imagining such improper conduct. But once in the car his stern façade disappeared and he broke into laughter. He complimented Mutt for the shiner he had put on Reese and praised Ruth for defending her brother. Then recalling some youthful misadventure, he held their rapt attention on the drive home.

But late that night, the pain came back and Ruth could hear him drilling Lizzie on things she must remember to carry on the business. Incapable of sleeping, he walked the floor insisting that he was doing them no good this way.

The next day, Lizzie hid his gun and told Ruth to watch him carefully.

"Seeing you draw or work with clay always seems to calm him," Lizzie remarked.

That afternoon, while modeling a figure, Ruth was relieved her father seemed content and pleased. When the statue was almost finished, he observed it critically and nodded approval.

"My little girl is going to be a great artist one day," he said.

But the next day, he suffered another attack and her brother Ed drove him to Othermama's home in Marshall...

At that point, Ruth felt a sharp jolt. That was it! "My little girl's going to be a great artist some day" were his last words to her! Her father had answered her question.

"Thank you, Daddy," she whispered softly.

V

Starting Point

As creditors carried off their finest furniture, including the Oriental rug her father had given Lizzie, Ruth felt a pang of pity for Christine seeing her piano carried out. A few friends made perfunctory visits but quickly distanced themselves, no longer calling or dropping by. Through it all, Lizzie maintained remarkable composure and dignity.

But when Ruth's closest friend never came by, Ruth went to her home, standing determinedly on her front doorstep until the girl opened the door.

But instead of the usual welcome, the girl's expression was cold.

"I can't play with you," she said curtly.

"Why?"

"Because your father killed himself and he and all his family are going to hell for that."

It came like a slap across the face, and Ruth slapped her back. Minutes later, the girl's mother was at their door demanding that Lizzie tell her children that their father committed suicide and what her daughter, Fannie Beth, had told Ruth was the gospel truth:

"The sins of the parents are visited on the children and Ruth can't go around slapping people for telling her the gospel truth!"

When the woman left, Mutt put his hand on Ruth's shoulder and whispered, "Ruth, don't feel bad about what Fannie Beth said. She goes out behind the barn with the boys." Ruth was not sure what this meant, but it had a consoling ring.

"In bad times you *sho-nuf* learn who your real friends are!" Mary, their cook, declared. "And certainly Mary stood by, taking care of baby Janey shopping in shantytown where food and vittles were cheaper. When Lizzie showed concern about Mary's taking Janey with her into shantytown, Mary replied, "Mizz Liz, no one's going to touch my little Punch. They all knows I carry a *raahzor* in my stocking."

On coming home from school, Ruth and Mutt could always count on Mary's leaving them a biscuit and molasses in the cupboard; and on going out to hunt, they found necessity quickly sharpened their skill. Soon they were bringing in enough game – feathered or furry – for their own and Mary's family too, ever mindful of Mary's warning words not to go near places like Cuthand Bottoms..."where strong men are known to go in those muck swamps but not always come out."

Sweet Grandmother Rebecca, always caring, opened her cedar chest and gave Ruth her paints, brushes and palette, showing her how to arrange colors and mix them from the edges.

Try as she might though, Ruth could never learn anything about her father's death. Lizzie simply would not talk about it. It puzzled Ruth that no one showed any curiosity about his illness, accepting his suicide as proof of madness. Ruth did not believe this. The bravest of men, the most loving of fathers would never kill himself unless he had suffered *real* pain. She had seen it in his eyes and knew it to be so.

As the chill of winter deepened and storekeepers began filling their windows with Christmas displays, Lizzie explained they could not expect any fine gifts under the tree that year. So that Christmas morning, seeing there *were* gifts for everyone – a shiny red wagon for Mutt and a doll for Ruth – all were surprised. Only Ed, smiling the broadest, had no fine gift.

It did not take Lizzie long to solve the mystery. Ed had bought the gifts with money earned from extra jobs, ignoring that his coat was worn thin and no longer fit.

"With winter coming on," Lizzie explained, "Ed could get pneumonia and die." He was their only breadwinner. They could play with the toys, taking care not to damage them, but everything must be returned the next day.

On Christmas day, Ruth and Mutt looked out to where children were playing, and speculated on their plight.

"If we go out they'll ask to see our gifts," Mutt commented.

"Someone might scratch your red wagon, maybe even wreck it."

"Or break your doll."

"If we go out empty-handed, Fannie Beth will say we didn't get gifts cause only *good* children get gifts on Christmas," Ruth remarked miserably."

"*Who said there wasn't any Santa Claus?* Ruth scribbled on this first Christmas illustration, never imagining her Christmas art would one day circle the globe.

For months, they had heard nothing from Othermama. Recalling how her eyes would light up on seeing Preston, Ruth tried not to think of it. But in April, Othermama called and asked to speak to Ruth.

"I'm going to San Antonio, to the Alamo," she said. "And I want you to go with me."

They went in Othermama's automobile chauffeured by Old Tye, timing their mealtime stops at relatives or friends as Othermama was prone to do. Old Tye was a special person in the Conerly family. As a boy, he had carried the warning to her grandpa Buxton that Yankee carpetbaggers were planning to kill his mother and take over the farm. After the Civil War, Tye came to Texas with Buxton, staying on with Othermama after Buxton's death.

On the drive to San Antonio, Othermama told Ruth about the Battle of the Alamo and how her father, John Collins, had actually known Colonel Travis, commander of the Alamo.

"Pa was about sixteen then and Mr. Travis was in his twenties," she explained. "Pa always called him Mr. Travis."

Entering the Alamo, Othermama looked all about with awe akin to reverence.

"Pa often talked about this," she whispered, "about what a fine man Mr. Travis was and what a terrible thing his dying that way and all those fine men with him." There were tears in her eyes and for a moment Ruth felt she could almost see the battle raging about her, ghostlike forms locked in mortal combat. It was an eerie sensation and quickly gone. But that evening on mentioning it to Othermama, Ruth was surprised by her reply.

"People used to say that for years after the battle, folks were afraid to come here. Legend has it that on a quiet night, the sounds of bugles and shouts and the cries of the dying could still be heard. Somehow I felt this would impress you. I always thought you had a special sensitivity and that it was important for you to come here."

Ruth was grateful, and proud too that of eight grandchildren Othermama had asked her to go to the Alamo. On their return home, Othermama questioned Ruth about her plans for the future. When Ruth said she was thinking about sculpture, Othermama thought it a good idea.

"Why don't you come and stay with me in Marshall a while?" she suggested.

It did not take much prodding for Ruth to accept. Roxi, Othermama's cook, served an abundance of good food and the Marshall pottery was within walking distance. Clarksville clay at White Rock Creek was of acceptable quality, but Marshall clay had a finer texture and the Marshall Pottery had kilns and firing equipment with people willing to share their knowledge.

That summer, Ruth spent her days at the pottery, modeling her statues on an upturned ten-gallon jar, using the crudest of makeshift tools: a nut pick, a razor blade, a penknife. As winter came on, the pottery became so cold her clay figures would freeze and crumble overnight.

One evening, on finding Ruth there working and touching her icy fingers, Othermama offered her the use of a room off the back porch with a heater.

The boarding house proved a good place for working *and* exhibiting her statues. And Othermama had a keen eye for business, what was going on and how to amalgamate the two.

When Lieutenant-Governor Thomas Whitfield Davidson, old friend and former resident of Marshall, started campaigning for governor of Texas, Othermama suggested Ruth do a statue of him. Finding a photograph in the local paper, Ruth set to work. When the piece was finished, Ruth took it to Clarksville where Butcher Drug Company on the town square put it in their front window. As people debated Davidson's chances of being elected governor of Texas, the statue generated a news article. And a sale! But on being shipped, the statue shattered.

Crestfallen, Ruth pondered on artist Samuel Morse, who in a rage of frustration threw down his brushes – and invented the telegraph. Clay was a fragile medium and breakage was high. In the drying process or final firing, a figure might easily crumble into pieces, as one indeed had, *four times*. Gradually though, Ruth became more adept at methods to prevent breakage – such as keeping her figures moist to prevent cracking and working out air pockets to prevent a figure from exploding in the kiln.

When Lieutenant-Governor Davidson came to Marshall, he posed for Ruth in person and was so pleased with the results he offered to buy it. His wife, however, was of a different disposition and made no effort at hiding her displeasure.

"Twenty-five dollars for that dead-looking thing!" she exclaimed in front of the mortified Davidson and fledgling sculptress. "I wouldn't have that in my house!"

Thus, the statue reverted to its original customer, who was delighted on hearing that Lt. Governor Davidson had posed in person. Ruth refrained from telling him the wife's opinion.

**Thirteen-year-old Ruth's statue
of Lt. Governor Thomas Whitfield Davidson.**

VI

Never Trust A Man!

Boarding houses were always a good place to learn the latest goings-on in small towns, and the Widow Conerly's establishment was no exception. In fact, lately Ruth and her cousins Mabel and Martha Jane were finding Othermama's parlor a wellspring of information on a topic of ever-increasing interest – men!

Specifically, Othermama had a group of friends: Mrs. Jack Allen, Mrs. Cynthia Spencer and Mrs. Mathis, dubbed "the chums," who on taking afternoon tea were a virtual sieve of information. And from behind Othermama's sofa, Ruth and her cousins learned much about life, men, their gallantries and evil ways. The secret lay in not giggling – extremely difficult whenever Mrs. Cynthia Spencer sat at the piano and sang, "Last night I dreamed someone kissed me!" going up with loud trills on the "kissed me" until the cousins' muffled snickering turned to red-faced gagging. After that, the ladies would inevitably lower their voices to discuss the *interesting stuff.*

One afternoon in 1923, as these ladies were sipping tea, Mrs. Jack Allen in a most casual way broached a subject she claimed was "causing some speculation in town," namely Othermama's new boarder, Mr. Thurmond. A rather fine looking man, didn't Myra Jane think? And exactly what business had brought Mr. Thurmond to town? Certainly well mannered and attentive, always rising from his seat so gallantly that way whenever Myra Jane came into the room. Just being courteous, of course, a strapping man like that, hardly older than forty-five. And wasn't Myra Jane now in her sixties?

Ruth and her cousins restrained a gasp. Crouched behind the sofa, they stared at one another holding their collective breath until their eyes bulged. Never had not laughing posed such a challenge. All were aware of the cat and mouse game *the chums* played, trying to hide their own ages while pinning down each other's. At that moment, Ruth vividly recalled how she had transgressed on this most unpardonable sin in Othermama's long list of strict rules.

Ruth was on her way to the pottery when Mrs. Jack Allen rushed out of her house and called out melodiously.

"Why, Ruth, my dear, how *are* you this morning?"

"Oh, I'm fine, thank you, Ma'am."

"That's nice. And tell me, my dear, isn't today your grandmother's birthday?"

"Yes, Ma'am."

"My goodness.. And how old is your grandmother, Ruth?"

"I don't know, Ma'am. About 60, I guess."

It was a bad mistake. When Ruth got home, Othermama was at the door with a cup towel in her hand. You could always tell Othermama was *madder than hornets* when she had a cup-towel, pulling the edges back and forth crisply that way.

"What do you mean telling Mrs. Jack Allen I'm sixty years old!"

"Well, I thought you were.. about sixty."

"I am not! I was born in 1860. I married your grandpa Buck when I was fifteen and your father was born in 1878. Now you wipe that bewildered look off your face. I'm fifty-nine for your information!"

"Well, I said you were about sixty."

"Young lady, there's a big difference between fifty-nine and sixty, and when you get to be my age, you'll realize it! In the meantime, you just keep your big mouth shut about people's ages. Particularly mine. Do you understand?"

"Yes, Ma'am"

Crouched behind the sofa, Ruth made silent mental calculations, born 1860, it was now 1923. Great guns! Othermama was sixty-three! Handling her age well, as people said. Ever explaining the why and wherefore of this. Her complexion, void of any wrinkle or blemish, Othermama attributed to never exposing her skin to the sun's damaging rays, never going out without a hat. *"Ruth, Mabel, Martha Jane, wear your hat out!"* Her eyes, remarkably blue, would still glisten in the presence of an attractive man, with a lift of the eyebrow, a sidelong glance or lowering of the lashes.

The language of the eyes was an art, she maintained, important to perfect. But it was carriage, Othermama insisted, that was of paramount importance. Just as men judged the breeding of a fine horse by its port and step, the quality of a woman was determined by the way she carried herself!

If all these teachings seemed to imply that a girl's major objective in life was to make herself irresistibly attractive to men, another rule, supreme to all, precluded this:

"Never trust a man! Nor a woman either, when dealing with a man."

In the next weeks, *the chums* seemed to be ever dropping by, showing an insatiable curiosity about Othermama's new boarder, Mr. Thurmond. When Mrs. Mathis suggested that Othermama's cheeks had taken on new color and wasn't that a new dress she was wearing, Othermama replied that she was a practical person, not frivolous and harebrained, or filling her mind with ridiculous tomfoolery!

But incredible as it seemed, Mr. Thurmond proposed and more incredibly still, Othermama accepted.

Needless to say, the marriage of the widow Conerly to Mr. Thurmond hit Marshall like a bomb. Some openly speculated that Mr. Thurmond was an opportunist and the marriage could not possibly last. But Othermama was happy. She went more frequently to the dressmaker and milliner, and on Mr. Thurmond's urging she bought a new car, which he enjoyed driving about town. When Mr. Thurmond invited Ruth out for a drive, she didn't think it amiss, but nevertheless refused. Not long after, her cousin Mabel said Mr. Thurmond had asked *her* out for a drive and had looked at her with a "lascivious eye."

A meeting of cousins was called. On comparing stories, they decided Mr. Thurmond was a rake and a scoundrel, and a fortune hunter to boot! They would avoid him, although perhaps it was best not to mention all this to Othermama, happy as she seemed.

Unfortunately, a young woman working at Miss Lula's beauty salon was not so discreet. When a customer asked if she was the one seen driving about with Mr. Thurmond in the widow Conerly's new car, the young woman – known more for her extravagant hairstyles than for what was actually in her head – replied, yes, that she and Mr. Thurmond had been seeing each other. And as a matter of fact, he had asked her to marry him. On being reminded that Mr. Thurmond was already married to the widow Conerly, the young woman ceded the point, countering that Mr. Thurmond had confided to her that he was only biding his time waiting to see how much money he could get out of the widow Conerly, at which time he would divorce and marry her.

It was not published in the newspaper, nor announced from the pulpit, but within hours everyone in Marshall seemed to be commenting on this incredible chicanery and speculating on what Othermama would do when she found out.

Word was not long in getting back, and, as might be expected, Othermama did the *appropriate* thing. She chased Mr. Thurmond out of the house with a broom, which was considered his just desserts. He left town with her new car, without the girlfriend, and was never seen in Marshall again. Nor the car either.

By 1924, nearing age fifteen, Ruth's ability in sculpture was drawing a growing clientele and her statues – whimsical children and historical personages – were bringing in a modest income. Washington, General Lee, Lincoln with his gaunt suffering features and French Commander-in-Chief Foch with his flamboyant mustaches were all popular subjects. Foch, who had saved Paris during World War I, was a great favorite and his phrase, "Outflanked on the right, outflanked on the left, am going to advance!" was still being quoted in classrooms and on town squares where old men whittled.

Ruth's ability in sculpture had been receiving considerable notice in an expanding radius of East Texas newspapers, all describing her as "a child genius," when one day a representative from Sullins College in Bristol, Virginia, came to see Lizzie. The representative said Sullins would like to offer Ruth a year's scholarship.

Lizzie gazed at the brochures showing magnificent buildings set on broad lawns with lakes and graceful trees, and then questioned,

"What are the conditions?"

"There are none," the representative replied. "Ruth is an exceptionally talented young lady and we feel Sullins might help her in achieving her goals that might well be notable. If in future interviews Ruth were to mention having attended Sullins, we would consider it ample reward."

Lizzie was of a mind to accept on the spot, but again her traditional caution took hold. The thought of Ruth's going so far away – a doe-eyed young girl on her own in these permissive times – made her conjure up all sorts of villains and pitfalls. Remembering that the daughter of a wealthy Clarksville businessman attended a fashionable college in the East, Lizzie asked his wife for advice.

But instead of dissipating Lizzie's fears, the woman stared at her in amazement.

"Why, Lizzie, you'd be crazy to send Ruth there."

"Why do you say that?" Lizzie asked.

"To be perfectly candid, Sullins is one of the most exclusive schools in the country. Those girls spend a fortune on their clothes. Ruth would be totally out of place there."

"She's not going to model clothes," Lizzie replied. "She's going to study."

"And you'd be educating her far above her station in life or any economic means she could ever aspire to. She'd be miserable for the rest of her life!"

That did it! Lizzie no longer doubted. Ruth would go to Sullins!

Sullins College in Southwest Virginia

Ready for Sullin's
Illustration by Ruth Conerly age 14

VII

With Sails Unfurled

Boarding the train to Virginia that September morning, Ruth was gripped by a sense of destiny fulfilled. Dressed in the new slim line of the mid '20s, copied from a figurine in the Ladies Home Journal, her red hair clipped in the new Flapper styling, Ruth was confident there was little to set her apart from wealthy girls on their way east to fashionable schools.

The Journal's August edition had proven well worth its ten-cent cost. Along with advertisements for Old Dutch Cleanser, fountain Coca-Cola at five cents, a Ford Runabout car at $250, were articles directed to the college girl:

Look a darling with only a $500 budget, which includes necessities such as this fur-trimmed winter coat at $85 and slicker raincoat at $6.

That a family would spend $500 – twice the value of a car – for their daughter's college wardrobe did not escape Ruth's attention. Recalling the few dollars spent on fabric, which she and her mother sewed, Ruth considered it a triumph of making do. And among her purchases she had actually bought one of the recommended items – the slicker raincoat!

As the train clicked rhythmically along, Ruth focused her attention on her magazine. On its first pages was a magnificent painting of a ship by N.C. Wyeth. A sleek clipper with sails unfurled as it tipped the wave crests, it brought to mind Wyeth's masterful illustrations for "Treasure Island" and her father's explaining how artists' illustrations attracted people to buy books and magazines. The ship seemed symbolic of this moment in her life when she too was unfurling her sails. With a thrill of anticipation, she turned to the lead article, *Modeling my Life* by sculptress Janet Scudder.

A foremost sculptress of the day, Scudder's statues adorned America's largest estates: the McCormicks, the Pratts and Rockefellers, and the article appearing in this issue seemed to bode well for her chosen profession – sculpture.

Within minutes, Ruth was so engrossed that she scarcely heard the voice from across the aisle until he repeated the question.

"Where are you going?"

Looking up, she recognized the blue-eyed young man as one of two she had noticed on boarding, decidedly the more handsome.

"Sullins," she replied. "And you?"

"Virginia Military Institute... also in Virginia." They had barely exchanged a few sentences when his companion walked by, nudging him and signaling him to follow.

"Her father went crazy and committed suicide!" the friend whispered too loudly.

"And what does that matter?" the blue-eyed young man replied. But he did not return.

Strange, she reflected, that after four years, words like these could still cut deeply, bringing back all the ostracism, sidelong whispers and aloof glances so painfully imprinted on her mind. Teetering precariously on the brink of tears, she recalled her father's contagious enthusiasm, wishing with all her might he could be there now to bid her good sailing. Before the image faded, she could almost hear his voice: "My little girl's going to be a great artist someday."

"I love you too, Daddy," she whispered, brushing aside the tears and reopening her magazine.

Located in picturesque Southwest Virginia, overlooking the Allegheny Mountains, Sullins College in 1924 had a hundred-acre campus of stately buildings with Georgian columns, promenades, lakes and broad lawns. Its two year college program offered what was considered a wide variety of options for the young lady: general studies, art, music, drama, languages, home economics, education, secretarial and commercial sciences, as well as equitation, swimming, volleyball and tennis. Having not yet completed high school, Ruth was not eligible for the college level and a special curriculum was outlined for her: English, French, History, Math. For sports, she chose equitation and swimming. Miss Christine Bredin, who had studied under the great French sculptor Auguste Rodin and was head of the art department, would schedule her art courses. Also, it was explained, she must work in the library as part of her scholarship duties.

A library considered a *duty*? Ruth reflected. More like throwing Br'er Rabbit into the briar patch.

Far from the traumatic experience predicted for her, Virginia was like coming home to ancestral roots. The wooded countryside and familiar Southern accent reminded her of East Texas and whenever stories of the Civil War were evoked, Ruth delved into her own arsenal of stories. Her grandfather Buxton's account of the Battle of Fort Gregg became a great favorite, which Ruth could tell with great effectiveness:

"Fort Gregg, close to Richmond, was little more than a battle-scarred earthwork in the final days of the Civil War. But as the South's army was retreating across the Appomattox River, it was the site of a terrible battle. To cover the army's retreat, two hundred and fifty Mississippians were sent to hold off five thousand Northern soldiers.

'HOLD AT ALL HAZARDS!' General Robert E. Lee ordered, which meant they must fight to the death so that General Lee would not be forced to fight with the Appomattox River at their back – or worse still – see the South's army massacred in mid-river."

At that point, Ruth looked around the room. Then, assured of everyone's rapt attention, she continued.

"While hurrying to Fort Gregg, the Mississipians picked up extra rifles scattered over the field, loading them as they ran. At Fort Gregg, they found a deep ditch surrounding the fort with cannon balls, grapeshot and canister stacked inside. On taking up positions and looking out, they could see the enemy, thousands of them, bayonets glistening in the morning sun. As the enemy's lines advanced toward them, the Mississipians' commander ordered, `Steady, men. Hold your fire until you see the whites of their eyes'. On shouting 'Fire'! great gaps appeared in the enemy's lines. Reaching for the extra loaded guns at their sides, it gave an effect of repeating rifles.

"Two terrible charges were driven back. But seeing hundreds of their comrades trapped in the ditches, the

Yankees came running to their rescue in a third massive attack. Surrounded by thousands scaling the walls, the Mississippians threw down cannon balls and solid shot and even bricks. But finally the Bluebellies flooded up over the walls, shooting and killing until only twenty Mississippians were left. On being marched away my grandfather looked back to where his colonel lay shot in the head."

Ruth's English teacher considered it remarkable that someone that young could describe a battle with such detail and drama. One composition so impressed her that she asked Ruth to read it at a college assembly.

That morning, stepping up to the podium, Ruth felt her knees go weak and was certain her voice was gone. Seeing a glass of water and recalling how her grandfather Dr. Davis would calmly take a sip, she did so. Her legs stopped shaking. Looking out over her audience, she found her voice was still there.

"Blame the South for the Civil War? And forget the North's tariffs, more impoverishing than any levied by England against the colonies and considered just cause for the American Revolution?

"Blame the South for slavery, forgetting it was Northern ship-owners who brought them to our shores in miserable ship-holds? The South had no big shipping trade.

"No. The South's great sin was its refusal to sell its agricultural products for a pittance and daring to buy better, cheaper goods elsewhere, as the constitution then guaranteed. And for this, the North was sure its numeric and industrial superiority could crush a few rebellious farmers.

"But when two million forcefully recruited Northern boys could not reduce a half million farm boys to subservience, more desperate means were considered. Perhaps by freeing the slaves in the South – not those in the slave-holding states of the North – this would bring economic ruin to the South.

"But when the slaves stayed on, running blockades to get cotton through to European markets, infiltrators were sent to urge them to revolt. When this did not bring the South to its knees, the North sent Sherman's army to burn and ravage – and the crime of this will haunt Yankee-doodle-dum until the crack of doom!

"And yet.."

Ruth paused and looked out on her audience.

"Out of it all, our great nation came together, mending its wounds. And while we must never allow anyone to stigmatize the South for the Civil War and much less for slavery, we must be thankful for that coming together and pray that our great nation will forever stand united."

In the ensuing silence, Ruth's heart pounded and her cheeks flushed red. Then as scattered claps swelled and people began standing, applauding in a thunderous ovation, Ruth felt her cheeks redder still.

The little redhead from Texas, great-grandniece of John C. Calhoun, had proved a worthy advocate of trampled Southern pride.

The next day, Ruth's English teacher decided that Ruth's ability for writing rivaled her talent in art and that she should give serious consideration to switching to a career in journalism. This provoked a swift retaliation from Ruth's art teacher.

"Over my dead body!" the deceptively fragile Miss Bredin responded. It was a declaration of war! The next day Miss Bredin offered Ruth the position of artist for the Sullins' annual.

Ruth was thrilled. With her reserves almost gone and winter setting in, she was beginning to feel how important a wool coat with a fur collar could be. Maybe a *necessity* as the Ladies Home Journal had said.

"It will mean a lot of work and there'll be no money in it," Miss Bredin clarified, "but it will be valuable experience for your portfolio."

Ruth's smile vanished. Arming herself with valor, she explained her present situation and how her mother had told her she must be supporting herself after this year at Sullins. And asked outright how she could earn a living in art. To this, Miss Bredin replied that the secret lay in learning to draw a figure quickly and professionally. And doing this meant *anatomy and practice*... anatomy and practice. And more anatomy and practice."

In spite of doubts concerning art as a profitable career, Ruth decided against changing ships in mid-sea and began to wonder what she could do to supplement her depleted reserves. Sculpture and paintings were *not* things college girls coveted. They spent money on clothes, maybe a fancy doll for the top of their bed, a Southern Belle. Ruth had long ago learned that if she were to have a doll, she had to make it. She knew how to form a head of unglazed bisque, paint a beguiling face, make black or golden hair from silk thread and stylish clothing from scraps of material, lace and ribbon. Ruth set to work.

Thus SUZIE FLAPPER, THE SULLINS' VAMP came into existence. It was all there – short skirt, beaded eyelashes, the epitome of the raging twenties. From the moment Ruth set the magnificent Suzie on her bed, everyone wanted a Suzie too. Soon Ruth had two girls helping her make Suzies and there were orders for Suzies in a downtown store.

Then Ruth went a step further. Using her slicker raincoat, she painted front and back views of Suzie dancing the Charleston. Suzie's wiggling backside created instant, squeal-provoking delight with the result that Suzie raincoats quickly became the school rage – *a wardrobe must* – with the advantage that Ruth could knock off Suzie raincoats with their wiggling backsides in rapid succession. Miss Bredin's adage on anatomy and practice proved solid advice!

By December, Ruth's financial status had done a *flip-flop* and the new economic buoyancy brought important changes in her lifestyle. Her first purchase was a wool coat with a fur collar. Next, she visited an orthopedic specialist, who fashioned a lift for her shoe, easing the strain in her hip and making her limp almost imperceptible. In December, she bought a ticket home for the Christmas vacations!

Come Spring, as young men began driving by Sullins, a list of rules was posted, reminding the girls that a brief conversation was permitted. But it was totally forbidden getting into a car or driving away. Aware that a misstep would mean the loss of her scholarship, Ruth buttressed herself with Ohermama's axiom, "Never trust a man," and the still stronger – "Remember Pretty!" This prime example of male perfidy doing in feminine virtue was a real slugger, like *Remember the Alamo!*

All were proud that September when Pretty, daughter of Othermama's cook Roxi, got a scholarship to the leading college for blacks. This was Pretty's big opportunity. She must be careful not to let any fancy-talking boy turn her head. But come spring, Pretty was home, pregnant, and the scalawag, from one of Marshall's prominent black families, refused to marry. *A wife might distract him from his studies.*

"Distract him from his studies," Othermama mocked as she and Roxi sat stern-faced side by side in Othermama's car with Old Tye and his wife Annie equally stern-faced in front. The drive through town was as grim as the Earp brothers heading for the OK Corral. Shotguns proved unnecessary.

Recalling Pretty's wedding with Othermama and Roxi in the front pew, Ruth had paid little attention when two girls wandered down the hill and began talking with several boys. Until they called to her. The boy at the wheel, compellingly handsome, was looking straight at her and patting the seat beside him. Seeing the girls jump into the car, Ruth shook her head and was gesturing for them to come back, when suddenly two figures leaped out of the bushes behind her. They were the principal and the dean of girls!

The next day, Ruth was back on the Sullins stage, held up as a paragon of virtue. The applause was weaker than before, but thereafter any girl wanting permission to go into town knew it would be granted if Ruth accompanied the group. The weight of her sword of virtue might have become unbearably heavy had her year at Sullins not been coming to an end.

In years to come, Ruth would look back on that year at Sullins with nostalgia and gratitude. Christine Bredin was an excellent teacher. The library provided invaluable experience in researching a subject, and the college annual gave insight into the rush, ink and deadlines of the publishing world.

Ruth's illustration *Texas Roping Knowledge* for the Sullins annual showed a knack for action and a whole attitude toward life. Her illustration of a young lady on horseback symbolized the importance of *doing things properly* like riding, speaking French for that trip to Paris she hoped one day to make, hearing fine music. When Irish tenor John McCormack came to Sullins, Ruth thought his the most beautiful voice she had ever heard. And if at Sullins table manners were considered the hallmark of the well-bred young woman, Ruth's table manners became impeccable.

Othermama was pleased. Little Janey, Ruth's sister, was awed, but confused on hearing the Victrola going full blast and finding Othermama, Roxi and Ruth, arms and legs flailing as they danced the Charleston, and the even more risqué Black Bottom.

But Ruth realized how proud Othermama was of her that day when Mrs. Jack Allen said, "Why, Myra Jane, Ruth's becoming awfully pretty." And Othermama observed Ruth judiciously and nodded.

"Yes, Ruth manages quite well with what she has. In spite of all that red hair and freckles like her mother Lizzie!"

Important to do things *properly*

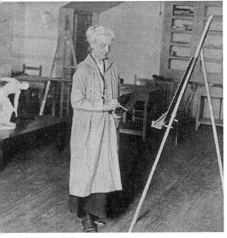

ver my dead body!" Miss Bredin,
Ruth's art teacher, declared.

Ruth's Suzzies brought
a warm coat with fur collar

College Specials

President	Art Reporter	Secretary
Catherine Collins	Ruth Conerly	Josephine Bond

Texas Roping Knowledge
**Ruth's illustrations for the Sullins annual showed an early knack
for action and a whole attitude toward life.**

VIII

The Red River Bank Robbery

The year 1926 was a time of notorious bank robbers like Bonnie and Clyde, and the little town of Clarksville with its twenty-six millionaires must have seemed an easy touch. F.H. Caldron and A.E. Flintworth (not the real names) had planned the robbery for over a month, finally settling on what they considered the most propitious time for a bank robbery: 12 noon.

There was just one flaw in their plan. They failed to take into consideration that nothing was ever secret in the little town of Clarksville. In fact, plans to thwart the attempt were already being laid in the back room of The Conerly Garage, and Ed Conerly had even paid for an advertisement of the Conerly Garage in the following issue of Clarksville Times, calculated to be a sellout. More inauspicious still, on arriving at the bank, the robbers failed to notice that Sheriff Hickman and three deputies were sitting in their car a half block from the bank at precisely high noon, eating their lunch.

And not entirely by coincidence, some twenty men were at the second floor windows of the buildings surrounding the bank, rifles cocked.

The only astounding thing was that, if so many people knew the robbery was to occur, why did all this not get back to Caldron and Flintworth themselves? But apparently it did not, because on leaving the bank with their booty of $33,125, they were met by an onslaught of gunfire unequaled in peacetime history. Within seconds, the robbery was snuffed and the robbers' riddled bodies lay on the front sidewalk, awaiting the arrival of reporters from Dallas. Sheriff Hickman felt that a broader coverage of the event would serve to alert other prospective robbers that Clarksville was not a town to be played with. (And indeed, there has never been another bank robbery in Clarksville.) He also felt the delay would give the citizens of Clarksville time to meander down to the Town Square and see what an efficient job the local authorities had done.

Ruth's little sister, Janey, could not remember who took her down to see the macabre scene, but as she was learning to tie her shoelaces at the time, her attention became focused on the robbers' shoelaces and how neatly they were tied. When a reporter asked her opinion of it all, she promptly pointed this out.

"Yes, of course," the reporter agreed indulgently. "But what I meant was, what *moral* lesson has been taught here today in Clarksville? What did you *learn?*"

Six-year-old Janey furrowed her brow and risked a guess: "That when you tie your shoelaces in the morning, you don't know what the hell's going to happen to you in the afternoon?"

The reporter smiled weakly and moved away.

Ruth was in Marshall at the time of the robbery but considered it a disgrace, exemplary of Clarksville's baseball bat justice. Over the years with each retelling of the story, she would add new touches of pathos. The robbers were young boys, newlyweds, one with a "poor little pregnant wife" who had gone to the sheriff to beg him to discourage them. Ruth's sympathies, clearly with the robbers, seemed to reflect more an unresolved love-hate relationship with Clarksville than fact. And although by 1926, the Conerly family's situation had undergone a decided improvement, Ruth's feelings toward Clarksville were still wrapped in ambivalence.

It was a many-faceted year for the Conerly family.

"We won't ever see her again," Ruth lamented as they laid sweet Rebecca to rest in Atlanta, Texas, beside her husband Dr. Davis, and little Janey, not totally happy about Rebecca's winging her way to heaven, burst into tears.

But all were proud that the Conerly family could afford a proper funeral for Grandmother Rebecca. Six years after their precipitous fall, Lizzie and Ed had brought the Conerly enterprises out of debt and were enjoying the Bull Market of the twenties. The Conerly Garage was not only a hub where people brought their vehicles for tire vulcanizing, fueling and repair, but where farmers and merchants wheeled and dealed. Testimony to the family's new prosperity, Ed bought a farm, making innovations that would win him an award for producing the largest yield of long-staple cotton in Texas. Prosperity brought a husband for Christine, an engineer from MIT, while Preston Jr., adept at tennis, had won a scholarship to Texas Tech. Girls considered his nickname *Mutt* cute.

Ruth's brother Preston, adept at tennis, won a scholarship at Texas Tech.

The year 1926 also brought a husband for Lizzie – the widower Joseph Augustus Tate, a six-foot-four giant of a man, owner of a thousand-acre farm of fine woodlands and a lumber mill. Only one person voiced any criticism of Lizzie's new marriage – Othermama. She could not *understand* how Lizzie could marry again after having been married to her Pressie.

1926 was proving a good year for Ruth. On her return from Sullins, she had fixed her course on sculpture, hopeful that herein lay a means of comfortable support. She had acquired a familiarity with the Greek and Renaissance masters, the great Auguste Rodin and Americans such as Gutzon Borglum, Augustus Saint-Gaudens and Frederic Remington. Of more weighty consideration, sculpture was a field in which *women* had made their mark. Nellie Verne Walker had become famous for her statue "Her Son". Elizabeth Ney, by age thirty, had sculpted Europe's royalty before immigrating to Texas in 1890. Ruth's imagination was stirred by stories of the redheaded, free-thinking Ney, whose ashes had been spread on Texas soil in 1907, only one year prior to her own birth.

That year, Ruth spent most of her time in Marshall with Othermama, a strict disciplinarian. Not even Othermama's errant cat, Bummy, escaped her iron-clad rules. Whenever Bummy appeared with chewed ears and missing patches of fur, Othermama would drop him, clawing wildly, into the washtub, where amid snarls and thwackings, he was scrubbed, combed, and warned, "You're going to get your fool self killed in some fracas!" Othermama was less tolerant if Ruth failed to keep her room straight and clothes picked up.

But Othermama's ability to muster support for a cause proved a special boon for Ruth that year when Marshall's most prestigious social group, the Sesame Club, sponsored an exhibit of Ruth's sculpture. Ruth worked hard, preparing seven pieces for the exhibit. Two hundred and forty persons attended and the Marshall Morning News described the event and each piece of sculpture in glowing terms.

Ruth was helping to serve the guests when her hostess took a plate from her. "You're our guest of honor. You must let us serve you." It was a heady moment. Recognition in one's hometown had a sweet taste. That day, Ruth sold three pieces and the Sesame Club voted to purchase "The Passing Herd", a cowboy with his saddle to one side, for the Marshall Library.

Soon after, one of Marshall's most prominent citizens commissioned Ruth to do a fountain piece for her new home. This was barely finished when Mr. Edmond Key of the Key-Garret Bank commissioned a statue of his daughter, Constance. The resulting work so pleased him that he had it cast and gave Ruth a casting.

But little followed, and when an invitation came to exhibit her work at Grand Central Art galleries in Dallas, hope surged that the more metropolitan Dallas would offer a broader market. Acclaim was sweet, but sales were crucial and there was a limited number of people in Marshall who could afford twenty-five dollars for a statue. To cover expenses in Dallas, Ruth calculated she must make at least one sale there. Two materialized, including one from a Mr. George Hopkins, collector of Internal Revenue for a bust of President Calvin Coolidge for his office. At another exhibit in Dallas Ruth captured a gratifying amount of press coverage. As these successes reverberated back to Clarksville and Marshall, Ruth found herself somewhat of a local celebrity, receiving invitations to speak before groups.

The Banker's Daughter

Over the years Ruth forgot the name of this girl with the beguiling smile, never knowing she, Constance Key, married the widowed Lt. Gov. Davidson, subject of her early sculpture.

Slaves of the Jug
A vase with feminine figures

Even her high school principal in Clarksville – *"Ruth, day dreaming again?"* – invited her to address the graduating class, introducing her as "exemplary of what talent and initiative could accomplish." More amazing still, Aunt Mattie, who had said, "Mark my words, that Ruth will come to no good end!" now unctuously proclaimed, "I always knew Ruth would be a success, smart as she is and with so much spirit," making Ruth marvel at the power of retrospect. But when her cousin Reese knelt to pray over her polio foot, presuming to heal it by his loud intonations, the mortified Ruth decided she far preferred him mean and hateful.

Aware that personal appearance played an important role in attracting publicity and business, Ruth spared no effort in her grooming. She had a natural flair for fashion and an artist's eye for color and how to play up her best features. A true red, she found, accented her full, well-shaped mouth bringing out the red glints in her hair. Stillman's Freckle Cream was proving effective in fading the freckles, while lightly applied make-up created highlights of glamour.

Not surprisingly, Ruth found herself attracting a good deal of male attention. Nor were the men intimidated by little Janey who would sit on Ruth's lap, suck her thumb and stare at them fiercely. One young man, considered Clarksville's most eligible, proposed but quickly modified his proposal with the condition that Ruth would, of course, give up her career on marrying him.

Ruth refused.

When another young man in Marshall proposed and she told her cousins, Ruth was surprised to find he had proposed to them too. On calling him forth to explain, he said it was simple. As they were the most beautiful girls in town, he figured he would be happy with whichever accepted! He struck out on all three counts.

Only one boy – Foots Garrett of Marshall – made a lasting impression on Ruth:

> *"Foots could play the piano as though he could sense my mood and would always play something just right. All I had to do was hum a tune and Foots would play it. Then he'd add harmonies and frills, making it incredibly beautiful."*

Although their paths parted, Ruth could never sit at a piano and play, as Foots had taught her, without thinking of him.

Decidedly, potential husbands were not lacking, but none showed any enthusiasm about her working. It had always been something of a fad for young ladies of good families to dabble in art or sculpture, but from that to making a *career* of it, was something entirely different. It was expected that once married, she would settle down, have babies and forget all that *nonsense*. Proper society was tolerant, but up to a point!

Unfortunately, this way of thinking had repercussions. Since people *knew* a woman would marry and therefore not reach the top echelons in the art world, the incentive to buy her work was diminished. *Not a good investment.* Even now, there were hints of this way of thinking. Although Ruth was experiencing an inordinate amount of acclaim, she was aware of the paradox between the image she was trying to establish of a world-class sculptress and harsh financial reality. The time required for a sculpture along with the pieces requested as commissions or for donations to a community cause, the cost of room and board while attending an exhibit and dressing properly, left little for living. Pinched in from all sides, she had even begun to wonder if sculpture could *ever* provide the means for a comfortable, independent life with a home of her own.

Without these considerations, what happened next would seem illogical. One morning, seeing an advertisement in a Dallas newspaper for an artist, Ruth prepared samples and applied. Much to her delight, they hired her. But a week later she was fired. The pressures of a newspaper's fast-moving world quickly revealed her lack of experience, leaving her to recall her art teacher's adage, "Practice and Anatomy!" A chastened Ruth returned to her sculpture and began preparing for the upcoming Sixteenth Annual Exhibit of Texas Artists soon to be held in Dallas.

The day of the inauguration, she was standing by her two statues when a group of people came towards her. The man in their midst, to whom everyone listened attentively, paused before Ruth's two statues. Making comments suggestive of a person knowledgeable in the arts, he called her *Water Baby* "a particularly well-modeled little fellow," and her *Creation of*

Man "a primitive masculine figure emerging from a shapeless mass, well conceived and executed." Both, he said, showed "amazing knowledge of anatomy and animation." Several persons around him scribbled in a notepad.

On making inquiries, Ruth discovered the man was Franz Strahalm, an artist of considerable prestige. A third generation Austrian painter who had apprenticed under Friedrich Prinz, Strahalm was a master of impressionistic Texas landscapes.

"Wealthy Dallas socialites flock to his art school," one of the organizers informed her.

The next day, Strahalm returned. He said he considered her *Creation of Man* an excellent example of male anatomy, ideal for his students in painting. And bought it! He then offered her a position as apprentice in his studio.

Mrs. Strahalm, a motherly woman, who called out to her children, "Kommt her, meine Schatzis," (Come here, my treasures), sealed Ruth's decision to accept.

Under Strahalm's tutelage Ruth acquired more proficiency in drawing and painting and valuable experience in the *business* of art, ways to increase prestige and sales. Things like how to develop 'pot boilers,' variations of a painting quickly drafted to keep money coming in during slack times.

Strahalm put great emphasis on maintaining one's individuality, not becoming a *copier* of other artists' work or style. He considered Ruth's lack of formal education an advantage and the reason for her remarkable versatility.

"Artists who exclusively copy a particular artist stunt their development and originality," he maintained. "Imperative to have one's own style and create an aura around one's name and work. At every opportunity you must advertise yourself," Strahalm insisted. "Few people know anything about art. Most people simply want a painting that will one day be worth a fortune!"

In the next few weeks, Strahalm did much to enhance Ruth's aura, recommending her to reporters and authors. "A History of Texas Artists and Sculptors" by Frances Battaile Fisk and "Art of Artists of Texas" by Esse Forester O'Brian, all carried extensive write-ups on the upcoming sculptress Ruth Conerly. Even Holland's Magazine carried a full-page article on Ruth in its April 1928 edition.

The Water Baby

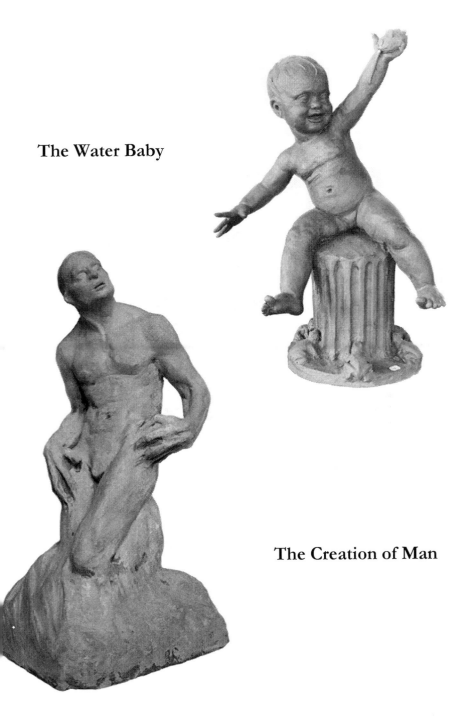

The Creation of Man

Holland's, The Magazine of the South, *April, 1928*

East Texas Girl! Wins Success as Sculptor

By
MARY K. ARMSTRONG

Ruth Conerly

EAST TEXAS clay, hitherto serving best as an incontrovertible argument in behalf of the liberal expenditure of the people's money for a system of good roads, in the hands of an East Texas girl, Ruth Conerly, of Marshall, bids fair to acquire fame out of all proportion to its rather homely natural attributes. For working in this medium, this nineteen-year-old girl has not only succeeded in obtaining enough commissions to make her self-supporting, but has also won the praise of eminent artists, who predict for her a promising career in the field of creative art.

Exhibiting two pieces of her sculpture at the sixteenth annual exhibit of Texas artists, held recently in Dallas, under the auspices of the Dallas Woman's Forum, Ruth Conerly immediately attracted the attention of artists and critics, who viewed her work, and has been designated by them as a coming artist in her medium. The young sculptor's instant recognition is all the more remarkable in view of the fact that she has had no training in modeling, and her only preparation for her work has been a year in drawing at Sullins College in Virginia.

Previous to the Dallas exhibit, except for one little flare of interest aroused by her lifelike portrait bust of Lieutenant-Governor Davidson at the time when he was in the limelight as candidate for governor of Texas, the girl's work had gone unrecognized until the fall of 1926, when a Marshall woman's club sponsored an exhibit of her sculpture, introducing her to the public.

Three of the seven pieces displayed at this exhibit were sold, and the artist began receiving commissions. For a while she worked in a dark corner at a local pottery, modeling her figures on an upturned ten-gallon jar, made of the same clay with which she was working. Later, because of lack of room at the pottery, she established a makeshift studio at the rear of her grandmother's home, where she had the advantage of a heated room, a necessity in the winter, since the clay figures in a cold room would freeze and crumble overnight. There, working with the crudest of tools, helped out by an occasional razor blade, or a penknife, Ruth Conerly in the last eight months has executed a number of interesting sculptures. Her finished work includes several vases; an Indian figure, which was sold at her first exhibit; a portrait bust of a child in which the artist has succeeded in a remarkable likeness, and caught a fleeting whimsical expression which is the charm of the subject; and a typical cowboy figure, "The Passing Herd," which has been purchased for the Marshall Public Library. She has just recently completed for the conservatory of a local patron a fountain which is a well-balanced composition, having for the central figure a beautifully modeled nymph. Except in two instances the sculptor has worked without models, and

practically all of her work is done from imagination.

Though it is only recently that her work has attracted the attention of the public, Ruth Conerly has been giving expression to her natural talent by modeling in clay since she was a small child. She tells of how she made her first figures — busts of Washington, Lincoln, and Lee, and other notables

"The Passing Herd"

— from pictures appearing in the pages of her school histories, and laughingly recalls that she made her first money from her art when in 1914 she modeled a bust of the Kaiser, and she and her brother charged the neighborhood children a penny to take a shot at it.

In addition to the clay modeling, Ruth Conerly has widened a decided talent for painting, and has two portraits and a landscape to her credit. In all of her work she shows a fine feeling for form, a rare sense of motion, and the gift of imagination.

Theodore Morgan, artist, who saw her two pieces, "The Water Baby," and "The Creation of Man," displayed at the Forum exhibit, commented upon her amazing knowledge of anatomy and her sense of putting animation into her work. "The Water Baby," a well-modeled little fellow, apparently delighted at the success in plucking a water lily and holding it out of reach of the frogs at his feet, was sold to a prominent Dallas artist. The second piece of sculpture shown at the Forum exhibit portrays a primitive masculine figure emerging from a shapeless mass. The head, arms, and torso are completely formed, while the lower part of the figure is only suggested. Another Dallas artist is negotiating with the sculptor

for its purchase with the expectation of using it in his art classes.

The Dallas exhibit brought the girl sculptor to the attention of Franz Strahalm, well-known Dallas artist, who became interested in her future to the extent of taking her into his home, and giving her a place to work in his studio. Before leaving her home in Marshall she completed two important commissions, and only recently, while at work in the Strahalm studio, has executed a portrait of her benefactor.

"Many times I am discouraged," she admits, "because, due to the medium in which I work, I very often have to do my figures over and over again, since much of my work is lost in the drying process or final firing."

That the young artist is possessed of an unfailing optimism and faith in her art, along with her great natural talent, is evidenced by the fact that when for the fourth time a beautifully modeled figure for her largest commission crumbled to pieces, the girl remarked to a sympathizing friend, "Well I knew I can make a better one next time."

An eminent artist, recognizing the girl's rare talent, and predicting for her a brilliant future, considers her lack of formal training an asset rather than a disadvantage, but Ruth Conerly, who already has won enviable recognition without any special training for her work, hopes soon to become a pupil of one of the foremost American sculptors.

That she will succeed in this ambition seems hardly questionable, in view of the point to which native ability, coupled with an undaunted persistence and love of her work, has carried her thus far in her chosen realm of expression. There is a self-confidence, an assuredness and certainty, about this girl that leaves those who know her with a feeling of equal assurance that her gifts will bring her to her goal. She is talented beyond the ordinary in her art and, too, she is blessed with that rarer gift of knowing what she wants and going after it.

In gratitude to her mentor, Ruth did a statue of Strahalm!

Franz Strahalm, sculpture by Ruth Conerly

Ruth loved sculpture, the medium she felt most capable of expressing the romanticism and pathos she saw in life. She loved the feel of the clay in her hands, seeing it evolve into something only lacking the breath of life. Her major concern was how to make it more productive.

Hardly could she imagine what one of America's greatest sculptors would soon tell her!

Ruth and Strahalm's daughter Julia frolic in costumes

IX

A Pragmatic Question

Gutzon Borglum, product of the rugged American frontier, trained in Paris under Auguste Rodin, had an uncanny flair for capturing the attention of reporters and public alike. His project to sculpt General Robert E. Lee's Southern regiments on Stone Mountain near Atlanta, Georgia, had ended in bitter controversy. On hearing that his patrons planned to use his plaster models and replace him with a less expensive sculptor, Borglum threw the models over the cliff-side and departed.

He was planning an even more formidable project for Mount Rushmore in South Dakota – four gigantic heads of American presidents, a feat of engineering for which no modern precedent existed – when with mustache and Stetson hat, he arrived in Dallas to judge a sculpture show.

On reading the front-page story hailing Borglum's arrival, Ruth could hardly believe it. This giant of American sculpture, the great Borglum himself, was coming to Dallas to judge an exhibit? There was no guarantee her work would be accepted for the exhibit, no guarantee that Borglum would so much as notice it. Ridiculous to think he might accept her as an apprentice. And yet so strong was the hope, Ruth confided it to a reporter - who promptly published it:

Ruth Conerly hopes to become a pupil of one of the foremost American sculptors and that she will succeed in this seems hardly questionable for one with such assurance in her goals.

For days, she berated herself for having made such a bold statement. But in spite of doubts, she could barely contain her excitement. Years later, the memory of what happened was still sharp...

"I was about eighteen and had taken a statue of a boy on a dolphin to a Dallas exhibit. But the woman in charge refused to accept it. She said they didn't take statues modeled in clay. Only cast in bronze or finished

in marble. She had turned her back on me when suddenly in walked Mr. Borglum. A well-built man, he reminded me of my deceased father.

He looked at the statue and said, 'Why can't this be admitted? It's finished sculpture and a very good piece of terracotta.' With that, it was accepted. Later he spoke to me aside. 'It's the best piece in there. I wanted to give it first place, but I would have had a war on my hands with that silly rule of theirs. They probably didn't know terracotta is considered finished sculpture. I gave it second prize just the same though.'

Later he asked me about my work, how much study I'd had and with whom. I told him my teacher Christine Bredin had studied under Rodin, which impressed him. It was then he asked me, 'Is your family wealthy or do you have to make your own living?'

'I have to earn my own living,' I answered. 'My father died when I was eleven.'

'If that's the case, you'd best look to commercial art for a living and keep sculpture for your own enjoyment. As a career, sculpture will break your heart and starve you to death. Do you have any idea how much I make?'

'You?' I exclaimed. 'Quite a lot, I imagine.'

'$25 a week after expenses, barely enough for room and board. Sculpture gets to be a passion with you. My advice is to get out of it while you still can!'

I was shocked. Twenty-five dollars! That was what I was getting for my pieces and that didn't fit my moneymaking ideas one bit. The next day, Mr. Borglum invited me to accompany him to a dinner the organizers were having and kept on advising me.

'People pay little or nothing for art. They find every excuse in the world to get you to work for nothing. Only businesses will pay an artist an honest price for his work. Commercial art is the way to go today.'"

Ruth's dream to apprentice under the great Borglum collapsed. But his advice to her had a momentous effect. With one question, "Are you from a wealthy family or do you have to earn your living?" Borglum cut through the trumpery and went straight to the bottom line. And although not in the way Ruth hoped, he changed the course of her life.

Whether by coincidence or due to Borglum's influence, on the last day of the show, three men – Tracy, Locke, and Dawson of the advertising agency of that name in Dallas – attended the exhibit. On seeing Ruth's sculpture of a boy, they asked her if she could draw children as well as she sculpted them. Ruth said she thought she could and accepted their offer to do several ads for their client, Imperial Sugar:

> *"The first illustration I did was Betty Bakes a Cake, then Caught Red-handed, a little boy raiding a jelly jar. Another illustration for the gas company was of a little girl sitting by a stove with a doll, warming the doll's panties. It looked every bit like my daughter Sharon, but she hadn't been born then. I didn't know about Norman Rockwell at that time, but the illustrations were a lot in that order. They paid me well.*
>
> *Marshall Roland was head artist then at Tracy, Locke and Dawson. He was a great artist. He showed me how to do a finish, how to balance darks and lights. When I started out, I knew anatomy, how to model in clay, but little about illustration. Marshall taught me how to do layouts and make billboards. He told me that on looking for a job, look in the paper. 'See what kind of ads they're running and see if you can do it better! And if you're doing a fashion figure, remember you're selling clothes, not just a figure!'*
>
> *I followed his advice and made some samples for Titche Goettinger's, a big department store in Dallas. They hired me right on the spot! They started me off in underwear and pots and pans. Then they let me do an ad on house dresses. They liked my work so well they moved me up to better dresses and pretty soon up to the good stuff!" (High fashion)*

Having a regular salary brought the economic security Ruth longed for. On renting an apartment, she followed her mother's suggestion that to live in a nicer and safer area, it was advisable to share the cost with a roommate.

**Ruth's first
illustrations
For Imperial
Sugar.**

Betty Bakes a Cake

Vollands April 1928
Page 39—

Amid clatter of crockery and much bustle and "busyness," Betty compounds her first cake. It must be quite as formal a procedure as when Mother makes it.

She has gathered her materials with care. Flour, eggs, spices, recipe book---and of course *Imperial* Sugar.

Betty is starting out right. She has had glistening, delicious *Imperial* Sugar heaped up on her bread and butter too many times not to know that here *is* something good.

Most likely Mother has been buying *Imperial* Pure Cane Sugar for fifteen or eighteen years. Back in the days when sugar was bought in a paper sack at the corner grocery she came to know its sparkling purity.

Now she is *sure* of getting *Imperial*. She buys it in the *Imperial*-marked bag. It comes direct from refinery to kitchen sealed against dust, moisture and germs.

Most housewives now prefer to buy their sugar as they buy their coffee, flour, shortening and other articles of food in an individual package or container.

If you would have Pure Cane Sugar of the highest grade---of known quality and cleanliness---insist on the *Imperial*-marked bag at your grocers.

IMPERIAL SUGAR
COMPANY
Sugar Land, Texas

The interesting story of this wonderful sugar is told in "What Becomes of Your Sugar Dollar." A copy will be mailed you free on request. Address: Dept. H. Imperial Sugar Company, Sugar Land, Texas

IMPERIAL Sugar

[IN THE CONVENIENT DUST-PROOF BAGS]

* *"Buy your sugar by name---Say IMPERIAL and be sure"*

Elaine seemed a good choice for a roommate, but when Ruth began receiving charges for items she had never purchased, she paid up her accounts and abstained from charging. A few days later, she was making some purchases in the drugstore when the owner asked if she would mind settling her bill. Surprised, Ruth said she had purposefully stopped charging.

"Strange," he replied. "The delivery boy is on his way to your apartment right now with an order."

Ruth raced home, arriving just in time to see Elaine signing *Ruth Conerly* on the bill.

Stunned, Ruth demanded an explanation. And got it!

"Who wouldn't take advantage of you, you're such a little dope!"

"And you're a common thief!" Ruth fired back. "Now get out before I have you thrown into jail!"

With her latest salary increase, Ruth had no trouble paying the apartment alone. All things told, she decided, she was happier this way. It was just then when someone in the office asked if she had seen the news article about her.

"You never told anyone you were a sculptor! A child genius, no less!"

Far from complimentary though, the article entitled:

CHILD PRODIGIES AND WHY THEY NEVER AMOUNT TO MUCH! named her as its prime example:

> *Look at the case of Ruth Conerly! Extraordinary young sculptor of great promise – now just a hack illustrator at a Dallas department store!*

"Was that a blow!" Ruth recalled. "I remember feeling it so terribly. There was a sense of having betrayed myself. Luckily, I had just been made Art Director at Titche Goetinger's – quite a responsibility for a twenty-year-old."

And on taking inventory of her situation that October 27, 1928 on her twentieth birthday, Ruth felt the scale tipped favorably in the professional sphere. She was art director of Dallas's most prestigious store, living on her own, an enviable position from any point of view.

Only in the romantic sphere there was little interest. Well yes, she had met a few young men. One in particular was nice-looking, from a good family, doing quite well for himself. Lately, he had begun saying he wanted to introduce her to his family, which put her in a quandary. How could she explain why she always extended her hand so properly on saying goodnight? To tell a man he had terrible breath would sound like a Listerine ad! Finally, possibly convinced of the futility of his efforts, he gave up.

"They liked my work so well they moved me up to better dresses and pretty soon up to the good stuff!"

X

Ted

Theodore Smith was convinced that life would go well with him. Born January 24, 1909 in Temple, Texas, on the South side, deemed capable of inflicting a lasting social scar, Ted worried not. Had his father, a locomotive engineer for the Santa Fe Railroad, not moved to a more socially acceptable area, it would not have made a hill of beans. Ted had the good looks, charm and sincere liking for people that made him impervious to a snub.

His mother adored him. A devout Methodist, Lola spent her leisure time reading the Bible or listening to the Stella Dallas radio serial in her large sun-lit kitchen with her canary. Once, Ted's father gave her a tiny gold pin with a tiny diamond and her eyes filled with tears. He then committed the incredible blunder of saying it wasn't as though it was something store-bought or anything. He had just found it while out on a railroad run. Even so, Lola wore it always.

While such foibles in no way diminished Ted's respect for his father, it did make him aware that diplomacy, perhaps even an innocent lie here and there were essential in social graces.

For Ted, two events were memorable. The first was his discovery of girls at the precocious age of eight when his father relegated him to sleep on the back porch with the young housemaid. The second occurred at age seventeen, and this momentous event Ted recorded on the last page of his baby book in a firm hand:

> *Took first aeroplane ride 21, June 1926 — Some Thrill*

1926 was the golden age of aviation, of "barnstorming" and wing walking, when Charles Lindbergh had just flown from San Diego to New York. It was a time intrepid pilots earned extra dollars performing stunts and taking up adventuresome souls for a quick spin.

From that moment on, aviation became the essence of Ted's life, taking precedence even over girls and his club friends "Twenty Good Boys," with whom Ted shared roisterous adolescent adventures.

By 1927, determined to join the fledgling air force division of the army, Ted dropped out of high school and enlisted in the army in San Antonio. During this time, Colonel Billy Mitchell was court-martialed for insisting that Pearl Harbor was vulnerable to a Japanese air attack and America needed a strong and independent air force. Ted was in full accord with the insubordinate Mitchell and wanted nothing more than to be a member of this proposed Air Force.

In San Antonio, Ted acquired a good dose of discipline, a military bearing and a profound love for aviation. But a career in the flying cadets evaded him. Hoping to qualify for a West Point appointment, he returned to Temple and finished high school. But no West Point appointment was forthcoming.

So Ted set out to seek his fortune in the great metropolitan city of Dallas.

The position of art director of a major department store like Titche Goetinger's carried an intimidating amount of responsibility. Fortunately, Ruth had a good relationship with her co-workers and her advancement over artists of longer standing caused no apparent conflict. Virginia, one of her best artists and a close friend, made it clear she felt Ruth deserving of the promotion and harbored no resentment.

Mary, the copywriter, proved more problematic. Mary's striking good looks and facility of word, written and spoken, gave her a place of authority in the advertising department. And Ruth's promotion obviously antagonized her. It required no great shrewdness to perceive the cool glance and hasty salutation of a person wishing to erode the self-confidence of a perceived rival:

>   *"Mary was extremely bossy, always trying to take over," Ruth recalled. "Soon after my promotion, she came in furious and bawled out Virginia for punching in a few minutes late. Virginia started crying and I sailed into*

Mary, 'Don't you ever come in here and bawl out one of my artists. You get back where you belong!'"

If Mary seized on Virginia's remiss as a means to undermine Ruth's authority and competence, the swiftness of Ruth's retaliation took her totally by surprise. It was an error of judgment people not infrequently committed with Ruth, taking her soft manner as evidence of a quivering nature, a mistake Elaine had committed. Ruth recalled having once read a horoscope concerning her October Scorpio sign:

In character, you are honest and dependable, but when provoked there is no fury like your temperament and you lose your fine sensitivity, becoming biting and cynically astute.

Aware of a grain of truth in this and seeing that her point had been made, Ruth assumed a tone open to conciliation and hoped the matter would be forgotten. Due to an aura of attention Mary was receiving in another matter, she was of late in an unusually good mood. Romance often creates an atmosphere of speculation and titillation and everyone was excited about Mary's new boyfriend, commenting how good-looking he was. Amidst all the attention, Mary virtually glowed. What manner of man this might be, capable of contending with someone so bent on power, aroused only a passing curiosity in Ruth, but anything conducive to peace had her good wishes – especially at this busy time.

Christmas, traditionally a time of increased activity in the merchandising business, was only three weeks away and in spite of ominous predictions due to the recent "Wall Street Crash," Titche Goetinger's was busily preparing for the 1930 holiday season. That morning looking in on a group of young people putting up a Christmas display she had designed, Ruth was annoyed on finding them sprawled about, laughing and joking. When one young man, obviously the ringleader, called out, "Hey, Gorgeous, come over under this mistletoe," Ruth bristled and quickly made it clear what duties were expected of those who wished to keep their jobs. Everyone scrambled back to work.

Back at her desk, Ruth was putting the final touches on an illustration when a woman and her daughter came in. The mother was certain her daughter was an emerging Da Vinci, worthy of a job.

"She can sit on the back steps and draw everything out there!" the woman proclaimed, sweeping her arm across an imaginary horizon.

Viewing the girl's childish sketches, aware that her boss, Mr. Panders, would not have her, Ruth said it wasn't a matter of drawing *everything* out there and suggested the girl study their ads more carefully. Then recalling that the head buyer of ready-to-wear wanted to pow-wow on which of the incoming new holiday fashions would make a good Christmas ad, Ruth raced off.

She was just getting into the elevator when she almost collided head-on into "this incredibly handsome boy," a description later confided to artist friend Virginia. Actually the *boy* had already seen Ruth in the store and overheard someone comment, "Quite a dish, our new art director!" Now at close range, he could well agree with the term "quite a dish." Although on more careful consideration, he thought she looked more like one of those debutantes who went to finishing schools, rode English horses and received expensive art classes. Still, he was almost sure he had perceived a smile before she turned around to face forward. When she took another glance over her shoulder, he was sure it was in his direction and whispered to the friend beside him, "If that little redhead looks at me one more time, I'm going to marry her!"

And as Ruth was leaving the elevator, she looked back.

Returning to the office, Ruth was surprised to find an invitation to Mary's Christmas party on her desk. People were already commenting on the upcoming event and that Mary's parties were a thing not to be missed.

Correctly so, Ruth conceded on arriving at Mary's stylishly decorated apartment. Everything was perfection: the soft lighting and piano music, the canapés on silver trays and the punch in a crystal bowl. Mary herself in a fashionable gown was beautiful. Almost immediately Ruth noticed that the young man she had seen in the elevator was there. Tall and compellingly handsome, he was standing in the midst of a group explaining something of an apparently serious nature judging from the intent expressions of the group crowded about him. Seconds later, however, shouts of laughter made it clear he had hoaxed them with some joke – which had an immediate enlivening effect on the party. A second later, he glanced in her direction, excused himself and walked over.

"I'm Ted Smith," he said standing before her like an officer at attention. He had brown eyes and a boyish charm totally incongruous with the amount of male magnetism he projected.

"I'm Ruth Conerly," she replied, extending her hand.

"Far too young to be an art director."

"I was twenty-one in October."

He furrowed his brow. "Four months older than I am," he said gravely. "But don't worry, I find older women far more interesting." He was outrageous. But before the evening was over, he asked her for a date. And she accepted.

On the night of the date, Ruth had already decided what to wear but tried on everything in her closet before returning to her first choice. Ted's smile made his approval clear. Nor was he a person to defraud her expectations. Meticulously dressed, he reminded her of one of artist Leyendecker's suave male figures, causing the fashion artist in her to ask if he had ever thought of modeling.

"I'd have to think that over," he said.

They went to a restaurant and on exploring each other's backgrounds, were amazed at the similarities. Both were from small Texas towns. Ted's father was a locomotive engineer for the Santa Fe Railroad while Ruth's father had been an auditor with the Texas & Pacific Railroad, before starting his own business. Ted's maternal grandfather had fought in the Civil War, "For the Confederacy!" he clarified with a flourish of Southern gallantry. Ted's descriptions of his grandmother Julia Bessonette Wylie and her home with white columns brought recollections of her grandmother Othermama, always a source of anecdotes.

Ted said he enjoyed art, music, reading, and had once tried his hand at writing, "a couple of short stories that never got any publisher excited." He said he was much impressed by a new writer, fellow called Ernest Hemingway, with a tremendous descriptive force in his book, "Farewell to Arms." Surprised, Ruth confessed her own fascination for books and reading, how she had wanted to be a sculptor and had gone into commercial art because of the pay, but hoped one day to illustrate novels and books on history, like N. C. Wyeth did for "Treasure Island."

Ted laughed heartily. "Those nightmarish pirate scenes of Long John Silver and Captain Billy Bones almost scared the daylights out of me as a boy. Terrific marriage of great literature and fine art!"

He then shared his dream of how he was currently working in display but his real ambition was to become a pilot, have his own plane and aviation company.

"Just like railroads transport people and goods everywhere today, aeroplanes are the thing of the future!" he declared. "It won't be too long before planes will be taking people all over the world!"

He had a visionary's enthusiasm remindful of her father, which provoked the Lizzie practicality in her to warn, "Careful, careful!" But when the waiter brought the bill and Ted could not find his wallet, she readily paid and even accepted a second date.

On their second date, they went out dancing. He was an incredible dancer. He knew exactly how to hold a girl and guide her steps and gaze into her eyes. He even had good breath. And this time, he did not lose his wallet.

It was not until after their third date that Ruth learned something about Ted that left her dumbfounded and horrified. He was Mary's boyfriend. The one everyone in the office had been talking about. That she had not suspected this seemed incredible in retrospect. She could blame the oversight on her busy schedule or her rule of thumb to avoid becoming involved in co-workers' private lives. Certainly she was not one to deliberately steer her course into trouble. But whatever the excuse, the oversight now took on the most chaotic and horrendous prospects for office relations.

She couldn't even back down. She was in love. For the first time in her life, she was head over heels, smack-dab in love. And right now, her only interest was to know what he was going to do about the situation.

"I broke off with Mary after my first date with you," Ted said matter-of-factly.

"Does Mary know you've been seeing me?"

"I have no idea."

"Was your relation with Mary serious?"

"Whatever, it's a thing of the past. The important thing is that I've found the girl I want to marry."

For the second time that day, Ruth was dumbfounded – but not horrified. Try as she might to keep her composure, she felt her spine tingle, her toes curl and was sure she was being lifted lightly onto a cloud.

In the following days, they seemed to be constantly running into each other, not always by accident, and Ruth never knew what plan Ted might invent for their next outing, from a bus ride and hot dogs in the park to dining out at the elegant Adolphus.

But when Mary stormed into Ruth's office shouting, "You little snake in the grass! Do you think you can just take over everything?" Ruth had no doubt why Mary was madder than hornets.

"Mary, I'm awfully sorry," Ruth said weakly. "I didn't mean to take your friend away."

Mary's eyes flashed wide and incredulous. "Friend?" she mimicked sarcastically. "Why you priggish little ninny!" And after delivering a scalding assortment of contemptuous phrases, turned on her heel and stalked out, slamming the door.

Ruth was left with the clear impression that Ted and Mary's relationship had not been of the kindergarten variety.

On hearing the story, Ted could barely keep a straight face. Under duress, he admitted he and Mary had been living together.

"Living together!" Ruth exclaimed horrified and in a next breath accused, "You lied!"

"I did not lie," Ted asserted. "Not talking about others is not lying." He did not consider it gentlemanly, chivalrous, nor in good taste to talk about other women, as some men did. He defended his position brilliantly. And though it was all very persuasive, Ruth shook her head saying she needed time to get a perspective on all that had happened. In the meantime he should refrain from calling or asking her out.

During the following days, Ruth berated herself. Here she had let herself be swept off her feet by some boy who couldn't offer her any solid economic security. With his looks and charm, women would always be chasing him and probably vice-versa. She could think of a dozen reasons to break off and never see him again. But after three days of misery, no logic mattered.

And that day in the store when he grabbed her hand and whispered, "Don't tell anyone, but the building's on fire!" and led her to the fire escape, she ran docilely alongside. With one passionate kiss on the fire escape – like a thunderbolt sending electric current down to her toes – she knew this boyish Lothario was the romantic encounter of a lifetime. And when he looked into her eyes and said, "Marry me!" nothing else mattered. They were in love and it was totally illogical, insane and wonderful.

On March 22, 1931, The Dallas Daily Times Herald carried a large photograph of Ruth at the top of its Society and Clubs section bearing the title: *Miss Ruth Conerly became Mrs. Theodore H. Smith.* After a weekend honeymoon, Ruth returned to work, cheeks glowing. "Mary would hardly speak to me after that," Ruth recalled.

But the tense situation was not to be long-lasting...

XI

New York, New York

They had been married only three months when Ted announced they must go to New York.

"New York!" Ruth exclaimed in dismay.

"New York!" Ted affirmed. "Where the big companies are. A person who makes it in New York is tops anywhere!"

For Ruth, it was totally irrational:

"Mr. Panders, my boss, nearly had a fit. He said we were too young. I was top artist with them, but in New York I'd be just a drop in the bucket. Even the president of the company came to talk to me. 'Why Ruth, you have places to go here. You might even be a vice-president, you've done so well.' But Ted was determined. With the stock market crash, things were getting worse, he said – the bread lines, men without jobs. Ted felt New York was the place to go. I didn't know it then, but he had lost his job."

Reducing their belongings to a minimum, they packed the essentials in two suitcases and set out, hitchhiking.

"We had the time of our lives, especially in Virginia. It was beautiful. We rented a car and drove all over, then went back to thumbing. Once when a car was coming, Ted said, 'Ruth, stick out your leg – the good one.' And I almost fell over laughing."

But on arriving in New York, they met a sobering reality: they had only one hundred dollars left and it was getting cold. They rented a furnished room, bought a sack of potatoes and set aside the few remaining dollars for bus fare. Late that night, they looked out the window. It was snowing.

The next day Ruth set out with her portfolio of samples to look for work and could barely believe her good luck.

"I found a job!" she shouted coming through the door. "The very first place I walked into! Metro Associated Services, an agency I've long admired, and they hired me right off!"

Ruth and Ted shouted and jumped up and down until someone below rapped on the ceiling, then they ran out into the street and threw snowballs at each other.

In the following weeks, Ruth worked hard in Metro's fast-paced bullpen formed by staff and crew. Dave Shapiro, president and founder of the business, was a human dynamo. Meticulous, always stylishly dressed with custom suits and haberdashery, elevated shoes to build up his height, Dave had an exacting eye for detail. It was art in a hurry, fast-paced, demanding, challenging... and exhausting. But it made Metro number one in publishing and newspaper advertising services.

Coming home at night, Ruth cooked their meager fare of potatoes, washed and ironed Ted's shirt while he described his day looking for work. He made the miles walked sound like a comedy of windmills toppled and adversaries slain, but his thinning shoe soles testified to a different reality. Exhausted, they would fall into bed, snuggling close, as much in passion as to ward off the cold.

"At first I did mostly fashion for Metro, little compositions like I did for Imperial Sugar. One evening I had just finished a job and was standing off to see how it carried when I saw one detail I had to correct and took a brush and ink in my hand – and spilled it all over the illustration! I didn't as a rule swear, but I did then and this very nice lady next to me said, 'Mrs. Smith, would you please not use language like that!'

'Well, you would too,' I cried, 'if you'd done something so stupid and had to do this whole illustration all over again!' "

It was late that night as she walked home. She was approaching the corner grocery when she saw the young thug and was gripped with a queasy foreboding. Almost every night he would be standing there and just as she was alongside, he would whistle, a long lascivious, repulsive sound. Tonight, however, as she walked past, he made a vulgar pantomime and began following her. Heart pounding, she quickened her pace and as she was nearing her building, fumbling in her purse for the key, she could hear the sound of his breathing, feel its vapor at her neck. Then suddenly the door flew open and an arm jerked her inside.

"Stay here!" Ted ordered and went out. From inside the door, she could hear voices rising in a crescendo of angry words, then a loud impact and a thud. As the door opened, she felt terror, then overwhelming relief seeing it was Ted. Beyond him, she got a fleeting glimpse of her pursuer sprawled on the sidewalk outside.

The next morning, peering cautiously out the door, Ruth was startled when an elderly woman opened her apartment door. She said the fellow bothering them was a local thug who made everyone's life miserable. That day another neighbor gave Ted a fuller story. The fellow was the son of a local mobster, far worse than his father though, seeming to take pleasure in every kind of perversity, tormenting people just for the fun of it. Soon men were tipping their hats to Ted and the corner grocer said the whole neighborhood was talking about how Ted had knocked that thug cold on the sidewalk. "Just what he needed. You be careful though."

They were down to the last few potatoes when Ruth got her first paycheck. They bought food and were enjoying an evening meal by candlelight when Ted announced he had found a job in a department store, not far from where Ruth worked. It was a night to celebrate!

Ruth had been at Metro barely three months when Dave Shapiro, the president, called her into his office.

"Sit down, sit down," he said waving her to a chair. "Ruth, we have a rule here that when an artist is working out all right, we like to have them sign a contract. I thought you'd be pleased to know I want you to sign on with us for three years. It'll guarantee your present salary of thirty dollars a week!"

Ruth said she thought that was nice... not much money though.

Dave considered a moment, then nodded in agreement. "We'll add a clause to raise your salary from time to time."

On meeting Ted at lunchtime, Ruth told him about the contract.

"Don't you sign," Ted warned.

"But Dave made it sound as though they might not keep me if I don't sign. They have to be sure of their people, he said."

"Don't you do it!" Ted insisted. "Tell him you have to show it to your husband first."

Returning to the office, Ruth was afraid.

"I was scared to death I'd lose my job. But Dave let me take the contract home. After looking it over, Ted said, 'Tell them you'll sign, but only for a year and then agree on price after that.' The next day I was just sure I'd lose my job, but I stood firm. Dave acted as though I was being childish, but agreed to a one-year contract like Ted said he would.

The year was not yet up when I began to suspect my work was being noticed. One day one of the girls in the office asked if Dave had asked me to sign a contract. When I said yes, she said, 'That's quite a compliment. You and the top wash artist are the only ones with a contract.'

You mean you don't have a contract? I was given to think it was required of everyone.

The girl shook her head. 'Nah, they can fire me tomorrow.'

After that I began to open my eyes. At Metro I never knew which companies were using the illustrations I was doing, but one day two of the girls brought in some newspapers. My illustrations were running in Stern's advertisements! That was a big fancy store. Next thing I knew, Stern's had called. They wanted me to deliver a drawing of theirs in person. Dave nearly had a fit! He didn't want me going over there one bit. But they were customers.

On arriving at Stern's, I was escorted right up to the executive offices, where they said, 'We understand you have a contract with Dave Shapiro for $30 a week and it's up. How would you like to come work for us for $250 a week?'

I could barely believe my ears. That was a thousand dollars a month! But before I could answer, they made an even better offer. 'Or maybe you'd prefer to free-lance at home and we'll guarantee you enough work to earn the same.' I accepted the offer to free-lance at home on the spot. Dave was really mad then! He filed a suit against Stern's for taking me away from him, but he didn't win. Later I did a lot more work for Metro."

On Ted's advice, Ruth hired an agent, Vanvalkenburgh, who brought in additional work. Not long after, Ruth hired another agent, Harvey Hepworth, who negotiated more work at higher prices.

> *"Soon I was getting more work than I could handle from all the biggest stores: Macys, Saks, Best and Company, Bloomingdale's, Gimbels, Bergdorf Goodman, and working faster than ever, money just rolling in.*
>
> *Not long after, we leased a larger apartment on East 28th Street and had it professionally decorated with carved furniture and white drapes. We hired a maid, Lovey, whose mother, Galloway, helped out with the cleaning. At Lovey's insistence we bought a car, an Oldsmobile, so Lovey's husband could drive it and wear a cap."*

Ted too was offered a better job with a large department store. "I am now the assistant production manager in the advertising department," he wrote home to his parents. "It's my line of work. I thrive at bossing people."

Impeccably dressed in new shoes and camelhair coat, Ted was barely settled at his new desk when the art director called him into his office saying he had a business deal to propose. If Ted would get Ruth to do their best artwork, they could juice up the price forty-percent and give him a kickback. "A kind of commission," he explained, "Only private like. All the art directors do it with free lancers."

"I don't think Ruth would accept that," Ted replied.

"I'm sure you can convince her."

"I wouldn't try. I am willing to forget this conversation."

Talking it over that night, Ted and Ruth agreed he had done the right thing. But the next day Ted found his belongings in a paper sack on top of his desk, a sobering moment coming at a time when jobs were virtually non-existent. But this only substantiated their conviction that the art director was an unscrupulous sort and Ted had done the *right* thing.

"You'll find another job," Ruth assured.

And surprisingly Ted *did* find another job. "With a large desk and all the amenities, just like I like," he proudly described to Ruth and in a letter home to his parents. "Telephone, memo-pad, all the little things that go to make a fellow a big shot."

His boss was a mess though – nervous, tense and harried. A middle-aged man in the throes of a divorce, his private life was a shambles and rendered him incapable of concentrating on business. With increasing frequency he would drop by Ted's office with more work and the latest episode in the ongoing saga of his private and legal entanglements. Ted's good-humored quips left him cheered and even laughing. An hour later he would be back, trundling some new crisis and more work.

Convinced that a home-cooked meal would cheer the poor fellow up, Ted invited his boss home to dinner. Ruth, ever amenable, planned a four-course dinner with flowers and candles. Lovey, their cook, perceiving the importance of the event, spared no effort.

The evening proved a total fiasco.

Tipsy on arrival, their guest downed two dry martinis in quick succession, then moved onto the subject of his decidedly sordid divorce. Sitting down to dinner, he asked for another Martini and in slurred speech came to the formidable conclusion that, "Women are all pussy with no brains!"

Ruth's condescending smile wilted. No Sullins etiquette had prepared her for such a jolt.

Ted's reaction was more direct and swift. "No one uses that kind of language in front of my wife," he declared and with one slug knocked him cold. After pouring a pitcher of water on him, Ted threw him out.

Reviewing the evening's events, they lamented the loss of the job – doubtlessly lost – but agreed that Ted had acted *appropriately*. Still, on looking for another job and finding none, Ted began to have doubts in himself. Day after day he went out, returning empty-handed and more discouraged. As the weeks slipped by, an ever-growing despondency began taking hold. The fact that thousands of men over the country were jobless and hungry, unable to provide for their families, somber-faced men queued up in breadlines, was of no consolation to his broken self-esteem. And on seeing Ted sink into a spiral of depression, Ruth felt her heart go out to him.

One evening hearing his heavy steps in the hallway and seeing him collapse into a chair, Ruth ran to his side. No longer capable of holding back, Ted poured forth a torrent of self-abasement and frustration, how he had imagined himself some golden boy, a magnet of success, and was little more than a panhandler, a gigolo, dependent on her. He felt useless, helpless, worthless. He didn't know what to do or where to turn. And seeing him there, the invincible Ted crying like a child, Ruth thought her heart would break.

Hadn't his decision to go to New York proved magically prophetic for her? Hadn't his Svengali-like advice catapulted her into New York's big league as a fashion illustrator? How unjust that his dreams and ambitions should lie in wreckage.

Her mind raced for something that might bring back the Ted she had known, good-humored, incapable of doubts.

Surely there was something he could do – something spectacular, they might do together. And seeing his eyes on her, she began enumerating qualities: how he was never fazed by challenge, always giving encouragement to others, making people laugh. Well, knocking them flat now and then, but only when justified.

"Why don't we just put on our thinking caps and figure this out!" Ruth exclaimed. "What can we do really well, the two of us together, that no one else can do?"

And soon they were tossing ideas about, speculating with ever-growing enthusiasm. Ted had a sense of humor and a flair for words. She had a knack for drawing a figure from any angle in correct perspective right out of her head. Many a time artists working beside her would ask her to do a sketch as a guide.

And suddenly the thought came! Why not publish a magazine, a *How To Do It* for the fashion artist? There must be hundreds of artists out there needing advice, ideas and encouragement. Ted could do the writing, and she the illustrations. It would explain basic techniques like wash, ink, light and shadow and how to *visualize* a figure in one's mind.

"Hey, that's it!" Ted exclaimed. "Why not call it The Visualizer!"

The next day Ted began writing. After two years of hearing art, his advice had the ring of authority tinged with his characteristic upbeat humor:

> *When your work reaches the point where it has a market value, you begin to look for a place to sell your skill more profitably. This stage is critical. The artist, a person of great sensitivity, becomes discouraged unless results are evident. Perhaps even hungry. A day spent selling artwork requires two to recuperate. As a result, the artist may decide to hire an agent – not bad business judgment at all. In touch with the market and adept at criticism, an agent earns a percentage of all work sold, giving him an inherent interest in your success!*

Script written, art incorporated, Ted secured a copyright. Naming himself publisher, he sent the first issue to press. Far from any colossal success, the first issue barely broke even, but people in the trade assured them that for a *first* this was remarkable. For the second issue Ted interviewed commercial artist Dean Cornwall and fashion illustrator Helen McDonald and secured an advertisement from Grumbacher Company, supplier of artists' materials. He also added a notice that subscriptions were available, checks to be directed to The Visualizer's office at 160 Fifth Avenue!

Not only did orders come in, Ted's debut in the publishing world brought a reverberating effect on Ruth's career. Reporters sought interviews and questioned her about the latest trends in fashion.

And the publicity brought more sales and checks.

"One day we just sat on the floor throwing the checks in the air. Wee-e," Ruth recalled.

Soon there were invitations to the Stork Club and new friends like composer George Gershwin and his brother Ira, lyricist, both amateur artists. Ted admired George, but liked Ira far more, a gentleman always, making Ted feel more comfortable having him around Ruth.

Newly-weds in mid-depression, they hitchhiked to New York arriving with $100 in their pocket.

Within two years, Ruth became one of New York's top fashion illustrators. With maids, agents and invitations to the Stork club, "We were like kids throwing the checks in the air!"

For two Texas kids, New York was revealing a compelling world of glitz and glamour. On returning from a cruise to Cuba, where they stayed at Havana's Hotel Nacional and danced to the magical musical of Ernesto Lucuona, Ruth saw a notice in the newspaper.

Someone was selling a farm in Connecticut. Fifteen acres with a stream running through it, it had an old house and the original deeds dating back to the American Revolution. It was love at first sight, responding to a deep-grained need. Success was temporal and illusive. Land was security. Ruth paid cash, negotiating a considerable price reduction.

Ted was pleased with the farm. "Quite necessary," he remarked, "to have one's *petite trianon* away from the city to fish, make martinis and grill a proper steak."

Undoubtedly they were sitting pretty.

Sitting Pretty

XII

Fame, Fortune and Disaster

They had managed on $30 a week that first year in New York. Hungry and barely subsisting, but they made it. It was illogical that success should cause trouble. But paradoxically success brought problems never imagined.

Away from her art board, dressed up and made-up, Ruth was a beauty and Ted a striking figure of a man. He had a compelling charisma and easy rapport with persons in the art world and cafe society. On entering a club or art exhibit, they caused a flurry of whispers. On the dance floor in Ted's arms, Ruth danced as she had always dreamed, under crystal chandeliers.

But businessman, Ted was not.

And in two major aspects they were at opposite poles. While Ruth had a dogged perseverance for work, and success augmented that perseverance, keeping her virtually glued to her drawing board, Ted had an uncontrollable itchiness to be constantly on the move. He was never so happy as when going places, meeting people and magnanimously picking up the bill. And when opportunity gave him access to large sums of money, his open-handedness knew no bounds. If some unforeseen expense arose, such as having forgotten to pay the printer, Ted would go to Ruth for the money saying he would return it, as soon as some check came in. The sums, however, were seldom repaid and when Ruth insisted on an accounting, he was incapable of understanding the importance of it. Why worry? Wasn't the money flowing in? And instead of putting order into his accounts, he would bring her a gift, like that exquisite replica of a diamond bracelet from Tiffany's that movie stars were wearing over elbow length gloves.

Opening the velvet case, Ruth could hardly believe her eyes. Suddenly memories came surging forth, of how at the worst moment her father had bought that gold thimble edged in tiny diamonds that Lizzie threw against the wall in tears. And how her mother's practicality could put a gloom on his heart. But Ted's expression was so full of boyish delight, anticipating her reaction, Ruth swallowed the lump in her throat and threw her arms about him, laughing and crying at the same time.

But by 1934, it was clear that they were living far beyond their means, spending recklessly, saving nothing. And that their brainchild, The Visualizer, had become the instigator of a lifestyle far in excess of the income it was producing. Swamped with bills, Ruth demanded that Ted reduce his expenditures. Either that or look for a job. When he replied evasively, elaborating on the many contacts a magazine required and the difficulties of finding a job in these hard times, Ruth wondered if it was an aversion to anything that might fetter his freedom to travel, socialize and enjoy life on a grand style.

Finally, with their reserves virtually gone and seeing how each check she received was already earmarked for an awaiting expense, it became clear that not even her own sizable income could cover the cost of it all. And as Ruth's frustration grew, her patience ran out, leading to anger, discord and recriminations.

The last straw came at the worst moment – when Ted's parents came for a visit. Ruth understood his wanting to impress them but the succession of restaurants and shopping sprees seemed never ending. The night before they were to leave, Ted and his father came home in the wee hours of the morning and Ruth awoke with a peculiar uneasiness about the $250 check that Ted had offered to deposit, almost too anxiously. On asking him for the deposit slip, she watched with sinking heart as he searched his pockets endlessly for it. Finally he admitted to having spent the money.

"For chrissake!" he protested. It was his father's last night! He would pay it back.

Right there, Ruth reached her limit. Had he lost his mind? They had lived on $30 a week and he could throw away $250 in one night? Take a check she urgently needed for art supplies and mindlessly fritter it away? And then lie about it?

It was precisely there, she insisted, where the major difference between them existed. While for her honesty was essential in any relationship, for him it was something to be used as a last resort, when all else failed. And at that moment Ruth decided she was totally disenchanted with Ted, her marriage and the whole shebang!

So great was the disillusion that she was incapable of hiding her anger and frustration. To the point that everyone around them – Lovey the maid, Yvonne her French model, Vanvalkenburgh and Harvey Hepworth, her two agents – was aware of the tension in the Smith household.

Especially Harvey. Well-dressed with a meticulously trimmed mustache, Harvey had brought Ruth many of her best accounts. A valued asset, Harvey could nevertheless be problematic. Only a few days earlier, while discussing a fashion figure, Harvey had begun elaborating on how a moderately hooked nose, classically called aquiline – much like Ruth had – was really very attractive. And was Ruth aware that the famous temptress Cleopatra had such a nose?

"Yes," Ruth replied. She was aware.

Encouraged, Harvey went on to elaborate on history's great seductresses and that Ruth might give some thought to the children they could have with her talent and his nose.

Reminiscent of Bernard Shaw's famous response to a similar proposition, Ruth replied, "And what if our children were to have my nose and your talent, Harvey?" and went back to work.

But Harvey would not be put off. Galvanized by Ruth's differences with Ted, Harvey threw caution to the winds and made still another more forthright suggestion: "Ruth, why don't you just leave Ted and marry me? Think what an incredible team we'd make!"

Ruth was not in a good mood. Turning around slowly and assuming her man-to-man business posture with elbow on knee, forewarning of trouble, she said. "Harvey, are you sure it's me you're really interested in? Or the style of life to which you'd like to become accustomed?"

Harvey's stormy exit was punctuated by a loud slam of the front door. An hour later his boss, the agency president, called Ruth. "Good God, Ruth, what did you say to Harvey this time? He absolutely refuses to work for you any more. I've never seen him so mad!"

Ruth regretted losing Harvey. He was a good agent, a valuable critic. She realized she could have handled the situation more delicately without blistering his ego that way. But she was not in a mood to retract now and other more weighty developments were soon to claim her attention. Minutes after Harvey's stormy exit, she got a call from Bert

Pagano of Pagano Studios, one of her best clients. Bert's major account was Sears and Roebuck with its catalogues. Complying with one deadline for Sear's, Ruth had done thirty-one figures in a day and night for the desperate Bert. It was a mutually profitable relationship.

So when Bert said, "Ruth, can you come down to my office now?" she knew it was something important.

She was barely seated in Bert's office when he came directly to the point, "Ruth, I want you to go to Paris!" And before she could catch her breath, Bert blazed on with the details. His best customers wanted to upgrade their catalogues with a section of *haute couture* designer fashions. Ruth knew all their lines, and as a top fashion artist for all the fancy stores in New York, she knew the snooty kind of thing his clients wanted to incorporate into their new catalogues. He wanted her to go to Paris and see what the Parisian *couturiers* were up to for the fall season to make it a smashing first edition.

"Ruth, few artists can capture the lines of high-styled clothes in a few brief strokes," Bert explained. "I'll see to it you have first-class accommodations on the next ship leaving for Europe. Can I count on you for this?"

Ruth's heart pounded. Paris! To preview the fall fashions in Paris, always at the vanguard of fashion! To study the techniques used by Parisian artists, adept in high style, would be an incredible experience! While studying art and French at Sullins, she had dreamed of going to Paris. She could visit the Louvre, examine at close range the brush strokes of the masters, see the sculptures of Auguste Rodin. Incredible! How could she refuse!

But refuse she must, of course. A married woman traveling to Paris alone? Totally improper! Ted would go in a minute, of course, but their economic situation, already in chaos, would collapse. And yet, somehow Ruth could not bring herself to refuse outright. Although not a person to procrastinate at the expense of others, she asked for twenty-four hours to consider, to at least hold on to the illusion overnight.

That evening on arriving home, she found Ted playing poker with Frank Owen. A gifted artist, originator of the popular comic strip, *Filibert,* Frank was from Clarksville,

Texas. Ruth sincerely liked Frank and his gentle humor and tended to overlook his inclination to drink heavily. But aware it was Lovey's day free and she would have to cook and serve dinner, she suddenly felt overwhelmingly tired with sore, aching feet, and fed up of working herself to a bone in this double-whammy role of dutiful wife and professional artist.

"Anything new?" Ted called out good-humoredly.

Laying her gloves and hat on the hall table, Ruth greeted Frank then replied, "Yes, as a matter of fact, I'm going to Paris." Later alone with Ted, she made still another revelation, "And on my return, I'm getting a divorce!"

Passport To Paris

"Ruth, few artists can capture high-style in a few brief strokes. I'll get you first-class accommodations on the next ship."

XIII

Paris, Fashion and a French Count

"I was sent to Paris to cover the fashion shows and bought myself a Schiaparelli original," Ruth told reporters on her return, giving the impression that nothing more transcending occurred that summer of 1934 in Paris...

Before her departure, Ruth wrote her mother telling her of the problems she was having with Ted and that she was considering a divorce. Realizing there had never been a divorce in the family, Ruth could only imagine what Lizzie's reaction would be.

Once aboard-ship, however, she felt an isolating comfort from her troubles. On seeing her suite in first class as promised, she was cheered. With decks and dining paired with the guest's level of accommodation, Bert Pagano obviously felt it important she get a preview of the atmosphere of *haute monde* she must transmit in her illustrations.

"Well then, Your Ladyship, step to it!" And while dressing for dinner that evening Ruth called forth all of her artistry.

Only a few clues remain of the man she met that first evening of her transatlantic voyage, other than his being French, a count, owner of a company that made soap and essences, and that they were introduced at the captain's table. In a never forgotten description to her sister Janey, then an impressionable fifteen-year-old, Ruth confided, "He had the most beautifully shaped legs. And when he stood on the deck, the wind would whip his linen pants against his legs in a most provocative way."

Once on land, however, Ruth put the moonlit evenings on deck aside, certain he too would promptly forget. He had his responsibilities and she must pay strict attention to her work, not let any romantic tomfoolery cloud her mind.

Her first day at work substantiated that decision. The Paris staff in charge of directing her steps was keenly attuned to the season's fashion shows and social events and briefed her extensively as to her itinerary. One staff member advised her to "always wear white," while another with a knack for making himself obnoxious, made it clear he was horrified they had sent someone so young.

"*Mon Dieu,* how could a mere girl from Texas comprehend art, fashion, Paris – a world so totally different from *Texas!*"

Turning her most withering Sullins look on him – as though looking down at some obnoxious, ill-trained dog, Ruth replied in impeccable French, a word she would never have uttered in English, *"Merde!"*

For long moments he stood dumbstruck, choked and then broke out laughing.

The next day the count called. And, try as she might, Ruth could not hide her delight. She refused his invitation to dine out, explaining that her work demanded getting a good night's sleep to be on her toes the following morning. He agreed entirely, secured a copy of her schedule and appeared everywhere she went. How was it possible she could be in Paris and not visit its many historical sights, savor a bit of *"la vie de Paris,"* necessary to embody her art with the true Paris spirit?

Adept in overwhelming any argument, he proved himself as agile with Paris traffic as in seeing she arrived punctually at each show and appointment. Knowledgeable in architecture, history and little-known stories concerning famous places and historical events, he took her to Versailles, the Louvre and Paris's tiniest park, where a young man was playing a lute in the misty rain. They went to an out-of-the-way Russian restaurant, ate caviar on egg halves and Russian salad to the music of a violin. He made her feel happy and totally adored.

Shortly before Ruth was to return to New York, he took her to meet his mother, who lived in a multi-towered home surrounded by gardens. Slender with white skin, dressed totally in black, she signaled a maid standing by to serve them coffee from an ornate silver service. And though gracious and cordial, she could not completely conceal her horror that her only son was determined to marry an American, an *artiste*, a non-Catholic, not yet divorced?

"Do you have any children, my dear?" she asked finally and Ruth could almost perceive her sigh of relief when Ruth replied, "No, I have no children."

That evening as they walked in the gardens of his home, the count took a cutting from a fern she admired and gave it to her. "Take this as my pledge of love to you," he said. "And promise me that regardless of any obstacle, you will return and marry me."

And Ruth promised.

She promised that on her return to New York, she would fulfill her professional obligations, divorce Ted and return to Paris.

That night at the hotel, the clerk handed Ruth a letter. It was from her mother. Almost fearfully she opened the envelope and read Lizzie's words:

> "*Regarding your intention to divorce Ted, in my experience, basic character never changes. And if Ted does not like to work and squanders everything you make, you should seek a divorce. But now, before there are any children.*"

At first impact, Ruth was amazed. Her mother's advice seemed totally at odds with the canons of behavior Lizzie had always inculcated in her children. But after thinking it over, Ruth was less surprised. Didn't Lizzie invariably reduce things to the practical?

On her return voyage, the count's fern tucked under her hatband, Ruth recalled the "unsinkable" Titanic and its fateful maiden voyage only twenty-two years earlier. Images of that night – the men at their cards, the women exquisitely dressed, the slight jarring, the questions building to poignant last scenes, the desolation of partings. All this seemed to transpose on the scenes in this crossing of 1934 with its more tailored lines and seductive clinging gowns, an elegance of its own. 1912 was an epoch immortalized by artist Charles Gibson with his famous Gibson girl and his beautiful, sad-eyed American heiresses forced into loveless marriages to old men with titles. In contrast, this 1934 was an epoch in which her fashion illustrations would be marking the trend that thousands of women would be copying. And how different her own story. Only the truest love could motivate a handsome French count to be so determined to marry her!

Ted breathed a sigh of relief. After multiple inquiries he had just learned that Ruth was on her way home. In spite of their troubles, he was sure he could win her back.

Their cook Lovey, sensing the precariousness of the situation, had everything readied with Ruth's favorite meal, squabs and wild rice by candlelight. After surveying the table setting and giving his approval, Ted went out and bought a dozen red roses. And a tube of toothpaste – proof he was prepared to give way even on the issue of where the toothpaste should be squeezed. On a card he wrote: *Greater love hath no man. Squeeze me wherever. I love you, Ted,* and propped the card against the toothpaste.

All to no avail. Ruth would not let him come close to her:

"I was determined to leave Ted. He promised everything under the sun, and I felt sorry for him, but I had made up my mind."

In the ensuing days, Ruth worked hard, paying no heed to Ted, thinking only of her count and trying to complete her work for Pagano quickly and return to Paris.

With Ted's every effort thwarted, his anxiety increased with each passing day. Finally, heartsick with despair, he confided to a close friend that Ruth was leaving him and he was at a loss as to what he might do.

"Get her pregnant," the friend, an obstetrician, advised.

"How can I get her pregnant," Ted countered, "if she won't even talk to me?"

"A bit of gentle persuasion, perhaps?"

Ted immediately discarded the idea. Totally unacceptable. Ruth had an innate earthiness, but force, when her mind was set, would never work. She'd never speak to him again. Besides for a gentleman, it was unspeakable

Sitting miserably at her dressing table, smelling the fragrances so remindful of her, Ted felt a vise on his heart like a dull ache. Opening a drawer, he saw a letter from Ruth's mother, Lizzie. Almost absently he opened it and read..

.. people don't change and if Ted does not like to work and squanders everything you make, you should get a divorce. But now before there are any children.

The words – *before there are any children* – virtually jumped out of the page, bringing his friend's advice vividly to mind. It seemed that the only chance to save his marriage was to get Ruth pregnant. He had no choice.

"I'm so-oo happy to meet you," the woman exclaimed, introducing herself to Ruth as the doctor's mother. "My son thinks so much of Ted and has told me so much about you, how talented and successful you are, such a wonderful artist. And just how much do you earn, my dear?"

Amazed at such a question, Ruth nevertheless answered candidly.

The woman's eyes bulged, then she smiled wistfully. "Oh my, isn't that a handsome sum yet. How I wish my son should find himself such a fine wife as you!"

Seconds later, the doctor, a close friend of Ted, opened his office door and greeted Ruth with effusive warmth. Talking animatedly, he ushered her into his office. After reading the lab report confirming that Ruth was indeed pregnant, he smiled broadly, making much to do about the event. Finally handing her a booklet entitled "Suggestions for care during

Pregnancy," he insisted she call him for anything at any moment. Ruth smiled stoically.

At home she recalled her mother's advice about divorcing Ted *before* there were any children. She recalled the count's mother and her question, *"Do you have any children, my dear?"* And suddenly, like Confucius, an Othermama story came to mind.

"And you never fell in love with anyone else, Othermama?"

"Yes, I fell in love once, very much so. We had arranged to meet by the train station. I had decided to run off from your Grandpa Buck. I had my suitcases and two children beside me and my heart was pounding as his carriage came toward us. But on seeing the children, his expression changed. And right there he turned around.

For a long time, I stood there, certain my heart would break. Finally I went home. After a time, I forgot about him... almost."

For days, Ruth could not gather the courage to write to her beloved count. When she finally made the decision, she stared at the empty page, wondering what to say.

Make it simple, she rebuked herself. No reasons, no putting him over a barrel, she had simply decided not to divorce Ted. In closing, she sent regards to his mother, asking him to thank her for her graciousness.

A few months later, the count came to New York and called. Could they meet and talk? By then, prominently pregnant, she did not want him to see her and overrode all his arguments. Yes, she admitted, she thought of him often. The piece of fern he had given her was growing and would always remind her of him.

In years to come, Ruth's recollections of her French count faded, but in spite of innumerable changes of home and cities, the count's fern survived and flourished. And whenever someone would exclaim over its magnificence and ask for a clipping, Ruth would oblige, often mentioning that it came from the gardens of a French count she had once known.

XIV

Baby Roses, Juggernaut, Catastrophe

The magnitude of his role of expectant father fostered a new resolve in Ted. Attentive to Ruth in every aspect, he applied himself to The Visualizer with renewed diligence. Gradually Ted's efforts to win back Ruth's affections began to have effect. She started laughing at his jokes and responding to his embraces. One night after going to a movie in which the heroine's name was Sharon, they decided that their next child, after this first boy, would be named Sharon.

Then in the early hours of May 10, 1935, Ruth awoke and nudged Ted. "I have a pain."

Ted sat bolt upright in bed. "A pain? Holy Mackerel!" His son was about to be born! Nervous and stumbling, he called the doctor and rushed Ruth to Murray Hill Hospital. All day he paced the floor, speculating on every horrible mischance. When the nurse announced he was the father of a fine healthy girl, Ted was a nervous wreck.

"A girl?" Ted repeated, "A daughter?" It took a moment for this unforeseen happening to register but after verifying that all was well with Ruth, he, the doctor and friend Ira Gershwin decided that after so wearying an ordeal, a celebration was in order. A real bash!

As the night and festivity progressed, more friends and well-wishers joined them, including, by one account, Ira's brother, George Gershwin, all calling Ruth from various bars and showing up in the wee hours of the morning, arms full of pink baby roses.

"We asked ourselves," they recited in slurred unison, "what more appropriate for a beautiful new mother and her baby daughter? And we all agreed – pink baby roses!"

The next day when the nurse asked what name they had chosen for the baby, Ted and Ruth replied, "Sharon."

"And the middle name?"

"Elizabeth, after my mother?" Ruth suggested.

"Most appropriate," Ted agreed, making a supreme effort not to show any sarcasm. That same day he went down to Macy's and ordered the finest baby carriage, embossed with gold initials and new uniforms for their maid Lovey.

Ted ordered the
finest baby carriage
with gold initials

And new uniforms
for nursemaid Lovey

Ted's enthusiasm was still visibly strong in his editorial for the Fall edition of The Visualizer:

"She's from Texas, she's redheaded and likes turnip greens. Started drawing at the age of five. Now it's gotten to be such a habit she can't quit. Never forgets anything connected with art, but can't remember names, telephone numbers or addresses. Likes to dance. Usually good-natured. Talks a blue streak except when she is working. Then won't hear a thing you say. Will be irritable if you bother her. Uses a model occasionally, but claims you can't put any imagination or feeling into a drawing by just working from a model. Ambition is to know anatomy so perfectly that she could subjugate the drawing for the feeling. Seldom uses "swipes." Feels other artists' work should be used merely as an inspiration and incentive. Works very fast as a rule. Many stories about her speed come back to her, such as making forty figures per day. Says it's exaggerated. Has done thirty-one once. Gets down in the depths of despair over her work or is up in the clouds. Hasn't much wit. But if she accidentally says something funny, she laughs the loudest. She swims, rides horseback. Is crazy about cats. Any flea-bitten forlorn specimen will do. Will go for weeks not bothering about her looks, ink, pencil marks and a worried look on her face. Then without a warning she will burst forth looking like a Park Avenue debutante and knock your eye out. What I mean is gorgeous. Plus a lot of poise. Leaves her clothes on a chair, except when her husband is around. Then she hangs them neatly in the closet. No concession with the toothpaste though. Squeezes the tube in the middle. Crazy about snow but hates the cold. Likes Havana in February and Connecticut in August. Has a baby girl four months old and a maid named Lovey."

"Will go for weeks not bothering about her looks…"

"Then without warning, she will burst forth looking like a Park Avenue debutante," Ted wrote for the Visualizer.

Things were indeed going well for the Smith family. A new page in The Visualizer, *Educational Books We Recommend,* brought an avalanche of letters, requesting more sketches and samples. Plainly, most artists could not *visualize* a figure and sketch it out of their head.

Ruth was not sure why she had this ability. Maybe it had something to do with the visual memory her father considered so remarkable or her multi-dimensional experience in sculpture. Whatever, Ruth realized that she had a unique gift. And while she might try to explain how to *visualize* a figure in mid-action, the average artist plugging away needed "swipes" to copy.

Thus came the decision to expand THE VISUALIZER to a book-size edition, full of swipes!

HOW TO DRAW FASHION FIGURES THAT SELL, published in 1936, made record sales.

In it, Ted wrote:

"An advertising concern has highly trained persons who do the overall plan for an ad. Your problem, as an artist, is to compose your figure so as to make the public STOP, LOOK, and READ. (And want to wear Stay-Put Supporters or what have you.) Whether in color or black and white, the illustration's mass of dark against light, rhythm and form must accomplish this. And the key to it all is **central interest.**

The viewer's eye must be drawn into the illustration. Even in a sidewalk scene, there must be one or two figures that catch the eye and stimulate curiosity. Design and Composition are prime factors. In drawing we call it **life action.** *Anatomy is fundamental, but far from all. A good anatomist may know every bone and muscle in the body, yet his figures can be lifeless.*

It is rhythm, charm, the carriage of the head, the action of the eyes, the slant of the shoulders, the movement of the hips. Books, a model, "swipes" are an aid, but your success depends on your ability to visualize and transcribe **life action** *in your own distinct way."*

**For their book edition, Ruth did scores of figures:
swimmers, divers, skiers soaring overhead.**

Ruth was not sure why she could draw a figure out of her head, whether it was the visual memory her father considered so remarkable or the multi-dimensional experience in sculpture.

HOW TO DRAW FASHION FIGURES THAT SELL did so well in New York art stores that Ted pushed circulation to other major cities in the United States. In 1937, a second book, 350 FASHION FIGURES, sold even more copies and by the end of 1937, they were working on a third book, THE NEW 1938 Edition of the VISUALIZER YEARBOOK, DRAWING THE FASHION FIGURE.

Drawing the
FASHION FIGURE

By Ruth Conerly
Author of "350 FASHION FIGURES" *and*
"HOW TO DRAW FASHION FIGURES THAT SELL"

The Success of three books out on the market gave Ted an enviable prestige in the publishing business and further increased Ruth's aura in the world of fashion.

Incredible to imagine that just when all their stars seemed in perfect alignment, the axle-pin of their well-organized world would break down. Never did they imagine that Lovey, a person on whom Ruth depended, would leave them.

"Lawsy be," Lovey declared. "I hate leaving that young 'un I love so, but my own need me."

The situation was desperate.

Incredible to imagine that the axle-pin of their well-organized world would break down.

A new maid, a girl in her twenties, brought a letter of recommendation and each morning arrived on time to take Sharon out to the park. But when a neighbor told Ted that two men had been asking about the neighborhood about their financial status, he went on high alert. The kidnapping of the Lindbergh baby had left a traumatic imprint on parents, and a series of copycat abductions fueled that concern.

Ted hired a detective.

The detective promptly discovered that one of the suspects had a police record and both had been seen talking to their new maid. The detective said he suspected the two were up to no good and that the maid was in cahoots with whatever schemes they might be devising.

"Frankly," he declared, "this smells every bit like a kidnapping plot!"

Under questioning, the girl started contradicting herself and finally confessed, "I didn't mean to do anything bad. It was my men-friends that made me."

Skeptical of her excuses, yet not wanting to publicize the incident, which might attract a more skilled attempt, Ted decided not to file charges. "But if I ever see you or your men friends around here again," he roared, "I'll see you rot in jail."

The girl left crying but that night on looking in his closet, Ted found his camelhair coat had been slashed down the back.

Ruth's sketches of daughter Sharon

The next maid, a buxom middle-aged woman, brought letters recommending her as a good cook. Immediately their food bills soared, but Sharon began to lose weight.

"Isn't she eating well?" Ruth questioned.

"Yes, Ma'am, she eats a lot." The woman assured.

But noting Sharon's limbs thinner each day and that she no longer ran about playing, Ruth took her to one of New York's leading pediatricians. Dr. Margaret Davis had impressive professional qualifications, but for Ruth there was one of prime importance: they were cousins. On the wall next to her medical diploma was the diploma of their grandfather, Dr. John Jones Davis III. It was Margaret's mother who inherited the Davis fortune, remarried and went to Europe leaving Grandmother Rebecca, Lizzie and her sisters in penury. Margaret, educated in Europe, was never held to blame though and Ruth's admiration of her was as sincere as Margaret's for Ruth.

Nor did it take long for Margaret to make her diagnosis: "Ruth, this child isn't sick. She's starving to death! She needs to be hospitalized immediately!"

Horrified, Ruth canceled all her work to be with her daughter, taking only enough time to fire the maid, who admitted her "food toting" might have been excessive.

Under Margaret's observation, Sharon was soon restored to health, leaving Ruth to reflect that the Davis fortune, in the form of Margaret's medical expertise, had come back to save her child. Life had its paradoxes!

Far behind in her work and with her faith in maids shattered, Ruth accepted Ted's parents' offer to have their grandchild spend the summer with them. Safety and an abundance of Texas cooking was guaranteed.

On the train trip to Temple, Ruth reflected on old dreams forsaken and the direction her life had taken. By the time she arrived, she was determined to make a change in her life. And to the news reporter waiting, she made a revelation his editor considered worthy of their front page.

FASHION ILLUSTRATOR 'TOPS' IN NEW YORK

At the top of fashion illustration, Ruth Conerly is quitting. She is determined to throw caution to the wind

and break into the field of art she has always dreamed of
*– **magazine illustration**. By fall, after intense study and*
practice, she feels her work will be on a level for
magazines like Colliers and Ladies Home Journal.

The die was cast. Returning to New York, Ruth dropped all
her accounts except Saks Fifth Avenue, secluded herself in
her studio and began working toward her goal.

Left with time on his hands, Ted too began to reflect on a
long suppressed dream. Perhaps he could take a little time off
and do some flying. Long Island had several airfields, where
aviators like Charles Lindbergh, Richard Byrd and Wiley Post
had made their memorable flights, and others were blazing
sky paths around the world.

After a few refresher lessons, Ted invited Ruth up for a
spin. "It's a Fairchild Kreider-Reisner," he explained. "A two-
seated biplane built in 1927, has a 90 horsepower Kinner
engine and maximum speed of 113 m.p.h."

**"It's a Fairchild Kreider-Reisner," Ted explained
on taking Ruth up for a spin.**

Before returning home, Ted asked her what she thought of Long Island. Plenty of fresh air for Sharon. He'd seen a place, selling for a song. Would she like to go see it?

It was a large home, in a fine old neighborhood, but badly in need of paint and repairs. Ruth argued that coming at a time when she had cut back her accounts and was trying to break into magazine illustration, a purchase of this magnitude would put them in a tight bind.

But Ted's enthusiasm proved effective. On a summer visit, Ted's kid brother, Christian, took away vivid memories of...

> *"going out from New York with a bed spring on top of the car to that huge, tumble down old mansion that Ted was going to fix up. It had a horseshoe drive, a bad furnace in a leaky cellar, and it would have taken ten years of his life to re-do. But Ted had hopes and plans and that fun, teasing way of saying, 'What do you think about all this?' He took me up in a plane and scared me half to death with wingovers or some turn. When I commented on how dangerous flying was, he said, 'I don't want to live to be an old man.'"*

In a letter to his parents Ted was buoyant:

> *"Yesterday was a big day in my life. I passed the test for my private pilot's license. The instructor said it was the best test he had seen, written and flying. I was and still am, thrilled. Tomorrow, weather permitting, a bunch of us are going out to the field and take hops over the Empire State Building and the Statue of Liberty.*
>
> *Ruth has been very sick with a bad case of the flu. Only now is she feeling better.*
>
> *Next month we expect to be in Havana for about ten days. We need a little warm sunshine and I am looking forward to sitting on the sunny side of a deck and having a steward bring me my Scotch and soda."*

Before leaving for Havana, Ted told Ruth he had been deeply concerned about her illness. The thought had even crossed his mind that if anything were to happen to her, he might not be able to take care of Sharon on his own. Did she really want to keep that Connecticut farm in her name alone?

Ruth had not considered her illness that serious, but the thought that Sharon might be in jeopardy troubled her. After consulting with a lawyer she decided to give Ted *co-ownership*. With this, the lawyer explained, Ted could not sell without her signature.

Havana was wonderful. They visited the capital building, went to a party at the home of the owner of the Tropical Beer Company and danced to favorite pieces of Ernesto Lecuona.

No sooner were they home though, a man called, asking Ruth for the deeds to her farm.

"Why?" Ruth questioned.

"Ted sold it to me."

"He couldn't have sold it," Ruth countered. "Not without my signature as co-owner!"

But it soon became clear that Ted had sold her farm, without her signature and for less than half its value.

Unable to understand how he could have done such a thing, Ruth demanded an explanation.

Ted mentioned house repairs and how he felt she needed a vacation, finally admitting he had unforeseen expenses.

"What expenses?" Ruth pressed. It was like extracting teeth. Finally the story came out. Flying lessons and plane rental had been more expensive than calculated. So as not to have to keep on renting a plane, he had bought one, that Fairchild KR-21. And now they were pressing him for the money. If he didn't pay, he'd lose all he'd invested, and the plane to boot!

While listening to this litany of excuses, Ruth recalled Ted's concern about her illness, which now seemed only a ploy to get her to sign away her farm. The whole thing was so ludicrous she could only stare at him in dumb disbelief, as though watching someone sawing the floor out from under her.

How could he have been capable of such deceit! Her farm for some lousy flying lessons! All his insistence on moving out to Long Island just to fly some damned airplane!

Realizing how little in control of her life she was and how some compulsion of Ted's could at any moment wipe them out financially, she felt overwhelmed with frustration and rage. But what made her more furious still was why in the name of heaven was it so difficult for Ted to simply tell the truth!

And finally, recalling her mother's words, "people never change," she wept.

Ted felt terrible. He could not explain his compulsion to fly any more than he could explain his need to breathe. It was not the camaraderie of men together, exchanging the adventures and challenges of flight. It was flight itself, taking off in the morning's first rays, seeing the earth spread out beneath him in its ever-expanding magnificence, feeling the lift of the wings and the rudder respond to his touch, making him as free as a bird. A feeling as close to ecstasy as he could imagine!

As each day brought new wondrous accounts of things going on in the world of aviation, he felt himself in the midst of history in the making. Howard Hughes had just gone around the world in ninety-one days. A friend was off flying the hump, taking supplies over the Himalayas into China, while another friend had gone off to Spain where there was a revolution. Even that writer Hemingway was in Spain now. With a few more flight hours he too might volunteer.

"Go to Spain?" Ruth exclaimed. "What in heaven for?"

Ted did not try to explain. The soul of an adventurer could not be encaged in words.

But much as Ted soulfully longed for adventure, to be off on some death-defying mission, he could not imagine it was soon to be delivered to his very doorstep, making him wonder if the wrath of God had come down to make him aware of his transgressions.

At that very moment far south, tropical breezes were being transformed into winds, pushing up the North Atlantic coast. In Halifax, Nova Scotia, people were surprised to see hordes of salps – transparent sea creatures – swarming into the harbor. A scientist in Canada speculated that it might be a warning of some kind.

But no one imagined that a powerful, roaring juggernaut was about to strike the New England coastline.

That morning of September 21, 1938, Ted left early to go into Manhattan. The rain for the past few days had made visibility extremely poor. Not good flying weather.

Ruth was at her art-board concentrating on an illustration when the maid peeped in timidly and said, "Mizz Smith, there's quite a wind out there."

"Um-hum," Ruth murmured in vague agreement without glancing up. A half an hour later the maid was back.

"Mizz Smith,"

"Hmm?" Ruth replied paying little more attention than before.

"The wind's really blowing out there."

"Um hum."

Minutes later, the maid came running back screaming. "Mizz Smith! Mizz Smith! Look out there! Just look!"

Annoyed by this emotional outburst, Ruth nevertheless looked out – to see the enormous tree in the front yard being lifted from the soil as if by some giant invisible hand. It poised briefly in mid-air, then crashed outwards over the road.

Immediately cars with wild-eyed drivers began swerving into their horseshoe drive, trying to skirt the obstruction. In the midst of the mayhem, three-year-old Sharon ran down the stairs and out the front door into the tumult of wind and veering cars, happily shouting, "I can fly!" In her tunnel vision it was the storm from the movie The Wizard of Oz they had seen a few nights ago come to take her off to a wonderful Technicolor land of flowers and adventure with Judy Garland singing *Somewhere Over the Rainbow.*

Horrified, Ruth ran out after her. Just as they were about to be blown off, Ted drove up and managed to catch hold of both. Back in the house, they scrambled down the stairs to the cellar where the maid sat trembling in the darkness.

As the wind roared, the old house above them swayed and groaned under the grinding of its own timbers. Huddled in the damp darkness, they feared that at any moment it would collapse about them, or fly away with them in it.

Suddenly realizing an important member of the household was not there, Sharon shouted, "Daddy, where's Tizzy?"

"Tizzy'll be fine," Ted assured. "Cats have nine lives, remember?" In spite of his apparent calm, Ted was not sure that any of them would survive.

In a letter to his parents, Ted described the terrifying ordeal:

> "It was a wind like nothing I have ever heard in all my days. I got a 'ringing in me ears' and knew that bad weather was ahead, so I got into the car and rushed home. Twice I was blown off the road and the car drowned out three times. The full force of the hurricane struck shortly after I got home. A tree had fallen across the main road right in front of our house and all the traffic was plowing through our driveway and some just drove across the lawn. All the while Mr. Rufino's trees – I suppose you remember what a forest he had in his front yard – were falling and snapping. The havoc and destruction you see in Hampton's further east and the South Shore is pathetic. Lovely homes just disappeared. Boats were washed two miles inland. Scores drowned and still missing. Whole towns devastated with signs of absolutely no human being ever having lived there. It was something that made you want to make peace with your Maker. Fortunately we all survived. Even Tizzy."

With hundreds dead or simply disappeared in a storm considered the worst ever to hit the New England coastline, Ruth and Ted could readily believe news reports that said the storm had "turned time backward a generation, radically affecting the lives of seven million people."

They were grateful to be alive, but financially they were wiped out. The old mansion had withstood the storm, but was too seriously damaged to warrant repair. Ruth's farm was gone and Ted's plane had been blown away.

Faced with the urgencies of the moment, Ruth put her dream of becoming a magazine illustrator on a back burner. They moved back to New York and Ruth went back to fashion illustration.

Conerly illustrations from the 1938 Visualizer Year Book

Jane Conerly

"And who but Ruth wou
be interested in her littl
sister's success!"

Portrait of Jane by
Ruth Conerly

XV

Ghostly Image, Promise Broken

Janey could hardly contain her excitement. After a year at Texas Women's University, she eagerly awaited Ruth's summer visit and the prospect of going to New York. She was determined to be an artist like her sister, Ruth.

From childhood, Janey had followed Ruth's rise to dazzling heights as a commercial artist, darling of the world of fashion with fancy New York stores clamoring for her work. Illustrations bearing the Conerly signature in newspapers and fashionable women's magazines, three art books out on the market. An artist sent to Paris to cover the fashion shows, pursued by a French count, hobnobbing with oodles of glamorous people, invitations to the Stork Club, cruising off to Cuba with a handsome husband – only in fairy tales could anyone find such romance and success!

Going through her scrapbook on Ruth, Janey read the article Ruth had written for the Clarksville Times just the year before, all about emerging style trends for 1939. She was awed that Ruth had predicted exactly what everyone was now wearing!

FORMER FASHION ILLUSRATOR
TELLS OF NEW STYLE TRENDS

Women's clothes make one of the largest industries of the world and much effort is put into selling them. The best way I find of analyzing the new trend is to find what the public is tired of and take the opposite road. For instance, we have had in the past few years, the young severe, strictly tailored person and the glamour girl. Now the trend swings to the lady, a beautiful, exquisite person with every detail of soft perfection. Romance has come back, the romance of the 1830s, 1860s and gay nineties. It's in the flowers you wear on your hat and in your hair, pulled softly back with little-girl curls as in the 1830s. It's in the veil you wear with a tipped-down shallow sailor hat, pillbox, and saucy Watteau covered with flowers and perched over the right eye. Turned-up hats, Fedoras, birds, bows, ostrich feathers and flowers make the new hats delightfully silly, alluringly feminine.

The short, tight jacket continues to be popular and new. Coat-suit jackets are longer and more loosely fitted. Daytime dresses are 12 to 14 inches from the ground. Evening dresses sweep the floor. Hips are unbelievably slim. Busts are back, and slim waistlines.

To put it briefly, the woman today is a lady, gracefully, delightfully, a lady!

Janey sighed, convinced that Ruth was a genius, endowed with magical powers of clairvoyance in the world of art and fashion.

And who but Ruth would be interested in her little sister's success? Who was in the position with maids, models, agents, apprentices hanging on her every word, to take that little sister under her wing as favored *protégée*, endowing her with the secrets of success and influencing her career in art. It was mind-boggling!

"I'm in a low now financially," Ruth said matter-of-factly, not meaning to discourage Janey, only to impress on her that they would not be living in some fairytale world with maids at their beck and call. "You'll have to buckle down and work."

While visiting Othermama, Ruth was surprised to see how frail she had become. With moist eyes, Othermama hugged Ruth close. "You'll probably be working so hard you won't even have time to come to my funeral when I die," she accused. To this, Ruth vehemently protested: "Never!" Never would she do such a thing!

At the train station, Ruth asked for an overnight stop in Washington, D.C.

"There's someone I want to see that's producing an incredible amount of illustrations for all the top magazines," Ruth explained to Janey. "Ritchie Cooper."

It was obvious that Ruth's dream of getting into this area requiring a high degree of skill and creative imagination was far from dead.

"Ritchie has a virtual art factory with her father and assistants, turning out a huge amount of paintings and illustrations for all the big magazines."

After Ruth's glowing description, Janey was surprised when they found this luminary of the art world scrubbing the kitchen floor. But she and Ruth were soon bantering remarks about how women, no matter how talented, were never free of menial chores. As Ruth hiked her skirt and rolled up her sleeves, joke followed joke and the two of them ended up down on the floor in the suds laughing.

Later that afternoon Ritchie took them to a barn with a long central corridor bordered on either side with wooden slots holding hundreds of illustrations. Going down the aisle, she took out paintings, explaining techniques of work, preferences of editors and clients. When Ruth showed special admiration for one, Ritchie wrote a dedicatory on it "To Ruth and Ted" and gave it to Ruth. She then removed a second painting of a young couple in a convertible and gave it to Janey.

In New York, Janey was impressed by the entourage of people coming in and out of Ruth and Ted's apartment: agents, a French model called Yvonne and a Russian count who had fought for the Czar and spoke French to Yvonne. On meeting Janey, the count declared himself vanquished by love at first sight and since Ruth had refused to marry him, he would marry her beautiful sister.

Exciting as it all seemed, Ruth had not lied. There was work, an inordinate amount with Ruth spending hours at her art board, often forgetting entirely about food or sleep. By the end of the summer, Janey was exhausted and her enthusiasm about becoming an artist somewhat tempered. She consoled herself that she had done an illustration for Meyer Both Art Services and a figure for Lord and Taylor, and was happy with the portrait Ruth did of her.

Especially she liked Ted's suggestion they go to the World's Fair. It was September and the whole shebang would soon be closing down, Ted insisted. Incredible that Janey should miss it. They stood in awe of the tower that hoisted people high into the sky and parachuted them to earth. Ruth was fascinated by a thing called television that supposedly could transmit images for over fifty miles, reminding her of her father's prediction that this twentieth century would bring unimaginable things.

The next day Ted left on a business trip and Jane and Ruth stayed up late telling stories, things like how Ruth once drove off to town in Othermama's car with her cat, Thomas Jefferson, on top. They laughed about how there always seemed to be an Othermama anecdote for every situation in life.

"But she suffered terribly," Janey said. "I'll never forget when I was about five and she took me to the cemetery to put flowers on Daddy's grave. We were standing there when all of a sudden she fell down and began ripping up the grass, crying "Oh, my Pressie, my dearest Pressie."

For long moments, they sat in silence.

"What was he like?" Janey asked. "Daddy."

Ruth paused a moment thinking back. "He had light brown hair with a little reddish glint in it. Blue eyes, like yours. He always had time to tell some funny story. Even at the end, when he was suffering so."

"Is it true what they say, that he went crazy?"

"He never seemed so to me, only that his stomach hurt. At times he would double over and cry out. Doctors never seemed to know what was causing it."

"And that story about our being descended from King George, have you ever found out anything about that?"

"No, not really. Only what the family book says, that while Prince of Wales, George married a Quaker girl named Hannah Lightfoot. One of these days I'm going to look into it, just for the fun of it."

Ruth was sound asleep in her bed and Janey on the sofa nearby when Ruth suddenly awoke, aware that someone was standing by her bed looking down at her. As her eyes became adjusted to the darkness, she recognized the person. It was Othermama. Startled, she called out to Janey just as the image faded.

"Did you see that?" Ruth questioned.

"Like a shadow just briefly," Janey replied. "What was it?"

"It was Othermama," Ruth said. "She was standing right here by my bed."

For a long time, they sat there. Ruth was sure she was not dreaming, but finally she conceded there could be no other explanation. The next day though, on receiving a telegram from Marshall, even before opening the envelope, Ruth had a chilling premonition.

OTHERMAMA PASSED AWAY EARLY THIS MORNING.
CAN YOU COME TO THE FUNERAL?
COUSIN MABEL, OCTOBER 20, 1939.

Reading those lines, there was no longer any doubt in Ruth's mind about the image she had seen the night before. It was Othermama. She had come to say goodbye.

But the question "Can you come for the funeral?" posed a soul-rending decision. For Othermama, attending someone's funeral was a sacred last homage, never denied to someone truly loved.

With a sinking heart, Ruth looked at her art board holding a major illustration and three deadlines lined up to follow it. She tried to convince herself that Othermama would forgive her. But memories of how Othermama had helped her and the many stories she would tell came flooding back.

Recalling Othermama's last words, "When I die, you'll probably be too busy to come to my funeral", Ruth was overwhelmed by a sense of remorse, betrayal and guilt.

A week later a letter from her cousin Mabel gave a full account:

"Even on her deathbed Othermama was flirting with her doctor. You know how she'd move her eyes. And the funeral, unbelievable! So many people, cars, flowers. We were all sobbing and blubbering, when Martha Jane remembered how Othermama and the chums would count cars and people at all the funerals and compare them with others. At that moment, Mary Lavinia cried out, "Othermama would just love it!" And right there in the middle of the funeral, we all whopped and couldn't stop laughing. Just kept on laughing and crying until .people turned around looking at us as though we were out of our minds.

Reading Mabel's account, Ruth laughed and then cried and laughed again. At least Othermama had gone out with well-deserved pomp!

1939 – a year of flashing movie marquees when the World Fair heralded unimaginable things – had come to an end.

Immersed in their daily lives, few showed concern that a man with a funny Charley Chaplin mustache had now taken over Czechoslovakia, Austria and Poland. That December, Ruth and Ted went to Atlantic City to celebrate the New Year.

"I had to do some work there, so for New Year's, Ted and I got all gussied up to go to a night club. As we walked into the club, the orchestra struck up an introduction and flashed lights on us while they were seating us. A few minutes later the master of ceremonies came over and asked for our names.

When Ted said, "Mr. and Mrs. Smith," he chuckled and said, `Yes, yes, but who are you, really? People here would like to know."

They never believed us but sent over a magnum of champagne and a bottle of French perfume for me."

That night Ted looked into Ruth's eyes over their glasses of champagne and whispered, "Wonder what the poor people are doing tonight." And Ruth laughed, amazed at how deeply she loved this man!

XVI

Chicago, Chicago

In 1940, Ruth's illustrations were appearing in all the major magazines throughout the United States. Not the art she dreamed of, dealing with epic events of history, but good commercial art, nevertheless, for America's top ranking firms.

Warwick & Legler required Conerly illustrations for Tangee Lipstick in its pages of Harper's Bazaar and Woman's Day. Lord and Taylor was using Conerly illustrations for its Mary Barron slips. A popular pulp magazine had commissioned an illustration for PLAYING THE GAME OF HOLLYWOOD LOVE and a Conerly illustration had marked a history-making *first* in the world of manufacturing: *Man Made Fabrics!*

As Japan moved into Malaysia menacing United States' rubber supply, American ingenuity responded with *synthetics*. Catalina swimsuits incorporated ControLastic, a product of Firestone into its new *form-molding* swimwear selling at Bloomingdale's. And Ruth illustrated the fact for magazines like *Mademoiselle*.

If Ruth's accounts read like a Who's Who of name brands and companies, the name Conerly was also being noted. So much that many people just assumed Conerly was a man. An executive at one major company had impatiently *insisted* he wanted to speak to *Mr.* Conerly and went mute when Ruth replied, "I am Conerly. Ruth Conerly."

True, there were unfulfilled dreams, but she was moving up, producing a wide range of art, succeeding and supporting herself comfortably.

It was precisely then when Ted dropped a bombshell.

He had sold the rights to The Visualizer. In a next breath, as if perceiving the reaction this would bring, he announced that he had been offered a job with Grumbacher, Inc., a leading firm making art materials.

Ted basked momentarily in Ruth's surprised admiration. Then flashing his most captivating smile, he dropped another bombshell.

His new job required them to move to Chicago!

"PIGTAILS, BUCK-TEETH AND FRECKLES...

I had 'em all"

"WHEN I WAS 16 and ready to graduate from the awkward stage, I bought my first lipstick...Tangee NATURAL. *And I've used Tangee Natural ever since!* I'm always thrilled by the way it *changes* from orange in the stick until my own most flattering lip-tint of warm blush rose is produced."

"ON MY WEDDING DAY I gave each of my bridesmaids a beauty kit...a Tangee Natural Lipstick, the harmonizing rouge, and their own correct shade of Tangee Face Powder. To each of them Tangee Natural Lipstick gave a different lip color."

"TODAY, my 16 year old daughter and I both use Tangee Natural. Its pure cream base keeps our lips soft, smooth and attractive for hours. Is it any wonder, then, that Tangee NATURAL has always been my favorite?"...Send for FREE generous size Tangee Natural Lipstick. Address Tangee, Dept. C, 417 Fifth Avenue, New York City.

TANGEE *Natural*

...FOR LIPS THAT ARE ALWAYS "SWEET SIXTEEN"

SWITCH TO *Mary Barron*

It's "sheer" risk to wear an ordinary

WHEN A *Slip* BECOMES A SOCIAL ERROR...
SWITCH TO *Mary Barron*

don't risk a slip broadcast...

Conerly illustrated products as familiar as Tangee Lipstick and Mary Barron slips.

JUST FRIENDS AND LOYAL
TO THE LAST EMBRACE

'ROUND AND 'ROUND

PLAYING
THE GAME
OF
HOLLYWOOD
LOVE

THE MULBERRY BUSH

"JEEVES, JUST WHO DID I GET ENGAGED TO LAST NIGHT?"

By HELEN BEATTY

THE individual who contributed to a stunned world the statement that love is a funny thing, committed the prize misstatement of all time as far as Hollywood is concerned.

Love is not a funny thing in Hollywood. Love is a serious, complicated series of maneuvers, complex as the festival rites of Borneo head-hunters, and just as clear in meaning to civilized onlookers.

But never under any circumstances is it funny. Hysterical, maybe — yes. Funny? No.

Love in Hollywood is an intangible something that happens to people who behaved as everyone else, as far as emotions and social decorum were concerned, before they landed in Hollywood. But the minute the travelers swing down the mountain grades and behold the orange groves of California, something happens to them. They suspect the change immediately. They are almost certain of it when they get a load of the snow capped mountains behind the oranges. (three dozen for a quarter). By the time they glimpse Catalina on a clear day, they don't even stop to think about it at all. They're in it up to their ears. Hollywood love, I mean, not Catalina.

The thing that renders the Hollywood variety of the well known emotion so different from the species found elsewhere is, that in Hollywood things only begin where they leave off elsewhere.

If it sounds a trifle confusing, don't let it throw you. The truth is, it *is* confusing and so the breaking point half the time. In fact the natives who participate in the game of Hollywood love are often themselves confused to the point where they can't distinguish their wives from their fiancees or their husbands from their fiances.

For instance, now, the normal course of romantic procedure for a young man in Detroit, say, is to meet a young lady, fall in love, court her, propose and if lucky, marry. That, I say, is the usual order of events leading to Marriage in Detroit or even Pittsburgh. Or was last time I was there.

But things don't happen that way in Hollywood. Out here, before the gentleman ever begins his courting, he quite often gets married to someone else and then hops to his courting like a wild man. Roses by the arborfull are sent. No, no,

**In tune with popular movies and pulp magazines,
Conerly captured the romantic light mood of the day.**

Catalina suimsuits announced its history-making venture with a Conerly illustration on Madamoiselle Magazine's first page.

**Ruth's painting of Ted's sister Zelda
showed masterful ability in darks and lights.**

Ruth's smile vanished. "Chicago!" she exclaimed. "I can't go to Chicago. You've got to be out of your mind!"

The idea of uprooting from New York where her career was well established and moving to Chicago because of a job Ted might leave at the drop of a hat did not attract her one bit. Moreover, she had perceived a pattern in Ted's wanderlust and inability to put down permanent roots.

But Ted's enthusiasm was unshakable, much the same as his conviction that Ruth would achieve even greater laurels in Chicago. Curiously, a few days later, Ruth had to make a business trip to Chicago. And while there, she learned that many artists lived in Chicago, namely the great Andrew Loomis – America's most famed and highly-paid commercial artist.

By fall of 1940, Ruth and Ted were settled into an apartment in Oak Park, a suburb of Chicago. Ted was happy. His new job with Grumbacher involved selling art supplies and sales promotion, which meant traveling and meeting people. There could hardly be anything more perfect for Ted. Compounding his happiness, he was getting paid well for it.

Ruth soon found most of her qualms concerning the move were unfounded. She managed to keep most of her New York accounts while adding a new one, the mighty Marshall Field & Co. On walking into Chicago's largest and most prestigious department store and introducing herself, art director Frances Owen hired her on the spot.

As Christmas, always a month of intensive work in the merchandising field, was just around the corner, Ruth hired a maid and model-assistant. Although the fetch and carry of picking up outlines and taking in finished work usually fell on her assistant, now and then Ruth would go in personally to pow-wow with the art director or deliver an illustration she felt especially worthy of interest. And whenever Ruth came in, people in the art department and executive offices would crowd around her, making excited commentaries as art director Frances Owen reverently lifted the illustration's tracing paper veiling.

The move to Chicago not only proved favorable to Ruth's career, but gratifying to her ego. Chicago boasted of a prosperous and socially active artist colony and the Conerly reputation had preceded her. That Chicago was the home of the great Andrew Loomis had already impressed Ruth and she was pleased on being warmly received into the inner elite circle where Loomis was the recognized king.

"Loomis was a wonderful illustrator. He worked for Coca Cola and was famed for drawing out of his head although he admitted to using models. When I moved to Chicago, Andy gave a big party for me. He lived in Winnetka and had a beautiful home with columns. He liked to entertain and played the piano very well. One night at a dinner party he asked me to go down to his study to talk art. Like many artists, he was interested in how I could draw out of my mind and wanted to know all about that. Several people came down to call him back to the party and finally his wife came down, saying he was neglecting the rest of his guests, but he waved her away. 'You invited all these other people,' he said. 'I told you I wanted to talk to Ruth. Now you go keep them entertained.' "

Ruth never hinted that anything other than professional interests and mutual admiration lay at the root of her friendship with Loomis. Even so, Ted became reluctant to accept Loomis' invitations, finally refusing altogether to go.

"They're too wealthy for us to feel comfortable with," Ted said, not entirely convincing from someone hardly known to be inhibited by wealth or social status.

Ruth (right) at a party in Chicago

MEET ME UNDER THE CLOCK
Illustration by Conerly, Courtesy of Marshall Field's & Company

That summer of 1941, before America was swept into World War II, would always be remembered as *The Summer of Alma*. As Ruth herself later recorded it...

"It all started when my husband Ted had to go on a business trip and I went to visit my mother in Clarksville, Texas. Unlike our Oak Park apartment building, playmates for my daughter Sharon were scarce in Clarksville and Mother suggested Alma. One of eight children, Alma was used to looking after the younger ones and Mother thought that for fifty cents a day she might come over and play with Sharon.

Alma was twelve with wide orbs of eyes and skin black as ebony. Arriving in a starched white apron dress, eyes full of "Don't tell!" and "Did you know?" Alma opened up a whole new world for Sharon. They marked off a house in the dirt and furnished it. Rocks, pieces of glass and twigs were their materials, the game of scavenging and evaluating their finds, an adventure in itself. By the end of the week, they had decided that Alma must go back to Chicago with us for the summer.

My husband Ted was not enthusiastic about the idea, but on putting his suitcases down in the hallway entrance and calling out, "Well, where's Alma?" two big eyes and a blue dress advanced from the shadows. "Heah I is!" Alma replied shyly. Ted was a pushover.

Our colored maid, Hattie, took Alma under her protective wing but insisted she did not want her going out to play with that bunch of rowdy white children. But I insisted and almost immediately Alma's talent for imaginative games and quiet authority for settling disputes brought order to chaos. Soon children could be seen scurrying on various errands. They collected wooden crates, nailed old roller skates on them forming a train called the Hootenanny Special, going in and out the entrance tunnels and around the building. They sealed off a stairwell and created a haunted house with relics of Halloween. A sign announced, **One Cent - Prohibited To Sissies!** *Parents, surprised that this summer was not another headache of fighting children, looked out in the evenings and were amazed to see* *children seated in neat rows playing school. And sometimes Alma would sing in a bell-clear voice, songs called 'spearchels,' like the one about 'Dan'l in the Lion's Den. And de bees made honey in de lion's head.'*

But one morning Alma said her tummy hurt. Fearing appendicitis, I rushed her to the hospital.

"No emergency," the doctor assured. "Alma has simply come of age. I've spoken to her and she understands." But coming out of his office, we were confronted by a policeman and two women shouting, "That woman with a Southern accent brought in a little black girl all doubled over with internal injuries!"

The doctor quickly explained, but that evening when Alma said she just might be convinced of staying on with us and going to school in Chicago, I said, "Alma, you can't do that. Your mother would miss you something terrible." As we had reservations at a lake resort in Wisconsin, I told Ted we should send her on home.

"No," Ted said, "Alma's never been to any place like that. Besides Sharon will mope around the whole time if we don't take her."

At the lodge, Alma loved fishing and going out to paint with me. One morning she and Sharon were at the lake with Ted fishing when Ted called back, "Alma, Sharon, look at that speed boat!" The boat was coming toward them at a fast clip on the lake's mirror-like surface. Suddenly one of the boys in it stood up, pointing and shouting, "Look at that girl! She's black all over!"

Alma's smile vanished. She turned and ran from the water. Back at the cabin, Ted and I tried to talk to her, but it was no use. On our return to Chicago, Alma refused to go down to play. I asked her if she wanted to go home but receiving a negative, I hated to insist. I was in my studio working on an illustration when Sharon peeped in. "Mommy, Alma's crying again." Putting down my brush, I went to her room.

"Alma?" I said sitting down beside her. No more was needed. Alma flung herself in my arms sobbing. "Mizz,

Smiff, why did God make me black? And if he had to, why so black?"

"Alma," I said hugging her. "You're twelve. When you're twelve the world is a total tragedy. Your feet are too big, your knees always skinned and you think you're the ugliest duckling in the world."

"But the ugly duckling became a beautiful white swan and I'm never going to become white."

"That doesn't mean you won't be beautiful."

"You are... and white."

"That's sweet of you, Alma, but few girls suffered as much as I."

Alma looked up in amazement. "You.. suffered?"

"Don't you see these freckles.. and this leg skinnier than the other? I used to wonder why God let me have polio, while other children could walk and run so fast. My idea of heaven was to have two beautiful legs. But God gave me this, and maybe that's why I became an artist."

"I never noticed anything," Alma said looking down.

"That's because I've learned to use padding and a lift with my shoe. You learn little tricks to make the most of things. Why, you have beautiful legs and walk like a little queen, so straight and fine. I wouldn't be surprised if you weren't descended from some African queen that lived a long time ago."

Alma put her head down. "No, I'm not," she said. "I just come from slaves, that weren't nothing special."

"A lot of people, black and white, were once slaves. Back in historical times after a war, whole cities with their kings and royal households were sold into slavery. Some of the wisest men, like the great poet Horace, friend of the Roman emperor Augustus were descended from slaves. Course, people can't go around with their nose in the air because of some great, great grandking, any more than get down in the dumps for being some great, great grandslave."

Alma laughed. "Mrs. Smiff, would you honestly not mind if you'd been born black like me?"

"Alma, I thought God did a terrible thing making me freckled all over like a guinea egg and why couldn't I *have a white skin like some people, but I guess He just couldn't make everyone all the same, or maybe He thought variety was nice. Or maybe He just didn't think the color of our skins was as important as we do.*

"And if you were poor, sometimes without enough to eat?"

"When I was your age and my father got sick, we had a terrible time getting enough to eat. Come Christmas watching everyone with their fine toys, we didn't dare go out, afraid they'd say `Santa doesn't bring things to bad children'. But in time you learn to do things, imaginative and creative, like you do. I've found in life, if you can do just one thing really well, it gives you confidence and commands the respect of others. Take the things you know, for instance, the way you have with children. You would make a fine educator. Or a great singer. Do you have a music teacher at school?"

"Yes'm"

"Has she noticed your voice?"

"Yes, ma'am. And she lets me sing solos sometimes! And sometimes I sing in church too."

"You see! With good grades you might even get a scholarship and go to college! I can see you now, dressed up in an evening gown, singing before a big audience, your mother and father out there watching you so proudly."

"And you'd come to watch me too, Mizz Smiff?"

"I certainly would. Mr. Smith and I and Sharon will all be sitting out there in front, so proud of you!"

Alma smiled broadly.

"Now you go wash your face and go on out. All the kids have been driving me crazy wanting to know when Alma is coming out to play."

The next day, a neighbor gave her a birthday-going away party. That evening Ted and I watched Alma coming back across the court, her arms full of presents. On coming in the door and seeing us waiting, she dropped everything and ran to us. "Mizz Smiff, Mr. Smiff," she cried, tears streaming down her cheeks, "they gave me a b-b-birffday party!"

That night Alma sat for hours taking out each gift, placing it back in her suitcase, tying the ribbons carefully in place. The next day she was gone.

I never knew if the bright picture I envisioned for Alma came true. But I often find myself thinking about her, wondering whatever happened to Alma."

Alma in Wisconsin showing the day's catch

Ruth paints Alma busily sketching two girls.

XVII

Wings of War

On Sunday, December 7, 1941, Ted turned on his Philco radio and, straining against the static, heard the news already being shouted in the streets — Japan had attacked Pearl Harbor! Thousands of men had gone down to a watery grave and America's Pacific fleet anchored there had been virtually destroyed.

"Holy Mackerel! Great jumping Jehosaphat!" Ted shouted, giving rein to the maximum of profanity he permitted himself in the sanctity of home. Ted never understood why Japan's invasion of China awakened so little commentary in the United States or why Hitler's aggression in Europe aroused only a determination to stay out of Europe's squabbles. Austria and Czechoslovakia had been taken over in a seemingly peaceful manner, but the invasion of Poland, divided up between Hitler and Stalin, had been a brutal thing. Next came Norway, Denmark, Belgium, Holland, then France, Yugoslavia and Greece. And now Hitler's armies, virtual masters of continental Europe, had turned on Russia and were at the very gates of Moscow! Only England was still putting up a determined resistance.

A man could be sure of nothing in this complicated scene, but Ted was willing to bet that this attack on Pearl Harbor would make the United States take its head out of the sand. How could anyone ignore that the war was now at their very doorstep!

That the attack had come by air reminded Ted of his youth-time hero, Colonel Billy Mitchell, who was court-martialed for insisting that Pearl Harbor was vulnerable to an air attack by Japan and how a strong, independent air force was needed to contend with the danger. It was likewise clear to Ted that, just as Billy Mitchell had predicted, aviation was going to play a decisive role in this war.

And that his moment in life had come!

He must go to San Antonio, update his flying skills, subject himself to the most rigorous training and enlist as a fighter pilot. They must pack up and go to San Antonio immediately!

"San Antonio!" Ruth exclaimed. "Why not think things over more calmly instead of making a decision on the spur of the moment?"

But Ted was adamant.

In their hurried departure, Ruth vehemently protested the scuttling of her player piano that Ted considered unnecessary flotsam, while six-year-old Sharon was miserable on loosing her collection of ballet tutues and Classic Comics.

In the early months of 1942, San Antonio's population of 250,000 was fast swelling with the influx of military personnel converging on its military bases: Fort Sam Houston, Kelly, Brooks and Randolph. Songs like Deep in the Heart of Texas, San Antonio Rose and This is the Army, Mr. Jones were heard everywhere, while youthful soldiers visited the Alamo, the Long Horn Saloon and Brackenridge Park, that hurriedly renamed its Japanese Gardens, *Chinese Gardens*.

On arriving in San Antonio and presenting himself to the recruitment office, Ted was amazed to learn he was 4F – unfit for active duty. He had a heart murmur, the doctor said, suggestive of rheumatic fever. Not understanding how this could be – he had no memory of being seriously ill, nor was it mentioned in physical exams for his early training – Ted vigorously protested. Gaining nothing by this, he went from office to office trying to have the diagnosis revoked. Failing in this, he tried to enlist in every other branch of the service. All to no avail. And each negative only deepened his depression at not being able to join the thousands training to go off to war. To be considered physically unfit to defend one's country at age thirty-three was a wound more terrible than any enemy might inflict!

When Ruth arrived in San Antonio, frantic and sick with worry at the thought of Ted's going off to war, she found a husband crushed and miserable – and was amazed to learn the reason. On listening to the litany of his attempts to enlist, she was incapable of understanding why he should be so wretched at not being able to "go off and get your fool self killed" and thought he had lost his mind.

"Men must like war!" she accused. And Ted, convinced that no woman could understand the gonadal urge of any red-blooded man to defend freedom and country, merely replied philosophically, "There will always be wars. If there were no wars, there'd be things much worse."

Ruth could only feel an enormous relief that Ted would not be going off to war and turned her attention to finding a place to live. The scarcity of lodging in San Antonio became immediately apparent. Hotels and boarding houses were filled to capacity. Finding temporary lodging in a nurse's residence and space for Sharon in a nearby Catholic convent, Ruth breathed a sigh of relief. Ted, who miraculously had not lost his job with Grumbacher, left on a sales trip.

Assured of a home base, Ruth sent a telegram to Frances Owen, art director at Marshall Field & Company, reporting her whereabouts. Then taking her portfolio of samples, she went job-hunting. Joske's of Texas, a block from the Alamo and bearing the awesome addendum "The largest Store in the Largest State," was her first stop. In this unstable world, she was not sure work would be available, but on seeing her samples, the art director instantly hired her. That evening on returning home, Ruth walked by the Alamo, observing the familiar façade, recalling her long ago visit with Othermama. Strange that another war would draw her here. Maybe Ted was right saying that there would always be wars.

She had just walked in the door of the nurse's residence when a woman called out, "You Ruth Conerly? Long distance call from Chicago!"

After several ear-shattering clickings, Frances Owens's voice demanded, "Where in hell have you been?" Without waiting for an answer, Frances blazed on, "I've got the most important campaign in Marshall Field's history dumped in my lap and my best artist's gone to Texas? I need you! The damn store's going to war!"

Three days later, an envelope marked 'Special Delivery' brought a briefing on the situation.

After Pearl Harbor, Japan had swept through the Pacific in a rapid succession of victories, invading the Philippines, British Malaysia, taking Thailand and Hong Kong. The U.S. Pacific fleet was in ruins, General MacArthur was trapped in the Philippines with 12,000 men and no naval or air support. And America faced the monumental task of recruiting a vast army to fight on two fronts, Europe and Asia, and supplying that army with ships, planes and ammunition.

In his speech addressing the nation, President Roosevelt said, "We are now in this war. Every man, woman and child is a partner in the most tremendous undertaking of American history."

Money was needed. Vast sums of it. The sale of WAR BONDS could raise the needed funding, but this required a major publicity drive.

Marshall Field's top executives were wondering what they might do to cooperate with the war effort when a customer remarked, "With the world crashing down around our ears, thank God Marshall Fields is still here at the corner of State and Washington." Those words and the store's maxim, "The customer is always right," sparked the idea of a drive to sell War Bonds.

"My problem," Frances finalized, "is that I've been charged with launching this campaign with a series of institutionals!" (Illustrations to promote good will for a cause or institution). "And for this I need you, Ruth, and your ability with action: battle scenes, ships, planes, locked in combat. The War Department has promised full cooperation."

"Can I count on you for this?" Frances repeated on a follow-up call.

"You bet your boots you can count on me," Ruth shouted back over the static.

The next day, Ruth found an old adobe house downtown behind the Menger Hotel. There she set up home and studio and went to work. Her first illustration portrayed a group of Revolutionary soldiers in the bleak winter of 1777 huddled around a fire. Standing with only his eyes visible over a woolen shawl, was George Washington, a figure Ruth had often sculpted. The economy of line created the illusion of a misty past contrasting with the fuller bodied illustration beside it, showing modern day soldiers backed up with tanks and planes.

Ruth reflected that in 1777, George Washington was fighting the British, ruled by King George III, presumably her ancestor, with all those poor British boys such good targets in their red coats with white bands forming an X in front of their hearts.

A second illustration focused on the plight of Stalingrad currently under Nazi siege and how it would be if the same happened to one of our cities, like Chicago...

If only
**Washington could see
your boys now**

Washington's men were usually barefoot, hungry, poorly armed. During most of their war,
the had no training in how to protect themselves. He never commanded an army with well-organized
communications, intelligence, supply. Yet *Washington* at *Valley Forge* knew what America's army could
some day be. If only he could review your boys now — inspect their Garand rifles, know the bombsight,
see army kitchens, hospitals, touch the good warm wool of an enlisted man's overcoat — he would ks
his fight had been worth it. Once again he would say, as he did before the Battle of Long Island,
"The fate of unborn millions will now depend, under God, on the courage and conduct of this army . .
We have, therefore, to resolve to conquer or to die."

Illustration by Conerly, ©Courtesy of Marshall Field's

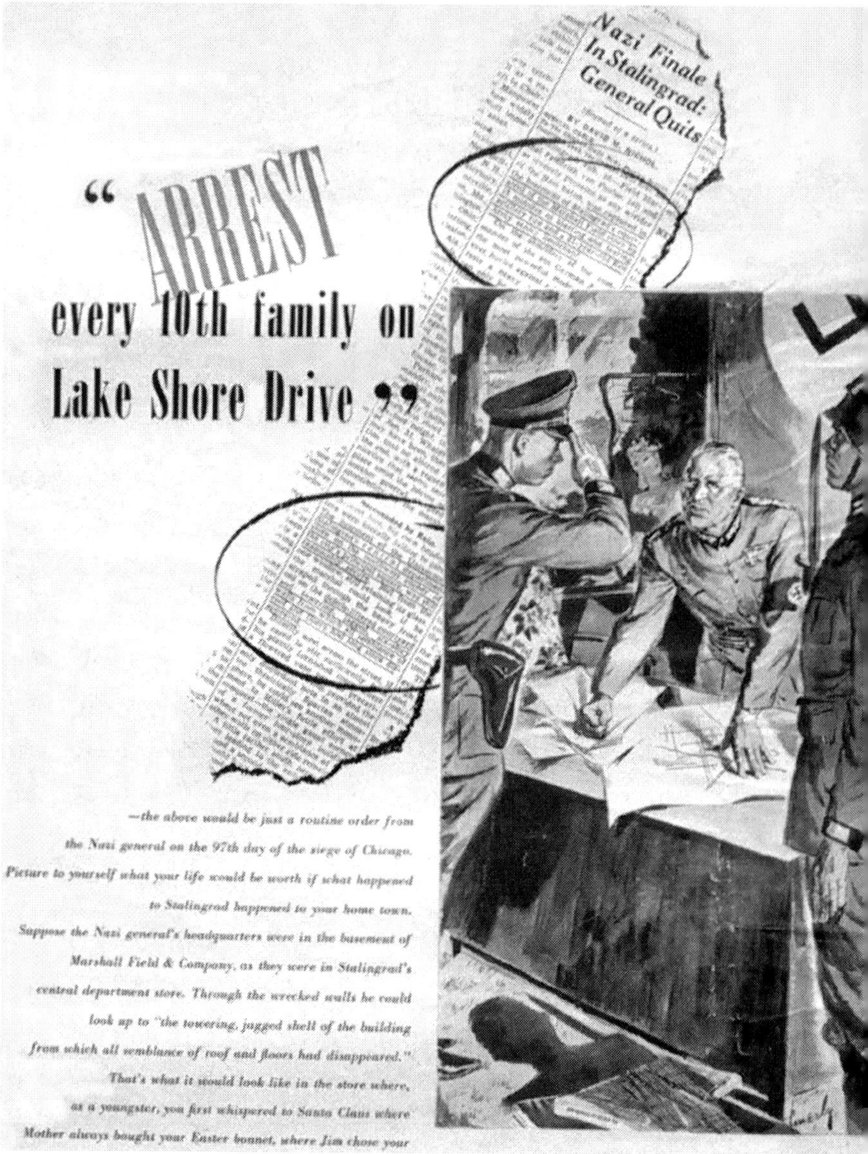

Illustration by Ruth Conerly, ©Courtesy of Marshall Field's

Illustration by Ruth Conerly © Courtesy Marshall Field's

Come Christmas, a series MOON AND CHRISTMAS called attention to the efforts of resistance groups in conquered European countries. As each country was overcome by Nazi rule, the leaders fled to England: King Haakon VII of Norway, President Raczkiewicz of Poland, Queen Wilhelmina of Holland, Queen Marie of Yugoslavia. When Hitler's invasion of Russia bogged down, partisans in the occupied countries initiated a mounting tide of sabotage. To support these groups, the Allies began dropping leaflets and encouraging them to adopt the "V" for Victory, painting it on buildings and ringing it in Morse code from bell towers.

For Greece's partisans, Ruth called on her love of ancient Greek history, architecture and sculpture and drew a Greek soldier standing beneath the towering marble columns of the Parthenon, a rebellious "V" painted over the Swastika. To commemorate Holland's partisans, Ruth drew a ghostlike figure etching a defiant *Merry Christmas* on a frozen canal, while a Dutchman made the sign of the "V". For Norway's partisans, Ruth drew a snowy mountain scene with a set of skis and an "H" crossed with a "7" for Norway's exiled king Haakon VII, fighting symbol of the Norwegian underground. In tribute to the Yugoslavian resistance force: a boat setting out on a nighttime mission with its flag, the skull and crossbones and motto "Freedom and Honor of Fatherland."

At times Ruth imagined herself a soldier, armed with a paintbrush. Curiously, at last she was painting historical scenes. History in the making!

As the war raged on, rationing, frozen salaries and the scarcity of housing made life increasingly difficult. In 1943, Ruth and Ted finally found a house. The weeds were high, the paint pealing, and its single bathroom was hardly adequate with Janey (husband Johnny off commanding a submarine) and maid, Eleanor (needing her supply of snuff). But at six thousand five hundred dollars, it was a deal and Ruth quickly transformed it from neighborhood eyesore to showpiece.

Not all was ominous. One boy, whose parents had a farm and cows, offered a pound of butter a week as payment for art classes, eliminating mixing color into the tasteless grease being used as butter substitute. A deal joyously accepted.

THE MOON and CHRISTMAS

it shines on brave people everywhe

Live forever, Greece!

V

This is first of a series of Christmas
Real Tributes to our fighting Allies.

The moon shines on Greece . . . on the marble whiteness of the Parthenon, floods the land

**For Greece Ruth drew a Greek partisan beneath the Parthenon,
a rebellious "V" painted over the Swastika.
Illustration by Ruth Conerly, © Courtesy of Marshall Field's**

For Holland, a ghostlike figure etches a defiant *Merry Christmas*
on a frozen canal while a Dutchman signals the sign of the "V"
Illustration by Ruth Conerly, © Courtesy Marshall Field's

HE MOON and CHRISTMAS

it shines on brave people everywhere

The moon shines on Norway . . . turns ski trails to rippling ribbons of shadow . . .

or Norway's partisans, snow-capped mountains and a set of skis
h an H crossed 7, evocative of Norway's exiled King Haakon VII
Illustration by Ruth Conerly © Courtesy Marshall Field's

**In tribute to Yugoslavia, a boat on a midnight mission,
its flag "Freedom and Honor of Fatherland" at the mast
Illustration by Ruth Conerly, ©Courtesy of Marshall Field'**

Always necessary, a bit of humor
Illustration by Conerly, ©Courtesy of Marshall Field's

Ruth's illustrations were now chronicling major battles in the Pacific. They heralded men like Claire Chennault, hero of the Flying Tigers now commanding the 14th U.S. Air Force, and Marc Mitscher, commander of the aircraft carrier Hornet, from which Colonel Doolittle's pilots took off to bomb Tokyo, their pilots knowing there was not enough fuel to return.

And a touch of Texas
Illustration by Conerly, ©Courtesy Marshall Field's

**Ruth's illustrations were now chronicling major battles
in the Pacific, heralding men like Claire Chennault.**
© *Courtesy of Marshall Field's*

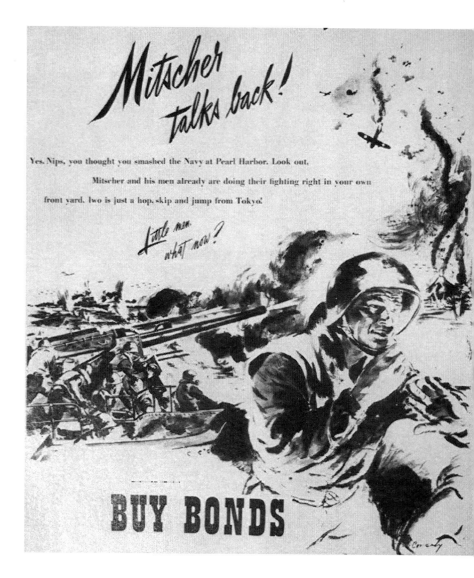

**Marc Mitscher, commander of the aircraft carrier Hornet,
from where Colonel Doolittle's pilots took off for Tokyo.
Illustration by Conerly, ©Courtesy Marshall Field's**

Increasingly Ruth met with other artists involved in the war effort. While visiting James Sessions, doing war work for Willy's Overland Jeep, Ruth was overwhelmed when Sessions gave her two magnificent paintings of his own, a battle at sea and a woman on a wharf. As Ruth was leaving, Session's mother said, "He'll do it every time. A pretty face and he'll give away his finest work!"

Abashed, Ruth insisted he take them back, but Sessions would not hear of it.

Artist Harvey Dunn in front of one of his paintings

Another artist with whom Ruth met was Harvey Dunn. A giant of a man from the prairies of South Dakota, Dunn's masterful paintings of early pioneer life were as much a part of American heritage as his illustrations while working as war correspondent during the First World War.

After meeting with Dunn, Ruth too was offered a job as war correspondent. Later when Sharon asked why she refused, Ruth responded, "And who do you think would have taken care of you, with your father off gallivanting around the country?"

If Ruth's expression implied that Ted might be doing more than selling art supplies while out on road, Ted firmly denied it. It brought to mind stories Othermama would tell of how during the Civil War, men became so scarce women actually chased them. And how Othermama's own father had been lured away...

"I was about five years old, sitting on the front porch with my mother, helping her to shell peas, when this pretty sixteen-year-old widow walked by, twirling her umbrella and flicking her skirts – a terrible insult in those times – and Ma whispered, 'There goes that little hussy! She's after your pa.' But the little hussy took Pa away, making me to do all the chores. Ma died of a broken heart, people said."

Ruth doubted Ted could be lured off. "Make a man comfortable and you can't chase him off!" Lizzie would say. Even so, as the war's toll rose and ever-younger men were being shipped off, the calls increased, until Ted openly jested, "A man's safer on the battle field than here at home."

One day though, hearing a familiar voice, Ruth held out the receiver, "Ted, it's one of your girlfriends!"

Ted took the receiver and after listening a few seconds, shouted angrily, "I'm sick and tired of your calling my home. There is *nothing* between us or will be. Is that clear?"

Ruth was satisfied, even more so that night when Ted whispered, "With a woman like you, how could a man ever look at anyone else!"

Soon after, Ruth left for Chicago to visit Marshall Field's VICTORY CENTER. Heart and pulse of the drive to sell War Bonds, VICTORY CENTER hosted a celebrity every week. Helen Hayes, Marlene Dietrich, Eddie Cantor, Groucho Marx, Sabu and his elephant, Betty Grable, Hildegarde, the cast of "Oklahoma", Maurice Evans and the King Sisters were just a few of the many who appeared in Marshall Field,s sponsored shows.

Colossal exhibits honored every branch of the United States Military Forces: Army, Navy, Marines, Air Corps and Coastguard and their feminine counterparts: Wacs, WAVES, WAFS and SPARS, along with Engineers, Amphibious forces, Sebees, Paratroops, Signal Corps, V-mail staffs, and war correspondents. Located on the first floor, new entrances had to be cut into the store to bring in airplanes, ducks (amphibious military trucks), big guns and major military equipment. Visited by millions, VICTORY CENTER had become the model for drives across the country.

Back home, Ruth found a pile of fan mail. One soldier wrote that he had hung one of her illustrations next to his Betty Grable poster! A great compliment as *pin-ups* were the coveted delight of fighting men. Al Parker, a leading commercial artist, was now famous for his girly pin-up posters. On meeting with Parker, Ruth was gratified when he expressed amazement at her ability to draw "out of her head."

"Sit here and tell me how you do it!" he urged. You don't mind my sketching you while we're talking, do you?"

Ruth Conerly sketched by Al Parker

As the war raged on, the government required ever larger sums to finance ships, planes and aircraft carriers – and a harder push to sell war bonds...

Illustration by Conerly, Courtesy of ©Marshall Field's

But Ruth felt a pervading sadness for so many dead and the wounded filling military hospitals. In spite of a heavy workload, she made weekly visits to San Antonio's military hospitals, giving art classes or just sitting beside some young man, sketching his portrait or just listening. And it was appreciated. One grateful soldier later sent a package with his letter - an exquisite pearl necklace.

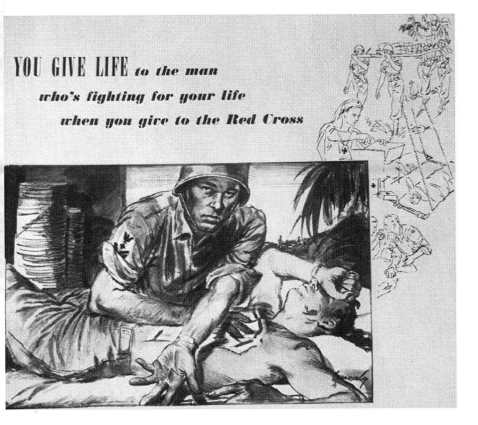

Illustration by Conerly, Courtesy of ©Marshall Field's

Although her personal life was often relegated to second place, Ruth never forgot her daughter. Ever since Sharon's near starving, Ruth supervised her meals carefully, seeing she had proper nutrition, swimming classes to avoid drowning, horseback to learn how to handle a horse safely and ballet for grace and form. "After all," she asserted over any protest, "you're my greatest creation of art."

When Sharon got a severe case of poison ivy requiring hospitalization, Ruth was terrified. One night on entering the dark hospital room and seeing her daughter covered with a sheet, she pulled the sheet back and was about to kiss her good night when she found her lips inches from those of a dead body. The hand holding the sheet went into electrified convulsions. Her screams echoed down the hallway. Ruth was still trembling when a nurse ran in and explained they had moved her daughter to a larger room down the hall, so this one could revert to its normal use, for bodies. She was still shaking on driving home.

General MacArthur's return to the Philippines – fulfilling his promise, "I shall return" – was a momentous occasion, requiring publicity. For it, Ruth received photographs of General MacArthur *and* General Wainwright with instructions that it was important to include Wainwright in the illustration. All knew that MacArthur had followed orders and escaped from the Philippines, but Wainwright had refused to leave the 12,000 Americans under his command, for whom there were no rescue ships. Thin and emaciated after the Bataan Death March and two years of captivity, Wainwright was a keystone in the upcoming offensive.

Important to show him and MacArthur affably reunited for the final push to victory.

Aside from briefings as to delicate political situations, geographical descriptions were also important. In March of 1945 U.S. troops took Manila and to give authenticity for the illustration commemorating the liberation of Manila, Ruth received a photograph of an old landmark church.

Similarly, in giving tribute to the mighty B-29, heavy bomber of the "Flying Fortress" type, it had to be well depicted with its turret-mounted machine gun providing defense against enemy aircraft.

MacArthur's return to the Philippines required publicity,
but important to include Wainwright in the illustration.
© *Courtesy of Marshall Field's*

For her illustration commemorating Manila's liberation, Ruth received a photograph of an old landmark church.
© Courtesy of Marshall Field's

But after Manila came the terrible battles for Iwo Jima
and Okinawa ...

Illustration by Ruth Conerly, ©*Courtesy of Marshall Field's*

Blast 'em, B-29s!

These blasts, little men, are just American drops in the bucket. The thundering cloud blotting out your Rising Sun is not rain from Heaven, Nips—it's a deluge of fire from the greatest air force the world has ever known.

Tokyo, here we come!

BUY BONDS

...BRING PEACE TO THE PACIFIC IN '45

To render tribute to the mighty B-29, this "Flying Fortress" had to be well depicted with its turret-mounted machine gun. Illustration by Ruth Conerly, ©*Courtesy of Marshall Field's*

After the Allied victory in Europe, thousands of war-weary soldiers were shipped home for a brief furlough before being sent to the Pacific, for what would be the most man-costly battle yet. The invasion of Japan, Operation Olympic.

Preparatory for this, Ruth had received an outline. But her illustration was never published. Instead, at higher levels another decision was made. Marked "Urgent," the new outline showed a single plane, leaving in its wake an image of a giant mushrooming cloud.

The war was over. Thousands of men poised for a battle estimated to be the most costly in lives yet, breathed a prayer of thanksgiving. One soldier in a Thailand hospital said, "When the news came over the hospital speakers, there was a long silence. Then from every corner, voices of the wounded could be heard shouting and crying."

FOUR FLAGS OVER TOKYO, the illustration symbolizing Victory over Japan, required Ruth to show four flags: the U.S., Soviet, Chinese, and British flags.

"Why the Russian flag?" Ruth questioned. "Russia never declared war on Japan."

"They just did," she was told. "Stalin's claiming Manchuria and North Korea as spoils of war."

"Interesting," she observed dryly.

Of the many war illustrations Ruth did, THANK GOD, showing a mother embracing her returning son, was doubtlessly the most moving. Symbolic of a nation welcoming home her sons, it caused an avalanche of requests for copies and reprints.

Marshall Field's WWII War Bond drive sold the largest sum in U.S. War Bonds during World War II. And Conerly's illustrations were a cornerstone of that campaign. Two illustrations won the 1945 Wartime Advertising Award and Ruth herself was given a gold medal **Victory Art Award** for excellence in illustration.

THE BATTLE THAT NEVER WAS
Ruth's illustration of the invasion of Japan was never published.
Instead, another outline was sent marked "Urgent, top secret."
© Courtesy of Marshall Field's

Four Flags over Tokyo!

The standards of free men are massed
in the skies of the East...heralding a thundering
might never felt before in all the world...signaling

"Why should I put the Russian flag?" Ruth questioned.
"Russia never declared war on Japan."
©Courtesy Marshall Field's

Thank God, published in major cities throughout the
United States received an avalanche of requests
for reprints and copies.

XVIII

Mansion on a Hill

It was a dream – an English manor on a hill overlooking the city of San Antonio.

"And with five bathrooms!" Ted quipped happily.

Built on speculation in the late thirties, it was drastically reduced during the war when gasoline rationing impeded living there. But as neither Ruth nor Ted required daily commuting, they acted on heart. Six months later, when the war and gas rationing ended, they realized they had made the buy of a lifetime.

In front was the home of Colonel Horner, owner of the San Antonio Light newspaper, which had recently published an article on Ruth. Next to him, lived the owners of the Dallas Furniture Company that had just commissioned Ruth to do a series of illustrations on their new line of patio furniture. The postwar was keeping Ruth busier than ever.

America's returning soldiers needed civilian clothes and WACS and WAVES wanted dresses and coquettish hats. Significantly, fashion was back. Bobby socks were out, replaced by heels and nipped waists. Not since the thirties was there such a demand for fashion and fashion illustrators!

Reconversion Center

We've streamlined our Men's Store to turn service men into civilians in jig time. Alterations are given top priority. Come in to Joske's and meet your old friends — in clothing: Society Brand, Worsted-tex, Goodman & Suss, Kentcraft, Goodall, Hyde Park; in shirts, Arrow and Wings, in hats, Stetson, Resistol and Mallory; in ties, Wembley, Arrow and McCurrach, in sportswear, MacGregor, Irby-Thompson, Pony Express, in shoes, Florsheim and Winthrop. Ex-service men in every section to help you. Rush here— we'll make you a "Mr." in a hurry!

Illustration by Ruth Conerly

Fashion Illustration by Ruth Conerly

Photograph of Ruth for a news story

Everywhere companies were expanding and new ones springing up, requiring advertising and illustrations – all bringing a roster of major accounts to Ruth's doorstep. Companies like Humble Oil, Lone Star Beer and Allied Stores.

Illustrations by Ruth Conerly ©Humble Oil and ©Lone Star

Ted too was feeling the buoyancy of the postwar economy. Increased advertising meant increased demand for art supplies. Having worked with Grumbacher throughout the war years, he was now much a part of the company's postwar expansion, traveling throughout the United States, opening new areas. After returning from a business trip to Hawaii with owner Walter Grumbacher, the two were reviewing company objectives over dinner at Ted and Ruth's new home when Grumbacher said: "Ruth, Ted is a born salesman. I've never seen anyone as effective! Whether landing a new account or smoothing over problems with a client... a word, a joke and it's magic!"

After fourteen tumultuous years and multiple uprootings, Ted seemed content in his work and lifestyle. Their new home had a size and boldness that spurred their imagination and its decoration brought a new excitement into their lives. The large entrance hall, bordered by an imposing stairway, led to a spacious living room with high ceilings and glass doors opening onto a terrace. Below that, they built a second terrace for dancing and parties, choosing patio furniture from the Dallas Furniture Company, a trade-off for Ruth's illustrations. On the north side, Ruth built a studio, with a north light.

To ease her foot in such a large house, Ruth ordered thick carpeting in the same pale beige as the walls, further increasing the image of lavish space. For curtains, she painted tropical leaves on tall panels of white chintz and sculpted her "Creation of Man" with an Eve, two nudes struggling up from their earthen bases. These she placed in the living room on either side of the sofa, explaining to her horrified adolescent daughter that in better society this was not considered vulgar and there was no reason she should feel embarrassed – even if boys did see them.

Only Eleanor, Ruth's cook and right hand of four years, objected to their new home. It was too big for one maid and, worse, her husband, "that black man she wanted nothing to do with", worked as bodyguard for their next-door neighbor, who couldn't be any great thing to have a gangster like him employed! Ignoring Eleanor's bent for drama, Ruth hired a girl to help with the cleaning and thought the matter resolved.

Wrong. A week later Eleanor's husband was shot. "Daid," Eleanor elaborated. Although this seemed to lend credence to

Eleanor's story, Ruth calculated with him gone, Eleanor had no reason to leave now.

Wrong again. Eleanor discovered she had inherited a fine downtown apartment building and a sizable bank account, requiring her supervision. A month later on paying a visit, Eleanor was a changed person. Fashionably dressed, she came in a Cadillac, chauffeured, and wearing a mink coat on a warm day.

"Kinfolk I barely know coming out of the wallpaper, telling me 'bout their woes and miseries, she lamented. "Makes me long to be back here where I was appreciated for myself, felt like family." After a lengthy visit, she dabbed a tear with a lace handkerchief and hugging Ruth, Eleanor pulled her mink coat about her and signaled her chauffeur. It was her finest performance.

Of the various friends and neighbors dropping by to observe Ruth's decorating and landscaping, next door neighbor Susan was the most frequent. Her place, she claimed, although of similar structure, was drab and depressing. Ruth went over. The house was indeed drab, but instead of considering Ruth's suggestions, Susan said she had already decided to buy a home in Alamo Heights. Maybe Ruth would like to go over and see it?

The house was indeed impressive. Not as large, well-built or with the amount of property of her present home, but exquisitely decorated and beautifully landscaped.

"The owner promised to leave everything just as it is, for only..." Susan quoted a price that almost made Ruth gasp. The owner obviously had an eye for color and design *and for business.* Ruth decided that fixing up and selling homes might well prove a profitable enterprise.

At that moment, the owner walked in. Tall, svelte and distinguished-looking, Mrs. Halvor McGrath was a striking figure of a woman.

"What a beautiful home you have!" Ruth commented.

Ann laughed. "I was barely through fixing it up when a real estate agent came by, wanting to know if I'd sell it. This is the third time this has happened. My husband Halvor says he's going to start calling before coming home – to make sure we still live in the same place."

Ruth laughed, extending her hand. "I'm Ruth Conerly."

Ann stared. "The famous fashion artist?" Ann exclaimed. "Of course! I thought I recognized you. There was an article and a photo of you in the paper just the other day. All about how today's top designers are beating a trail to your doorstep and swanky eastern stores fly down Lily Dache hats and Schiaparelli gowns!"

Ann then confessed that fashion had always fascinated her and she and her husband Halvor had even been thinking about creating a line of fashions.

"Well, if you like fashion, drop in sometime. I don't suppose I could talk you into modeling?"

"I'd love it!"

A week later, Ruth and Ann had worked out a business arrangement. Ann's chic made her an exceptional model and her discerning eye could pick the suit or gown which would make the most striking illustration. More important, Ann proved an excellent business manager. At first, Ruth was alarmed by what Ann wanted to bill for a particular illustration, but when the new charges brought no objection, Ruth conceded it was more in accord with what she should have been charging. With Ann's organizing skills, Ruth soon got down to what she did well – drawing, resulting in an increased volume and quality of work. And more time to spend with Ted.

Some of their favorite places were Port Aransas, famed for its tarpon fishing, and Mexico. In Monterey they rode donkeys to the falls and bought a chair with a bullet hole and blood-stained seat, where the salesman assured some governor had been assassinated.

On their return, Ruth took Sharon to have their pictures taken in the Mexican blouses Ted had bought them.

Then she decided to do a portrait of Ted. Now at age thirty-seven, his features had more depth and character, she felt.

"You are an exceptionally handsome man, you know," she remarked tilting her head and squinting while extending her paint brush toward him for perspective.

"Later I'll have to do a painting of you all dressed up..." Her voice trailed off as some technicality of the developing painting claimed her attention.

**Ruth and Sharon had their pictures taken wearing the Mexican
blouses Ted had bought them.**

Ted and Ruth
in Monterrey, Mexico

Painting by Conerly in
Monterrey

Husband Ted by Ruth Conerly

Swept into a world of renewed goals and illusions, they found themselves enjoying a new romance in their lives. Ted was an imaginative lover, always full of playful initiative, and Ruth, passionate by nature, responded with delight.

Always a generous spender, Ted loved to party and their new home was ideal for entertaining.

As San Antonio's Fiesta Week approached, Ruth did a series of illustrations publicizing the River Parade and other events with fashions by leading world designers. While attending the inaugural ball at *La Villita,* they met Eduardo Martinez, whose orchestra had just won first place in Mexico's Festival of Music. Eduardo's interpretations of their favorite pieces, *Brazil, Seboney, La Comparsa* were so beautiful that Ted asked him to play at their home to premiere their new terrace. That night, Ted's expertise on the dance floor made Ruth feel she was dancing *under crystal chandeliers.*

After their guests had left, Eduardo stayed on, telling stories of his youth and Ruth was fascinated to learn that he had ridden with Pancho Villa and actually been his bookkeeper.

"*Talvez* Villa considered a boy more trustworthy, or maybe it was simply because few could read or write then," Eduardo said with a shrug. "But after Villa died, I lived in constant fear. People thought he had left a great treasure hidden somewhere and threatened me and my family to tell where. But there was nothing left."

Amazed, Ruth told Eduardo about how, when she was a child in Kingsville, a group of Pancho Villa's men had ridden in and shot her friend's father as they were coming out of the theatre and that her father had killed several of the raiders.

Then alarmed, Ruth asked, "You weren't with them that night, by any chance?"

Eduardo shook his head and seemed puzzled. "I can't remember Villa ever attacking Kingsville. We operated more to the west. But many outlaw bands were active then and people just called them all Pancho Villa."

Eduardo's musical virtuosity, together with his knowledge of history, soon made him a favorite person in Ruth and Ted's home.

Hardly could Ruth imagine that Eduardo would one day bring her valuable information for one of her finest paintings.

"The World Comes to Texas"

Conerly art animates San Antonio's Fiesta Week

Glorious Gowns for the Gayest Fiesta

**Conerly's fashion illustrations for San Antonio's
Fiesta Week showed a mastery of movement and style.**

Nearing her thirty-seventh birthday, Ruth realized there was little chance of a second child. After six miscarriages, she had become reconciled to the fact. But on suspecting she might be pregnant, she dared to hope. Ted was exuberant! At long last, a son!

But two months later, the bleeding began. And in spite of Dr. Juliet Lampe's measured voice on calling the hospital, Ruth could sense an undertone of urgency. Then all went fuzzy. On awakening, Ruth learned the operation had saved her life, but she could never become pregnant again.

In the following weeks, Ted became more demonstrative in his affections. Whenever he left on a business trip, he would call out from the entrance hall, "I'm gone!" and Ruth would hurry to him for a farewell embrace. And whenever his "I'm home!" resounded in the hallway, she would tumble from her drawing chair to welcome him home.

While out on the road, Ted frequently wrote home, but one day Ruth received an intriguing envelope.

Dearest Ruth,
Keep this sealed until I get home. I want us to be on the terrace together when you read it. Love, Ted

And when Ted next called out, "I'm home!" Ruth ran to him, happy he was home and curious about that enigmatic letter. That evening while sitting together on the terrace, Ruth opened the envelope.

Dearest Ruth:
I've always wanted to sit down and write you a letter that I felt would do my feelings toward you a measure of justice.
It would be an attempt like all writers – or would-be writers make at one time or another to make the world stand still by the sheer power of words.
At some period in every man's life, there is one woman whom he feels would be the one thing above material things that is worth calling his. There is never a time that I have sincerely felt otherwise toward you. I am certain that few men find such sustenance and happiness in having a person who lives the qualities you have.

Remember this always – that if anything I've ever said or done or will do, may hurt you, it was done in a moment of thoughtlessness.

I realize, as you too probably understand, that those unpleasant phases of our lives together were stones that we have used to build a true and enduring shelter for the love we now share for each other.

Let us pray that we will have each other today, tomorrow and forever. I feel this way about you and only you.

> *Lovingly,*
> *Ted*

Ruth folded the letter. Never could she remember feeling so deeply moved or imagine that after fourteen years they could be so much in love.

Ted was convinced this was his big opportunity to at last have a plane of his own, maybe a whole new career in aviation. At the end of the war, all kinds of war surplus had become available at give-away prices and this Vultee BT 13 (Basic Trainer) was a bargain. His business trips for Grumbacher justified the expense. Even Ruth had seemed amenable to the idea. Plane bought, Ted found a leather jacket at an army-navy surplus store that hinted of many missions flown during the war.

At summer's end with some forty hours of flight time, Ted flew to Clarksville to bring Sharon back from her summer visit with Lizzie. The flight went well, but shortly after his return he discovered the plane needed some parts replaced.

The problem lay in finding the parts. As these planes were no longer being made, there were no spare parts either. The only option was to buy another plane for the spare parts.

"By doing the repair work myself, I can save on the cost of a mechanic," Ted explained to Ruth.

Not wishing to doubt Ted's ability, Ruth nevertheless was skeptical. Recalling that a neighbor was an executive in a company specializing in plane maintenance, she decided to ask his advice.

On hearing the story, the neighbor's expression reflected concern.

"Ruth, aviation is very unforgiving of mistakes. To play mechanic on your own plane is not a good idea. To begin with, those BT-13s are not the best choice Ted could have made."

"What's the matter with them?"

"On reducing speed at landing, they're known to stall. Start vibrating – Vultee Vibrator, they call 'em! The other day I heard they're considering recalling them. Been a lot of accidents with inexperienced pilots."

"But Ted said it was a trainer plane, safe for even beginning flyers," Ruth protested. "The government wouldn't sell something if it weren't safe, would they?"

"In anything you have to know what you're buying. Especially planes. A stalled jeep, you can walk away from. But not a plane. When a plane stalls on you up there in air, it's like sitting on top of a piano in midair. "

Ruth shuddered. "I don't suppose you'd talk to him, would you? I know nothing about planes. "

"Frankly, Ruth, I probably wouldn't have any more luck than you. I've seen men like Ted. Flying isn't a means of transportation for them. It's an adventure. Like car racing."

Ruth's heart was pounding. "There must be something I can tell him that would make a difference."

"Tell him what I said. Tell him to junk that damn plane."

Bracing herself for the worst, Ruth nevertheless decided to give it her best shot.

"Frank's very qualified in his work," Ted admitted, "but what do you imagine the manager of a plane maintenance company would say about a man's repairing his own plane? I made my first radio, put together my first jalopy and spend as much time under the hood of that plane as in the cockpit. I don't need advice on what needs to be done. I need seven thousand dollars to buy a second plane for the parts – a situation that could be dangerous if ignored too long." Then hugging her, he pleaded, "Please, Sweetheart, help me out on this. I'll pay you back, I promise."

"But Frank said several of those planes have gone down and the government's considering a recall. If there are no spare parts available, why buy another plane? It's like going down a dead end street."

Ted looked heavenward as though incapable of explaining things Ruth could not grasp. Ruth, fearing any more said would provoke a stalemate, dropped the issue. As weeks passed and Ted continued to fly, she presumed he had managed to fix whatever was wrong.

In December, Ted said he had to see some clients in Colorado and would Ruth like to fly up with him? It was beautiful up there this time of year. They could go through Temple, see his parents then fly through Amarillo and visit her brother Preston and his family.

Ruth was awed by the scenery. Colorado's cold crisp air was exhilarating, inspiring silly things like making angel wings in the snow and throwing snowballs. And taking movies of each other. They spent the night in a rustic old cabin with an iron stove and cuddled under a patchwork quilt. Vance Kirkland, head of the Art Department at the University of Colorado, invited them to an art exhibit and Ruth bought two of his paintings.

Ruth regretted having to return to San Antonio that Sunday, December 8, but several Christmas ads were waiting. Ted had promised some clients he would take them up for a spin that morning. But as soon as he was through, he would fuel up and fly home.

Stapleton was a small field on the outer edge of Denver. It was a clear day. Ted had just returned from taking up a man and his young son. He was shaking hands about to leave when another man who had held back decided he too wanted to go up. Ted readily accepted and they took off.

The plane made a short turn around the field and was about to land when something went wrong. Someone said it was a freak downdraft. Another said there was no wind. The plane simply stalled in midair. The controller in the tower said he could hear a loud vibrating sound in the background and Ted's voice shouting over the noise, "Sweet Jesus, hold it!" as the plane plunged downward eight hundred feet and plowed into the ground.

Rocky Mountain News

87TH YEAR: NO. 343   DENVER, COLO., MONDAY, DEC. 9, 1946   PRICE

2 PERISH AS DENVER PLAN FALLS 800 FEE

Two men were killed yesterday when a plane plummeted 800 feet at Stapleton Airfield. The plane crashed with such terrific force that was buried three feet in the ground.

Victims were Thomas M. Lyons, 38, of 2352 S. Adams st., and H. Smith, 39, of San Antonio, Texas.

The men were killed instantly. Firemen worked for some time gett bodies out of the wreckage.

Smith was pilo plane, a Vultee BT-1 taken several pers it during the morn nesses said.

Several planes w air when the acc curred. Smith appar circling in prepar landing, accordin nesses, when the p out of control and c most straight down

The motor dug a in the field, and the buried up to the for of the wings. The crushed in the cock was decapitated.

The accident occ the extreme northea of the field.

Smith had been vi Denver for several d his wife. Mrs. Smith back for San Antoni the fatal flight. A

(Continued on Pag

Force of a crash which killed two men yesterday at Stapleton Airfield is shown in this picture, taken a few | minutes after the crash. The plane struck at an almost vertical angle, burying its nose in the ground three feet.

—Rocky Mountain News Photo by Morris Engle.

The controller in the tower said he could hear a loud vibrating sound and Ted's voice over the noise shouting, "Sweet Jesus, hold it!"

XIX

Alone

Sharon paused in the hallway, undecided as to answering the phone. Their Swedish maid maintained it was *her* duty to answer the phone. But thinking it might be her mother, Sharon picked up the receiver.

For long minutes she listened to the information a man was giving her, but thinking there must be some mistake, she asked him to repeat. When he did, she was certain there was some mistake.

Mr. Theodore Smith, her daddy, could not be dead. He was in Denver with her mother. It must be some other Mr. Smith.

But the voice insisted – Mr. Theodore H. Smith of 322 Broadview Drive West in San Antonio was dead. His plane had crashed that morning in Denver, killing him and another person in the plane with him.

Stunned, Sharon was barely able to formulate the next question. "Who was the other person? Was Mrs. Smith with him?"

Suddenly a hand brusquely jerked the telephone from her. Incredulous, she watched as the maid replied with cool indifference and hung up.

"Is Daddy dead?" she cried out. "Who was the other person in that plane?"

"Your father is dead," the housekeeper replied laconically. "Your mother was not with him. She'll be here shortly."

On Ruth's arrival at the San Antonio airport, someone called her aside and told her about the accident. In a zombie-like haze she returned home, hugged her daughter and began making calls. Ted's father asked if Ted could be buried in Temple and Ruth agreed. All of Ruth's family came. Lizzie was there, Preston, Ed and Christine.

On returning to San Antonio, Ruth glanced through the stack of telegrams and letters of condolences. One from Mayor Gus Mauermann and his wife advised: "It is our hope that in the intense application that your profession requires you will find consolation and comfort."

Mustering her last strength, Ruth did the Christmas illustrations waiting. One showed two children standing before a large open window looking out to where Santa soared across the sky on a covered wagon. The script said "So long, Pardners. See you all next Christmas". Staring at those words, the reality that Ted would not be coming home for Christmas or ever settled into her mind. Never again would she hear his voice in the hallway calling, "I'm home!" or see him extend his hand to dance, coaxing with a few steps.

As the finality of it all engulfed her, she felt carried down into a whirling void of grief and remorse. If only she had insisted he sell that damn plane or helped him buy the extra one he wanted, he might still be alive.

She recalled their last outing to favorite restaurant La Louisiane, how while Ted went for the car a Gypsy had read her fortune, saying she saw tragedy and two marriages in Ruth's life.

"Never," Ruth whispered.

Then recalling Ted's letter, sitting on the terrace reading it, she wept bitter tears. Suddenly the house that so excited them was more like a mausoleum full of ghostlike memories of Ted and how life had been such fun. Everywhere her eye fell – their bloodstained governor's chair, Ted's portrait – there was a reminder of what was gone forever. Trapped in a vortex of misery spiraling her ever lower, Ruth locked herself in her

room refusing all visits or calls. Only close friend Dr. Juliet Lampe could breach her depression. But on failing to get Ruth to submit to treatment, Juliet was considering electro-shock...

Dr. Juliet Lampe in front of portrait by Ruth

"*So long pardners* see you all next Christmas"
Santa Claus waves a last farewell to his partners in magic... the children of Texas! He leaves the land of poinsettias, of golden days, and brilliant nights... to soar away to the bleak North Pole to begin his work anew... to work against another year-another day when he will return to spread joy in the hearts of childhood. Happy Christmas!

SO LONG PARDNERS
Staring at those words, the reality that Ted would not be coming home this Christmas or *ever* settled into Ruth's mind.

Then it happened. Alone in her room, touching Ted's belongings with a nostalgia akin to reverence, Ruth found the letter. From a woman.

Among the letter's tender words, one sentence stood out:

"This woman you mention who helps you in your financial matters, are you sure there's no sentimental attachment?"

More violent than any electroshock, Ruth hit bottom and rebounded.

"The louse! The Goddamn, dirty, two-timing louse!"

It jettisoned her out of her reclusion more effectively than a bomb.

Thin and sunken-eyed, Ruth found herself confronting the real world. A world totally unconcerned with the wreckage of her life. There also awaiting was a stack of letters. One from the funeral home demanded *instant* payment of a *triple* funeral bill for Denver, San Antonio and Temple. Other letters informed her of returned checks and that she must make *immediate* cash payment.

On calling the bank, she found they had frozen all her accounts – checking, savings and safety box.

"Why?" Ruth questioned bewildered.

"Policy. Not until the estate is settled can we allow a widow to access any account."

"But how am I supposed to pay funeral expenses and live?"

That was not their concern. No, this was not done to men, only to widows. She must understand, when the household provider died, a woman's financial solvency was questionable. No, it didn't matter if the woman was a professional artist and had her own money. It was a matter of *policy.*

When the grocery and pharmacy canceled her credit, she realized how little things had changed since 1920, when her father died. In this modern 1946, a widowed woman became *ipso facto* a social and economic liability. As a matter of policy.

Enraged, Ruth gradually calmed down and examined her options. Ted had never thought it important to buy insurance. But recalling the two annuities she had bought for Sharon's education, she phoned Prudential. The two policies were available and she could borrow on them, which proved manna in the wilderness. With that, she paid the funeral charges, the housekeeper, releasing her, and bought groceries. Thinking Ted might have something due in salary at Grumbacher, she called, but was told Ted had collected his last salary before leaving for Denver.

Minutes later, Walter Grumbacher called back, saying the employee was mistaken. Ted *did* have money owed him and he was taking it to her personally. Aged and visibly grief-stricken, Grumbacher said he couldn't believe it. Ted had been like a son to him. He wrote out a large check, insisting that this was truly owed to Ted.

Shortly before Christmas, Ruth went to Clarksville. On the drive up, she realized she had neglected her daughter. Yes, Sharon could keep those pieces of her father's watchband and the leather pilot's jacket he had been wearing. No, she had no idea who had sent them.

"I was about your age when my daddy died," Ruth recalled. "We were left in terrible poverty. Mother said I had to be earning my living by age fourteen.. No, no you don't have to go to work. Just keep helping me and we'll make it."

In Clarksville, Lizzie was waiting with open arms, and although on the trip up Ruth had talked optimistically, once at home with her mother she gave full rein to her grief and fears. And as the days went by, Ruth's despair grew more intense, defying all solace. It was almost as though Ted's death, more than a tragedy in itself had brought back all the fears, loneliness and ostracism she had suffered as a child with her father's death, a pain locked away these many years.

Finally when Ruth cried out, "How can I manage without a husband and with a daughter to support?" Lizzie told her!

"Do you think the world is coming to an end because you lost your husband and have a child to support! I was left with five children, a bankrupt business and a mountain of bills, and I got to work. You're a successful artist, capable of making more money than most men ever see in a lifetime. Now you pick yourself up and get on with your life. I did it, and you can too!"

Ruth stopped whimpering. Chastised and with new determination, she returned home, settled the estate and got back to work. Business manager and friend, Ann McGrath breathed a sigh of relief, as did Caroline Shelton, art director of Joske's. A small woman of swift movements and decisions,

Caroline had studied art and fashion illustration at L'Ecole Nacionale des Beaux Arts in Paris and was in her element with the surge of French designers.

"I thought our artistic complicity was ended!" Caroline declared, relieved to have Ruth back. "I'm sending out several outlines with valuable merchandise under armed guard."

Ann McGrath was there in a flash, thrilled to model "all that gorgeous stuff." Ann's enthusiasm stirred Ruth's professional zeal, reawakening her interest in life.

One morning, observing her reflection in the mirror, Ruth was stunned by the sallowness of her complexion and the gray in her hair. She made an appointment at the beauty parlor and started eating better and exercising. Encouraged by the improvement in her appearance, she bought some new clothes, and ventured out socially.

On attending a fashion show previewing the spring fashions, Ruth was surprised to see the walls on either side of the models' ramp held Conerly fashion figures, blown up to giant size. After the show, people pressed around, complimenting her on her work and appearance, making her realize that at age thirty-eight she was not just a successful artist, but an attractive woman capable of looking glamorous.

Not long after, a widower with whom she shared an interest in archaeology and ancient civilizations, invited her out, and she accepted. Then a friend, owner of an art gallery, called. He had a rare unsigned watercolor by Frederic Remington that the artist had left as payment at a boarding house. He wanted Ruth to have it in gratitude for the clients her recommendations had brought. He also wondered if she might hostess with him an art exhibition he was giving. Ruth said she would be delighted.

A few days later Caroline Shelton, art director at Joske's called again. "There's something big afoot!" she said excitedly and then lowering her voice conspiratorially, "Two executives from the New York offices are in town."

Obviously Caroline's recent promotion to vice-president of Joske's made her privy to secrets in top executive echelons. Ruth was well aware that Joske's New York offices meant Allied Stores, owners of Joske's, Stern's of New York, Jordon Marshes and hundreds more, comprising the largest chain of department stores in the United States.

"What's up?"

"This is strictly confidential, of course," Caroline warned, "but Allied is planning to enlarge Joske's. Make the Largest Store in the Largest State, even larger! And these two executives, their top store designers, are here to evaluate the feasibility of the project! Calvert (Joske's president) is all excited. He feels that if Joske's has a large enough parking area around it, the crowds will keep coming downtown instead of going to these new suburban stores. He asked me to personally see that these fellows are made to feel comfortably at home."

Then, as if just thinking of the idea, Caroline asked, "Ruth, why don't you let them stay at your home? They would hardly be noticed in that big house of yours and the company would pay for their living expenses. They're bachelors and awfully cute."

"No."

The next day when Ruth's housekeeper said that a Mr. Layne Carver of Allied was on the phone, Ruth recalled Caroline's maneuver with annoyance, but accepted the call. Mr. Carver said he and Arvid Zachrisson, had invited Mrs. Shelton out to dinner and wanted to know if Ruth might join them.

Ruth hesitated, but curiosity won out.

Layne Carver was tall with a debonair mustache and a devilish glint in his eyes. About forty something, Ruth judged. Arvid Zachrisson was shorter, more serious, until he smiled and his blue eyes lit up.

"People call me Zach," he said, then added that he had long admired and collected her artwork, making Ruth wonder if she had been a bit harsh in her judgment.

That evening at dinner, the two executives admitted that Allied was indeed considering enlarging Joske's to double its present size and Caroline, hard pressed to control her delight, kicked Ruth under the table.

It was an enjoyable evening. Not long afterward, Layne and Zach invited Ruth out again, this time as a threesome, and she accepted. On a third invitation she opened the door to find them in a heated argument.

Layne, trying hard not to laugh, explained that on the way out they had decided to buy her some chocolates.

"I decided," Zach clarified with annoyance.

"Correct," Layne granted condescendingly. "And I offered to go in the store and buy them."

"And here on the doorstep Layne gives me this lousy can of chocolate covered peanuts, while he.."

"Is tendering this magnificent box of Whitman's Sampler as his gift," Layne said smiling devilishly. "And that is what brought on Zach's rude and unsavory display of behavior."

Was this some kind of stunt, Ruth wondered? Were these two for real? Layne, decidedly the more charismatic, had a repertoire of stories. He said his father had been a horse trainer and a close friend of Buffalo Bill and that as a boy he loved nothing better than to eavesdrop as they exchanged bawdy tales of wild adventures, drank rotgut whiskey and matched wits with imaginative profanity.

Zach, a Bostonian of Swedish descent, was far more serious and reserved, although once, when one of Layne's anecdotes held Ruth too raptly attentive, he broke into a creditable soft-shoe dance. He said that as a boy he earned his first money in Vaudeville, before learning sign painting. From there he went on to gain skill in drafting which in time led to store planning with Allied Corporation. Zach said his progress in Allied was due in part to his "peace-making" ability, calming the turbulent waters of strained egos.

And once when Layne left the room, Zach said, "Especially I have to keep an eye on Layne, who doesn't always show seriousness in his work."

When Ruth mentioned this to Denny, Joske's chief store decorator, Denny firmly disagreed, saying that under all his funning, Layne had incredible creative talent, intelligence and practical sense. "Zach has remarkable ability too," he added, "reconnoitering a terrain, so both sides of the bridge meet in the center, you might say."

Ruth decided that Zach was a person of contradictions. A collector of old books, he admitted having little time to read them. And although his conversation reflected a fascination for the mysterious or unexplainable, when Ruth mentioned having met a wealthy Texan pursuing Big Foot and the Abominable Snowman, Zach called it a waste of good time and money.

"A fool and his money are soon parted," he opined sagely adding that he was a conservative person with a good deal of

stock in Allied Corporation among his investments, mostly
blue chips.

Layne showed a definite interest in Big Foot. "Ideal
opportunity to find out if women's fascination for... big feet is
well-founded!"

Layne was fun, while Zach was a paradox. Zach insisted
he loved art and enjoyed nothing more than visiting an art
gallery, but when Ruth mentioned that a friend, the owner of
an art gallery, had invited her to hostess a show with him and
would Zach enjoy going, Zach recoiled. He said he was
surprised she would consider anything so improper. People
might presume she and this *art salesman* were engaged! Or
worse!

Decidedly a contradictory person, Ruth decided. A bit
stodgy to boot!

Of the many vacation spots springing up everywhere,
dude ranches were fast becoming popular. And the nearby
town of Bandera, offering horseback riding, rodeos, Western
dances, hoe-downs and jamborees was a great favorite.
Responding to the new craze, stores pushed their Western
attire, requiring publicity and illustrations – all coming to
Ruth's doorstep like a California gold rush.

One Bandera ranch that had commissioned Ruth to do
the illustrations for its promotional campaign was preparing a
grand opening rumored to be the social event of the season.
On learning that Ruth was among the prominent invited
guests, Layne and Zach hurried to Joske's President Calvert
to secure invitations. They then visited Joske's western shop
for proper western attire.

It was a real bash, Texas style. After the rodeo, there was
a Western dance with band, Bar-B-Q and cowhands. From
handsome rope-twirling young men to bow-legged, tobacco
chewing old coots, all ready to show their talents in
traditional dances like Cotton-eyed Joe, the Schottische, and
Put your Little Foot.

When one, snaggle-toothed old toot sashayed up to Ruth
and, fanning his sweaty underarms, asked "Care to struggle
this one out with me?" Zach's face fell and Layne's devilish
eyes lit up on seeing Ruth daintily accept.

With the new craze for dude ranches, rodeos and Western dancing, stores pushed publicity for Western attire. Illustration by Ruth Conerly

At a party to greet the newly arrived engineers and designers from New York, Layne reenacted the scene and Ruth laughed. When someone told a joke about Texas, Ruth joined in. But then someone made a joke about the South, and Ruth's good humor vanished.

"I think it appropriate you learn your first lesion about Texas,' Layne pointed out. "Here in Texas you can joke about Texas and Texans will laugh along with you. But never joke about the South."

"Yang Dankees beware," Zach joined in putting his arm around Ruth.

Illustration by Conerly

Ruth Conerly, Self-Portrait

XX

Two Gallants and a Choice

By now it was apparent to Ruth that Zach and Layne were competing for her attention. Like two adolescent boys in a game of one-upmanship, they vied for her approving smile. If one of Layne's stories made Ruth laugh, Zach would soft-shoe. If Zach told some tale laced with tender sentimentality, Layne would simulate violin playing. But it was fast becoming clear to Ruth that of the two, Zach seemed far more determined, constantly trying to steal moments alone with her. His compliments and penetrating looks made her ever more determined to evade him.

Finally, tired of beating around the bush, Zach proposed outright. When Ruth refused, claiming her grandmother Othermama would turn over in her grave if she were to marry a Yankee, Zach replied, "Madam, rest assured. In our home you would never hear any sanctimonious Northern tripe!"

Surprised by this deft answer, Ruth nevertheless could not picture herself married to this pragmatic, unexciting man. And a few days later, when a call came from Dallas offering her a yearly base salary of $60,000, Ruth asked Sharon what she thought.

"What's holding us back?" Sharon replied.

"It would mean selling the house and moving to Dallas."

"Any problem with that?"

"Nothing I can see," Ruth agreed.

Even so, Ruth vacillated and showing an incredible naïveté, she asked Zach's opinion. Zach promptly found more problems concerning Dallas than its mayor knew about.

"And what about your loyalty to Joske's and Allied?" he questioned. "Joske's is counting on you to promote the new expansion."

It was precisely at this moment, like in some Broadway play, that Helene came onto the scene. Tall, skinny as a fashion model, twenty-five, and absolutely beautiful, Helene's appearance was abrupt and electric. Moreover, she made it perfectly clear in words and body language that she was in love with Layne. Nor was it possible for Layne to hide his fascination for her. He was like a man struck by lightening and Zach wasted no time in supplying Ruth with the details of their ongoing romance.

"They're one for another!" Zach concluded triumphantly. And if Ruth had been harboring an inclination toward Layne, decidedly the more handsome, interesting and fun, Zach now seemed the more dependable, the only one eligible for that matter.

Animated by his advantageous situation, Zach pressed his suit with new vigor. So much that Ruth began to vacillate. Might she be making a mistake in refusing Zach?

While pondering who might best advise her, Ruth's thoughts curiously turned to Ted's aunt, George Bridgers. Dorm mother and advisor of girls at Trinity University, George had always impressed Ruth as intelligent and sincere.

While listening, George showed no great surprise. She said that when she was first widowed, several men had become attentive and one had actually proposed, but imagining she had plenty of time and other offers would be forthcoming, she put him off.

"And I lost him," she said with an expression reflecting sadness and nostalgia. Then with a gesture brushing aside what was past, she added, "For a while, when you're first widowed, men flock around. There's an aura about a widow that men find irresistible. Remember that story artist Charles Gibson illustrated, of a widow and all the suitors thronging about? She becomes a nurse and they fill every bed in her ward. She goes to a costume ball as Juliet and they all come dressed as Romeo, all standing around frowning at each other. The only thing is, in true life, time slips by and before you realize it, you find you're alone with no one asking you out or offering marriage."

George's words were to wield a considerable impact on Ruth. Although not possessed of any overwhelming passion for Zach, she wondered if there might be an advantage in making a more weighted and mature evaluation of a marriage partner this time.

Zach was not a bad choice, really. She had not wanted to pry into his financial situation but imagined him to be reasonably well-off. He had mentioned being married once previously to a concert pianist. The reason for the divorce, he said, was that they had agreed to respect each other's religious preference – he was a Lutheran, she a Catholic – but no sooner had they returned from their honeymoon, she invited a priest to dinner. Zach packed his bags and left.

Ruth thought it a bit rash and wondered if there could be more to it, but having no radical denominational leanings, she foresaw no conflict in this area.

No one understood how Zach so quickly convinced Ruth to marry him. Layne seemed totally amazed. But on July 3, 1947, barely seven months after Ted's death, Ruth and Zach were married. A short time later, Layne and Helene were married.

For their honeymoon Zach took Ruth to Boston to meet his family. Anders, Zach's widowed father, a master cabinetmaker, had kindly blue eyes and gave Ruth an exquisite jewelry box of intricately inlaid woods he had made for Zach's mother. Zach's brother Carroll, a professional photographer, had flown many missions over Europe during World War II, filming strategic areas and had been an admirer of Ruth's WWII work. Zach's sister Svea, married to Ralph Colson, Director of Physical Education of Massachusetts was a close friend of someone everyone considered important in Massachusetts's politics, a fellow called Joe Kennedy.

"And this is my baby sister, Sanna," Zach said with obvious pride. "Librarian at Harvard!" Dressed simply without a trace of make-up, Sanna made Ruth long to show her how a touch of make-up and different attire could wield miracles.

Ruth listened to their stories about Zach, how at Christmas Zach's gifts were always the most generous. They joked about how a Swede never says "I'm fine! But answers solemnly, *"Jag kan inte Klagar"* meaning I cannot complain.

"And never expect a Swede to tell you what is wrong," Svea volunteered laughing. "He withdraws and pouts! The silent freeze-out. To make you feel guilty."

"Give the gift that lasts – guilt!" Sanna put in.

Ruth laughed delighting in it all. They gave the impression of a happy, united family with Zach as the beloved elder brother, his few idiosyncrasies, minor and laughable. Hardly imaginable that, deprived of this respect and adoration, he might be a very different person.

Almost immediately though, Ruth began to suspect she had married two men: one, good-humored and outgoing; the second, far more complex and capable of unpredictable reactions. Before their marriage, Zach would encourage her to talk about Ted, listening sympathetically. But as soon as they were married, he said she must not mention his name again. It was unhealthy to think of the past. When on their return to San Antonio she found a letter from Ted's father and mother wishing them well, Ruth was amazed when Zach forbade her to have any contact with them. It was dangerous to their marriage, he claimed. Ruth thought it cruel as it meant denying them any contact with their granddaughter. But she agreed.

When Zach's sister Sanna came to visit, Ruth was pleased. Intelligent, well-read, Sanna quickly endeared herself to Ruth. And when Ruth said, "Just for fun, let's make you gorgeous!" Sanna was all interest and cooperation. With touches of make-up and pointers as to fashion, the results were dramatic.

Observing herself in the mirror, Sanna turned one way and another, hardly believing the image reflected. That afternoon on introducing her to a neighbor's son, Sanna's mood was lively and outgoing and she rushed in to tell Ruth the incredible news.

"He invited me out to dinner! What should I say?"

"How about *yes*?" Ruth suggested. "He's from a good family, an only son, an engineer, very eligible."

"I won't allow it!" Zach protested vehemently on coming home. "Sanna, how could you even consider going out with a man you know nothing about?" And before Ruth's astonished eyes Sanna's glow and lightheartedness vanished. She virtually withered.

That night Zach made his displeasure even more evident. "What do you think you're doing! Sanna has a natural beauty. I won't have you ruin her, painting her up like some common prostitute, encouraging her to go out with men. She has enough on her hands with her work and taking care of our father. She shouldn't have come here. I'm sending her home tomorrow."

Ruth thought it unimaginable to deny a thirty-year-old sister the right to a life of her own, intimidating her that way. Sanna's expression of shame was pathetic.

Recalling the saying, "Give the gift that lasts – guilt", Ruth wondered if it was actually a joke. Or a veiled warning.

But Ruth agreed it was no affair of hers and promised not to meddle in matters of his family.

A week after Sanna's departure, Ruth and Zach drove to Clarksville where Lizzie had organized a family reunion. Some thirty family members were there for the homecoming luncheon at North Lake Country Club where Ruth posed with a rolling pin beside a smiling Zach for a family photograph. It went so well that Ruth decided to present Zach to her second family.

Artist Franz Strahalm had long passed away, but Mrs. Strahalm, now living on a farm near San Antonio, had her whole family reunited to welcome Ruth and her new husband. Recalling Ruth's love of horses and riding, there were horses saddled and waiting. That afternoon after lunch Zach listened to Mrs. Strahalm's recollections, plying her with questions.

"Tell me, what was Ruth like as a young girl?"

And Mrs. Strahalm, remembering how Ruth would dance and frolic with her daughters, searched her limited English and with a broad smile happily proclaimed, "Oh, Ruth was wild!"

Zach forced a smile. The change was so subtle no one noticed. But on the drive home his voice took on a satirical sweetness as he questioned female morality in general, moved on to intimate that no attractive young girl out on her own could remain chaste. Then shouting furiously, he accused Ruth of having been promiscuous as a girl and ordered her out of the car.

Ruth could not believe it. Finding herself alone on the highway, she barely managed to walk back to the Strahalm farm where humiliated and in tears, limping with the strain on her foot, she explained what had happened.

The Strahalms were horrified and united in their condemnation of this monstrous act against their beloved Ruth.

Try as she might, Ruth could not imagine what had gotten into Zach; all his excuses seemed inadequate. But finally she forgave, hoping that things would normalize allowing her to get back to work – ultimate catharsis for all stress.

But another far worse situation was about to occur.

Ruth had imagined there might be some conflict between Sharon and Zach. When a woman remarried, her children sometimes found it difficult to accept a new man. Anticipating this, she had explained to Sharon that it was important she have a father. A nice home and proper background were not sufficient. A father figure lent protection and respect.

"And I must think of my future," Ruth added candidly. "In a few years you will marry and be gone and I will be left alone without a companion in life."

Although not convinced of her need of a father, Sharon acknowledged her mother's right to her future and promised to accept the new order with good grace. In all truth, she had nothing against Zach. While courting her mother, he seemed quite nice, often talking to her in an amicable fashion.

Even so, at the wedding reception recollections of her father came surging forth. When the photographer started herding everyone together for photographs in the living room, in the exact place where her father had taught her to rumba, Sharon could almost see him demonstrating the steps. By supreme effort she controlled the urge to run away and cry, but a smile was simply not forthcoming. And the more the photographer insisted, the more stubbornly Sharon frowned. The camera, treacherously truthful, captured a happy group with a sullenly defiant child in the foreground.

Ruth opted to ignore the matter. Zach's father, the older and wiser Anders, advised him "be patient and more understanding of this unfortunate orphaned child." But ruining his wedding photographs was something Zach could not accept. He was convinced it bespoke an innate hostility to him and a danger to his marriage. A child needful of a strong disciplining hand.

People had warned him that a person of Ruth's professional status would be strong-willed and difficult to govern. He had frankly been surprised to see Ruth submit to his authority with such docility. But her daughter, although cordial, went on with her life as though he didn't exist, never asking his permission or consulting him. As an executive in a major corporation, he was conditioned to keep a cautious eye out for what was going on around him. And whenever he saw things happening about which he was not consulted, he took it as an inherent threat to his position of authority.

Not strangely, Sharon's upcoming slumber party with twenty classmates invited, without requesting his permission, made Zach *uncomfortable*. An all night party of twenty adolescent girls called a *slumber* party? The noise would not only keep him awake, but the task of controlling a house full of giddy girls would be horrendous at best. Overhearing that it was important Manuel, the gardener, do a good job for the party, Zach told him his services would not be needed that week. But Sharon mowed the entire acre and attended the gardens, actually doing a remarkable job.

On hearing that *boys* might be coming by, Zach was horrified. Determined to end the matter with one masterstroke, he ordered five trucks of horse manure spread thickly over the yard and watered down until the stench was intolerable. Unbelievably, Ruth managed to convince Sharon the manure had been previously ordered and that it wasn't anything intentional.

Most incredible, the party was not called off.

The twenty girls had barely arrived, when Zach announced he was going to bed. "To sleep," he emphasized. Fifteen minutes later he was back, face contorted with rage, a desperate Ruth trying to restrain him. Between gritted teeth, he told the amazed girls that if anyone spoke a word, he would personally throw them out of the house, even in the middle of the night. Immediately phone calls went out and parents rushed to pick up their terrified daughters. It was all over by nine o'clock.

Zach was sure he would no longer be ignored in this household.

But instead of the docility he imagined, the result was far the opposite. The next day Sharon curtly informed him that he was a rude and disgraceful person and she would never speak to him again. Unaware that in Zach's world, "not speaking" or "withdrawing" was a prerogative of men only, not women, much less to be tolerated in a child.

Tension mounted. Mealtimes became a trial of nerves where Sharon's silence was a reminder of her inconceivable insolence. Until one evening Zach seized her arm and began slapping her until she fell to the floor. Momentarily petrified, Ruth was about to run for a broom or skillet, when she heard someone running up the back steps. It was Layne. With one viselike grasp he seized Zach, shoved him aside and knelt beside Sharon, who even now, whispered, "I will never speak to him again."

In defense of his actions, Zach accused Ruth of being so wrapped up in her work she could not see that her daughter was a brat, needful of discipline. Although Ruth had barely restrained the urge to run him out of the house, uncertainty gripped her. Might he be right? Certainly the child she had always been able to manage with logic had turned perversely stubborn.

A few days later Ruth was still gripped by uncertainty when Zach's voice went into that silky mocking tone auguring trouble. He would not tolerate this disrespect any longer, he sustained. Sharon would either speak to him respectfully, or he would beat her until she did.

Seeing him leap after her, Ruth held his arm and shouted, "Sharon, run to your room. Lock the door!"

Ruth's legs propelled her as never before as she ran after them. By the time she got to the top of the stairs, Zach was lunging against Sharon's bedroom door. Suddenly, like at no other time, Ruth's Scorpion exploded.

Just as the door was about to give away, she grabbed his shirt and as he turned, her fist hit his jaw with a force she never imagined herself capable. For long seconds he stood dazed as blood gushed from his mouth.

"You knocked my tooth out," he said looking down at the tooth in his hand.

"Yes, and if you so much as touch my daughter again, I'll knock every tooth out of your mouth. Now you get out of my house. I want a divorce!"

That night, pondering his situation, his tongue exploring the empty space where his tooth had been, Zach realized that things were not going well for him. He had married a woman highly valued in Allied Corporation, where he worked, and where they were counting on her in promoting Joske's expansion. He was living in an elegant home with someone who went to great lengths to make him comfortable, entertain his friends and business associates. Paid more than her share of the bills, asked very little really in return. Except never say anything against the South... and now this new thing, never lay a hand on her daughter, a stubborn, obnoxious brat, but not without some merit, perhaps.

Less a tooth as he was, he might live with this. One thing for sure, that saying about Southern women having 'an iron fist in a velvet glove' was one hell of an understatement.

Never in his days of amateur boxing had he seen a right so effectively applied. Probably due to all that drawing and painting. Wonderful artist... good cook too. It might be a good idea to make an effort to control his temper.

But the next day Ruth gave no sign of a reconciliation.

"Let me tell you something you Northern men may not be aware of," she informed him. "Out on a farm you can walk through a pasture and likely nothing will happen. But never touch a calf. Don't even walk between a cow and her calf. Unless you want to die!"

He could believe that. And when Ruth said, "My father never laid a hand on me and I won't have anyone hitting my daughter," he believed that too.

But then she said, "At this moment I frankly would like you to leave, but if you can make your peace with Sharon and behave yourself, I'll give it some consideration." And Zach dared to hope.

At breakfast the following morning, Zach drew a funny clown with an expression of repentance on the manila covering of Sharon's notebook. Perceiving a faint smile, he drew another happy clown. Impressed by the caricature and amenable to the gesture, she said, "That's cute. Wish I could do that."

"I'll show you, if you like."

Things began to improve. On learning Sharon wanted to modernize her room, Zach showed her how to make a scaled plan and took her to Joske's warehouse of unfinished furniture. He then showed her how to sand down and finish furniture. The shared project brought a new comradeship and respect. Relieved, Ruth went back to work.

The postwar boom with its bonanza of marriages was generating a big demand for bridal gowns and Joske's Bridal Salon enjoyed world-wide prestige. So much that in 1947 when Britain's future Queen Elizabeth II married Prince Phillip, the *deshabillè* for her wedding night was ordered from Joske's of Texas. Made of forty yards of georgette and satin, with roses and bows, it cost the momentous sum of three hundred dollars – which the labor party pointed out as double the average British laborer's monthly salary!

Ruth wondered how the groom found his way through it all.

In 1947, Britain's future Queen Elizabeth II ordered the *deshabille*
for her wedding night from Joske's of Texas.
Illustration by Ruth Conerly

Everywhere companies were expanding and new ones
springing up, people showing amazing resourcefulness for
creating new things, such as Charga-plates, escalators and
missiles to the moon! All requiring publicity and illustrations.
It reminded Ruth of her father's words about the incredible
things this century would bring — and how illustrations
attracted people to buy things.

Shopping was a chore in 1873 . . . .

But in '48 with a Charga-Plate' it's a pleasure

People were showing amazing resourcefulness for creating new things like CHARGA-PLATES...
Illustration by Ruth Conerly

ESCALATORS...

AND MISSILES TO THE MOON
reminding Ruth of her father's predictions of the
wonders this century would bring. Illustration by Conerly

By 1948, Layne, Zach and the store planning division were busy enlarging Joske's. Allied Corporation had bought up a large swath of land for the new construction and surrounding parking area. Dozens of old adobe and limestone homes dating back to early San Antonio history succumbed to the economic expansion. Only the old St. Joseph's Church in the middle of the projected construction resisted.

Finally the planners had no choice but to build around it.

A diverse group of men, they enjoyed pranks and partying and Ruth's home soon became the favorite after-work site for cocktails and dinner. On one such evening, while commenting on the latest hit mystery film THEN THERE WERE NONE, wherein several persons were invited to an old English mansion and one by one imaginatively murdered, Ruth exclaimed, "Wouldn't it be a fun theme for a Halloween party for Sharon!" And all agreed.

With macabre imagination worthy of Edgar Allen Poe, Ruth wrote out. verses creating a blood-strewn trail throughout her English manor. As children followed the verses, finding murder weapons and bodily remains, bones in the chimney grate, meat and catsup in an upstairs tub, a skeleton borrowed from a college anatomy department, running feet and screams were heard everywhere. It was such a success, the store planners decided to make an even better Halloween party the next year.

And they did. Ruth illustrated and Zach scripted the invitations with blood red ink announcing a "Treasure hunt on Zachrisson Island." On the entrance walls, Ruth painted towering buccaneers with swords and knives drawn. Beyond that, a jungle island was created. For this, Layne raided Joske's warehouse trucking off life-sized animals – lions, giraffes, tigers, and elephants used in window displays at circus time. And on the back lawn, the store designers of America's largest chain of department stores built a life-sized galleon, with bosomy figurehead, a skull and crossbones flag and a plank for captured victims to walk.

Across the galleon's bow, Zach scripted *The Lady Sharon Smith* in bold lettering.

**Allied store designers Layne and Zach were busy with plans
to *double the largest store in the largest state.***

NOTICE to all Pirates and Other Shades of Jean Lafitte's times..

There is to be a RAID on the Blockhouse at Zachrisson Island...

OBJECT: THE BURIED TREASURE OF THE BUCCANEER SHIP "LADY SHARON SMITH"

For Sharon's party Allied's store designers built a lifesize pirate ship in Ruth's yard

"Some party!" Ruth exclaimed.

That Christmas Ruth's full page Nativity scene carried a hopeful message.

"On Earth Peace, Good Will Toward Men"

**Husband Arvid Zachrisson "Zach"
by Ruth Conerly**

XXI

A Need to Control

Ruth had always felt a special kindred with her brother Preston and when he and his family moved to San Antonio in 1949, Ruth was delighted. In childhood, a time the world seemingly turned against them, they bonded together protectively. As a man, Preston's expressive blue eyes and kind manner were sharply remindful of their father. Like him, Preston loved history and the little known facts behind historical events. Lately he had become particularly interested in the family tradition of their descent from George III and the Quaker girl Hannah Lightfoot. He had even come across a book suggesting that the marriage had actually occurred.

But that morning, when Ruth and Sharon stopped by for a visit, Preston had a new topic of interest. His new next door neighbor.

"He's from Costa Rica in Central America, Ruth. His father was a Chicago newspaperman, who went to Costa Rica in 1890, got into the lumber business and construction. Our neighbor married one of two sisters considered the most beautiful women of Costa Rica. The other sister married the president, named Calderon, who established labor laws, a social security system and started the University of Costa Rica. But last year a revolution overthrew their party so our neighbor, fearing for his life, brought his family here. Their five-year-old son plays with our daughter, Martha Jane, calls her *Martita,* and their two sons, well-mannered, nice-looking boys, go to Peacock Military Academy here in San Antonio."

As Preston walked Ruth to her car, he nudged her. "That's their oldest boy, Arthur, out in front now. Why don't we introduce him to Sharon."

On being introduced, neither showed any interest, but that evening Preston called Ruth. His neighbor had dropped by to ask if she might ask her husband if their son might escort their daughter to a dance at Peacock Military Academy. It would be properly chaperoned.

When Zach heard all this, and that he was being consulted, he loved it! This was Old World formality, the way things were *properly* done in Europe and among the better families in Boston. No boots and "want to struggle this dance out with me?" type of thing. Rising to the formality of the occasion, Zach told Ruth to find out more about the family's background. When an even fuller story was forthcoming, Zach, barely able to contain his satisfaction, approved.

Fourteen-year-old Sharon said that if this boy wanted to escort her to a dance, he should call personally. To this Zach threw up his arms, but granted that some concession to modernism was in order.

Ruth gave the matter no more attention. Her life was far too busy with an inordinate amount of work coming in. Fashion-wise Paris had re-established itself with designers like de Givenchy, Nina Ricci, Pierre Balmain and Pierre Cardin. Designers like Pauline Trigere and Maurice Rentner were also enjoying acclaim, but Christian Dior headed the list with his revolutionary "New Look." Impeccably structured suits with nipped waists, regal gowns and furs, all sent to Ruth's doorstep in armored cars with armed guard posted outside. In spite of Ruth's protests that it was excessive and more likely to attract attention.

By 1952, with fashion deemed "the embodiment of the age," Ruth was on a pinnacle professionally. Strangely though, the greater her success, the more hassle she got from Zach. Right now he was insisting she didn't need a maid. It brought memories of that day finding Ritchie Cooper scrubbing the kitchen floor, their bantering jokes about how men artists always managed to get a wife or mistress to scrub and cook for them, while women, no matter how successful, were never free of chores.

"For me, a maid is a necessity," Ruth insisted.

"My mother didn't have a maid," Zach affirmed in a tone precluding all argument.

"A fine person, I'm sure. But I have no intention of being worked to death."

"Did it ever occur to you that I might feel *uncomfortable* with a maid under foot?"

Ruth swiveled around her chair. "People are always curious why there are so few women artists in history! Shall I tell them?"

Zach made a tactical withdrawal.

Announcing the presentation of the
entire Fall 1952 collection
of the world's master of fashion...

Christian
Dior—New York

only at Joske's in San Antonio!

You are cordially invited to see the entire Christian Dior Collection for Fall 1952 at a luncheon presentation in the Colonial Room of the Menger Hotel, Monday, September, fifteenth at twelve-thirty o'clock and to meet Miss Mabel Glemby, Mer. Dior's representative in our French Room, Monday and Tuesday.

Sketched: Diorama: gold and silver lame strapless evening dress with a green faille stole, typifying Dior's "Campanile Look" ... a slender bell silhouette, molding the feminine figure to its natural beauty.

Joske's Famed French Room, third floor

Millinery by Christian Dior
Millinery Salon...Joske's third floor

Stockings by Christian Dior
Hosiery . . Joske's street floor

"Miss Dior" Perfume
by Christian Dior
Joske's Famous Toiletries . . . street floor

Jewelry by Christian Dior
Costume Jewelry . . . Joske's street floor

Illustration by Conerly

"Fact is women artists *have* been succeeding," Ruth fumed to her art board. "In spite of all the hassle they have to put up with! Much as she tried, Ruth could not understand Zach's need to reduce her to total domesticity. He was a successful executive. Why would her success be such a nemesis for him? But inevitably at any party if someone complemented her with enthusiasm, Zach might smile, but back home there'd be trouble. And heaven forbid if a reporter wanted an interview!

Of late Ruth found herself actually shying away from publicity for the sake of keeping peace, ignoring what her mentor Franz Strahalm had instilled in her, how fame was crucial to an artist's success, but ever evanescent, easily snuffed out. For a reporter to write a good article, the subject must cooperate with anecdotes and quotable phrases, be presentable, glamorous if possible for a photo.

At times the thought crossed her mind that Zach's first marriage to a concert pianist might not have ended in divorce for any religious differences, as he claimed, but because she simply refused to be bullied. In her most perverse moments, Ruth even wondered if Zach might have some compulsive love-hate attraction to accomplished women, pursuing them, then whittling them down.

It was difficult to understand. Ted spent her blind, but he was not at all like that. He wanted maids, agents and all the publicity possible.

While in this frame of mind, Ruth received an invitation from Witte Museum asking her to give a conference on art. She accepted. Then the McNay Art Museum asked her to give a conference and she accepted. When a leading university asked her to give a short course, she accepted that too. She had given such conferences before – in New York at the Phoenix Art Institute, in Chicago's Art Institute and enjoyed helping young artists.

The course was about to begin when a secretary called Ruth asking where she had gotten her degree.

"I went to Sullins College, but I don't have a degree," Ruth replied candidly.

A long silence. "Could I call you back?"

Later on calling back, the secretary was apologetic, but it was no longer permitted for someone without a degree to teach.

"That's quite all right," Ruth replied. "I'm far too busy now anyway."

"The stupidity of it!" Zach denounced "A perfect example of how people who can't earn a living at something, teach it! And are always afraid a ray of genius might break through their wall of academic protectionism!"

Zach's reaction amazed Ruth. Illogical he would get so mad about something he didn't want her to do in the first place. But as Zach told the humiliating story over and over, Ruth wondered. More than wanting to appear supportive, might it have something to do with *his* job as store designer, without a degree, and seeing this as a threat to *his* job?

In all truthfulness, she was not overly curious. After seven years of marriage, she was tired of the daily battle of trying to work and keep peace. And overwhelmed with boredom with this pragmatic little tyrant. Long dead her dreams of *great* art, romance and a man that might *truly* fascinate her.

Encounter with a man from the Past

XXII

William B. Travis, Alamo Commander

In January, 1836, Colonel William Barret Travis and twenty-five men of the newly formed Texas Army rode to San Antonio de Bejar with orders to take command of the garrison there. In San Antonio, Travis found the volunteer army that had captured the town from Mexican General Cos. There too were Davie Crockett and his thirteen Tennesseans and James Bowie with his thirty men – a meager few to contend with Santa Ana's fast approaching army of thousands.

General Antonio Lopez de Santa Ana, known as the *Napoleon of the West*, tactically recruited men from one region to fight those of another. Those who opposed him were summarily put to the sword. Rumors of his vengeance on the city of Zacatecas had preceded Santa Ana into Texas, gaining the calculated reaction of terror and indecision. The Texans had dealt him a humiliating blow in defeating his brother-in-law, General Cos.

Travis, Bowie and Crockett realized a retreat with the wounded would be futile. To abandon them and flee would be dishonorable. The Alamo, an old mission fortress, offered the only means of defense. Surrounded by a wide perimeter affording little cover to an attacking enemy, they might, with proper reinforcements, delay Santa Ana's avenging sweep across Texas. To the demand of surrender, Travis fired a cannon shot and dispatched his famous "I shall never surrender or retreat!"

For thirteen days they resisted, but Travis' last letter showed awareness of his plight, "I feel confident that the determination and valorous courage of my men will not fail them in the last struggle..."

The assault came at dawn on March 6th, 1836. By daybreak the Alamo's 186 defenders had perished.

"It was but a trifle," Santa Ana remarked viewing the body-strewn battle scene.

"Yes," replied his field commander General Almonte. "But another such victory and we are lost!"

That March morning of 1953, Ruth read the notice in the paper that The San Jacinto Association was looking for an artist to depict the death of Alamo commander, William B. Travis. A committee and members of the San Antonio Art League would make the selection and the chosen painting would be placed on permanent display in the Alamo.

As to the artist, two requisites were specified: the artist must be highly qualified and a Texan.

Born in Marshall, Texas, Ruth's Texas roots could be traced back to the early 1830s. The battles for Texas Independence as well as the Civil War had been fed to her with molasses and corn bread.

And she was qualified. Conerly's ability to depict action and men at war had been demonstrated in the campaign that sold the largest sum in war bonds during World War II.

But at that moment, Ruth could hardly consider a project of that dimension. No longer did she have any supportive staff. Husband Zach insisted that privacy was not possible with servants underfoot. The stairs of her home were not as easy on her polio foot as before, and attending Zach's many business associates working on the enlargement of Joske's left little time for her work. While seemingly proud of being married to a famous artist, Zach was highly jealous of her time, making it necessary to avoid an overburdened schedule.

Ruth had forgotten the matter when Claude Aniol, owner of a publicity agency for whom Ruth did work, called. Claude, now also the chairman of the Fiesta San Jacinto Association, was curious. Had she seen their ad in the paper? The committee was anxious that this painting be of exceptional quality. He had been hopeful that Ruth would submit an entry. A finished painting was not necessary. A sketch and samples of other work would suffice.

"I can't possibly at this time, Claude," Ruth protested, but even then memories came flooding back of how as a child her grandmother, Othermama, had taken her to the Alamo, how standing in the dim quiet of the mission, Othermama had looked all about in awe and whispered, "I remember Pa talking about this, about what a fine man Mr. Travis was, and what a pity he had to die that way, and all those fine men with him." At that moment Ruth had almost felt the battle raging about her.

Claude interrupted her thoughts. "You were born in Texas?"

"Yes, my great grandfather Collins actually knew Travis."

"It's destiny then! We can give you all the reference material you need. We have Travis' diary."

A few days later the San Antonio Express carried the story:

Ruth Conerly Wins Fiesta San Jacinto Painting Award

FIESTA SAN JACINTO Association award of $400 for painting to be reproduced in elaborate invitations to April fiesta is won by Miss Ruth Conerly (left), professional artist, who is showing winning sketch of Col. William Barret Travis in Battle of Alamo to Claude B. Aniol (center), association invitation committee chairman, and Arthur E. Baird, association treasurer.

Considering the time and work involved, the $400 prize award was not a large amount. The guns alone, bought to insure authenticity, cost her more – long-barreled rifles and flintlock muskets, Bowie knives and swords. How true Gutzon Borglum's words to her, "Sculpture and fine art will starve you to death. Get out of it while you still can!"

But it was her father's words "My little girl's going to be a great artist someday," that she still held close like an amulet. And although her talent as a commercial artist was firmly established, she longed for those youthful dreams, where heroes, legends and artists great enough to portray them still existed.

Ruth quickly immersed herself in her subject. As with any illustration requiring historical documentation, this required research. Not just obtaining a description of Travis, his attire, weaponry, the plan of the Alamo's fortifications, but an understanding of the personality of the man. Much the same as putting muscle on bone and flesh on that, the underlying character behind his presence needed to be understood in order to infuse his figure with life.

Books like "The Tempered Blade" by Monte Barrett, "Judge Robert McAlpin Williamson, Texas' three-legged Willie" by Duncan W. Robinson, "TEXAS, An Informal Biography," by Owen P. White, "The Texas Republic" by William Ransom Hogan, were perused for any story relating to Travis.

From the onset, certain minutiae concerning Travis attracted Ruth's attention. Travis was born in 1809, a curious inversion of her own birth-year, 1908. Travis hailed from South Carolina, an area thick with Scot-Irish Celts, a fighting people. Ruth's Scot-Irish ancestors, the Calhouns, were fighters and hailed from South Carolina. "Travis had auburn hair," one reference said, "and a temper quick and only fairly well controlled." She too had auburn hair and a mind of her own, some insisted. An expert marksman, Travis learned early to shoot a squirrel in the head and skin a rabbit; Ruth too had been a sharpshooter. From early childhood she learned that shooting for the head was not a display of showmanship; you did it that way or you shot it to pieces and there was nothing left to eat. Travis loved to dance. In his diary, which Ruth touched with awe akin to reverence, Travis alluded to a flurry of invitations and romantic trysts in those last days before going into the Alamo.

When word came that Santa Ana's army had been sighted, Travis was at a fandango, dancing. Ruth loved to dance. Difficult to walk long distances, but she could dance the night away, and would have loved dancing with Travis.

Another thing Ruth found of interest, Travis' nickname was Buck, the same as her grandfather who had fought at Fort Gregg. In that last battle of the Civil War two hundred ragged remnants of Mississippi's manhood went down fighting. Taking down her old family book, Ruth reviewed her grandfather's account of that famous battle and a news article written by a correspondent of the London Fortnightly Review, in April, 1865:

> *"Fort Gregg, manned by Harris' Mississippi brigade numbering 250 undaunted men, breasted intrepidly the tide of its multitudinous assailants. Three times Gibbon's Corps surged up and around the works – three times, with dreadful carnage, they were driven back with an admitted loss of six hundred men. When at last the works were carried, there remained of its 250 defenders but thirty survivors. In those nine memorable days there was not an episode more glorious to the Confederate Army than the heroic self-immolation of the Mississippians in Ft. Gregg, to gain time for their comrades."*

For Ruth, the situation of the men in the Alamo and at Fort Gregg revealed an uncanny similarity. In both, the men had hastily improvised protection from old, near demolished fortifications. In both, some 200 men faced an attacking enemy of thousands. In both, the commanding officer was shot in the head: Travis at the Alamo and Colonel Duncan at Fort Gregg. In both battles the men had bought strategic time for their comrades-in-arms at the cost of their own lives and against every normal instinct to preserve one's own existence.

Allusive to the nickname "Buck" both Travis and her grandfather shared, Ruth found several dictionary definitions: "Buck, a young blood, a younger son of poorer aristocracy, poor but aristocratic." According to family tradition, Ruth's grandfather, Buxton Conerly was the great, grandson of

Buxton Lawn, son of King George III and the Quaker Hannah Lightfoot, decidedly a young blood of poorer aristocracy.

In each assignment a commercial artist accepted there were many things needing consideration. Sometimes the action hinged on a person or historical event, wherein costume and location must be carefully depicted. Sometimes it required solving a problem of drama or the time it occurred. In the case of the Alamo, the battle occurred in the twilight of early morning.

Although Ruth realized models and photography rarely captured dramatic action, Pierce McGrath, son of Ruth's business manager Ann McGrath proved highly effective in his portrayal of Travis, as did the youth who posed as Travis' servant Joe. Ruth considered Joe an important part of the painting. Described as twenty-three years old, about 5 ft 11, of good build and countenance, he was the last surviving person to see Travis alive. Frequently asked about the events he had witnessed, Joe's stories would vary, but his account under oath to the United States' government representative and to Travis' mother were remarkably similar. Joe said he thought Travis was only wounded, but on seeing the enemy "pouring over the wall like sheep," he had run back into the Alamo, later insisting he was a slave, as Travis had instructed him. In the painting Ruth placed Joe in the center background to Travis' right. Both color draft and sketch testify that her visualization of the battle scene was firmly imprinted from the onset.

One day watching her paint, husband Zach confided that while excavating the foundations of Joske's – a short block from the Alamo – workers found two skeletons in what appeared to be a tunnel leading to the Alamo. On calling the New York office, he was told "seal it up, say nothing about it." Too much valuable time had already been lost because of the old St. Joseph's Church they had to build around, to risk becoming involved in an archaeological debacle.

Even so, Ruth wondered about those two skeletons, who they might have been and what their mission was. An attempt to escape? Someone carrying Bowie's maps of the San Saba mines presumed lost in the Alamo?

With a Herculean capacity for reading, Ruth created a file full of notes and descriptions of Travis, things that might explain his decisive stand.

Pierce McGrath was highly effective in his portrayal of Travis, as was the youth who posed as Joe.

Conerly's early color draft

Early color draft and sketch testify that her visualization of the battle scene was well imprinted from the onset.

"Are you sure you had the right?" his father would ask whenever young Travis came home with a black eye or bloodied nose. And if that was satisfactorily surmounted, there was always the inevitable second question, "Did you stick it out?"

Another Alamo hero whose courage impressed Ruth was James Bonham. Just arrived in Texas, Bonham could not have felt Travis' intense cohesion to the cause of Texas independence. And yet Bonham rode out through enemy lines in search of volunteers twice, returning that final second time fully realizing he was returning to certain death. Ruth's research uncovered a poignant reason behind such courage. Travis and Bonham had been boyhood friends in South Carolina. When Travis' family moved to Murder Creek, Alabama, Travis and Bonham swore to visit, but twenty years would elapse before the two friends were to meet again – in Texas. Bonham's loyalty to the cause of Texas was indeed desperate – but because of his loyalty to Travis, the boyhood friend he could not desert.

Putting together Travis' physical features posed a special challenge for Ruth. In 1836, photography was non-existent. There were descriptions of Travis. Travis' brother described him as having "a powerful frame, a natural leader in appearance and personality." There was an amateurish sketch done from life and a photograph of a nephew, considered a look-alike of Travis. The McArdle portrait, frequently used in books, was painted in the 1880s, forty-four years after Travis' death.

"I compared the picture with the sketch some budding artist had made of Travis from life," Ruth explained. "Both had a long nose, a steady look from the eyes and a set look to the mouth. Travis was described as six feet tall, 175 pounds, with a high forehead, white from use of a hat, his lower face ruddy-toned from sun exposure. Every man I met six feet tall, I'd ask how much he weighed."

Increasingly Ruth found herself captivated by Travis' personal life. Like many men who came to Texas there was a dark side in his past. At age twenty, Travis had married the beautiful Rosanna Cato; she was expecting a second child when a neighbor's wife told Travis that Rosanna had been unfaithful. Although the accusation was considered false, Travis challenged the man to a duel and shot him. Then taking rifle, horse, law books and frock coat, he joined a wagon train for Texas, never to return.

Several references described Travis as a bookworm with a love of history. "If there was a book in Texas," Stephen F. Austin, father of Texas Independence, said, "Travis would find it." Especially he loved the stories of Sir Walter Scott and Lord Byron. For Ruth, also a book worm, this disclosed a realm of meaning. Sir Walter Scott, creator of Ivanhoe, Waverly and Rob Roy had immortalized his mighty clan: "A bold hard fighting clan were the Scots of old, whose boast was:

By the sword they won their land
And by the sword they hold it still!"

Lord Byron, often described as *the incarnation of revolt itself,* was the creator of many a romantic hero. Curious, Ruth reflected, that both of Travis's favorite authors had suffered infantile paralysis, as she had.

Over the years Alamo heroes Davy Crockett and James Bowie had been more romanticized, but for Ruth, Travis was a person far more noble and educated and with whom she could empathize. His letters pleading for reinforcements were the most inspired, moving and pathetic documents she had ever read. While researching Travis, Ruth wondered at the bond she felt for a man dead these one hundred and seventeen years, yet taking on life and significance for her.

One evening remembering the charismatic orchestra leader, who as a boy had ridden with Pancho Villa and loved history, she wondered if Eduardo Martinez might know something concerning Travis. But on hearing about the painting, Eduardo was not happy. Instead of sharing her enthusiasm, he insisted she give up the project. It was dangerous. There were hotheads resentful of the way many Anglos twisted Alamo heroism against people of Mexican descent, forgetting that Mexican fathers and sons had fought in the Alamo and signed the Independence of Texas, and Anglos had held positions in Santa Ana's government.

"John Bradburn to mention one," Ruth exclaimed. "Commander of the garrison at Anahuac, Texas, who shackled Travis and threw him into prison!"

"You read!" Eduardo exclaimed. "Most people are satisfied with demagoguery. Simple is easy."

Eduardo's concern for her safety impressed Ruth, but she was too gripped by this commitment – to portray Travis with impacting realism and make his death the most faithful rendition possible. And seeing her determination, Eduardo gave way, admitting that he did remember something...

"There's a letter somewhere, written by a Mexican soldier who was at the battle. He was writing home to his family after the battle telling about the death of his colonel by an Anglo colonel at the north wall."

"*The north wall!* That would be Travis!" Ruth cried out. "Do you know where that letter would be now?"

"It was in a collection of letters somewhere. It's in Spanish, but if I can find it, I'll translate it for you."

Dare she hope, Ruth wondered heart pounding?

Ruth had studied the final days leading up to the battle in great detail. Many of the Alamo defenders carried Kentucky Long Rifles used with a refined accuracy. A revised 1776 Revolutionary gun with a 39-inch barrel and overall length of 54 inches, the Kentucky Long Rifle delivered a .45 caliber ball effective at 200 yards, depending on powder load. Accuracy was encouraged by the fact that the marksman had only one shot before having to reload. Another factor was the pecan tree at the north wall. Travis had ordered every tree surrounding the Alamo cut. The enemy must have no advantage of protection. Only one pecan tree did he spare. A sketch of the Alamo by a Mexican engineer depicted that sole pecan tree destined to play a role in Travis' death.

Not long after, Eduardo called back. "I found it," he shouted triumphantly. "I found the letter!"

And to Ruth's amazement, the letter gave a detailed description of Travis's death. In an article published by the Houston Post August 3, 1986, Ruth's memory of her research and that letter was still clear and vibrant:

> "*After a lot of research, I had the battle and Travis well set in my mind. An eyewitness account gave me the details I needed, including his uniform. The wall on the north side of the Alamo was considered the weakest, so the attacks on the south and west walls were only a diversion to keep the Texans busy. The main assault was focused on Travis' north wall.*

Travis' servant, Joe, said they were tired the night before and went to bed with their clothes on. The next thing he knew, bugles were blowing, El Deguello was playing, meaning no quarter would be given. Travis jumped up, grabbed his coat, putting it on as he ran, yelling, 'The Mexicans are on us! Let's give 'em hell!'

Travis manned the 18-pounder cannon only he knew how to shoot. The Mexicans, many of them young farm boys who had never shot a gun before, said the barrage was something terrible. The canon, designed by an engineer from Napoleon's wars, had been brought to Texas by General Cos. I studied everything about it and finally covered most of it up in the painting, except the wheel.

A letter written by a Mexican soldier to his family confirmed much of what I had read. The Mexican soldier said he was approaching the north wall where there was a 'terrible firing of weapons and cannon.' His commander, Colonel Mora, ordered a sharpshooter to 'climb that pecan tree and get that colonel by the cannon!' This confirmed that Travis was wearing a uniform with a colonel's insignia. The Mexican soldier writing the letter said he saw Travis fall, but pull himself up on the wheel, and run his own beloved Colonel Mora through with his sword, the two embracing and falling together.

As the only tree was that pecan tree, I knew Travis was shot in the right lobe of the brain. But to know exactly how to pose him, I called a doctor friend who had been in World War II. I have to explain here that I often work late paying no attention whatever to the time. When the doctor answered, I said, "How does a man act when he's shot in the right lobe of the brain?" And the doctor shouted, "My God, Ruth, have you killed Zach?" (my husband)

"No, I'm working on this Alamo picture. Commander Travis is shot in the right lobe and I want to know what his position is as he runs his sword through a Mexican officer."

"Ruth, do you know what time it is?"

"No."

"It's ten o'clock. I went to bed early so I could get up for an operation at six."

But since he was already awake, he answered my question. "In the first place," he said, "he's dead immediately. Killing the Mexican officer is only a muscular reaction to a thought that was last pictured on Travis' brain before he was shot. Now, is he near something he can lean on? The cannon wheel? OK. If he's been shot in the right lobe, his left side is giving out, but he'll still be able to use his right arm to run that colonel through... "

It all fell into place. On observing the completed painting, Ruth was satisfied. A news article said, "With action all about him, Travis in the foreground is a figure of powerful isolation."

In years to come, President-elect Dwight D. Eisenhower, commander of Allied forces in WORLD WAR II, stood at attention before the painting and saluted. John Wayne enlarged it to giant size for the New York premier of his movie THE ALAMO and dignitaries from around the world posed before it. But for Ruth, the most memorable tribute came from a man in officer's uniform who standing before it cried out, "By God, this is a painting done by a man who knew war!"

Death of Col. William B. Travis, Alamo Commander

from the Panhandle to the Rio Grande . . . it's so easy
order by mail when you have a Joske Charge Accou

Ruth's illustration From the Panhandle to the Rio Grande
won a national award in advertising.

XXIII

Speak Softly

Over the years, Ruth had learned to be wary about too many triumphs. "Speak softly, for the Gods are jealous," the ancients would say. And personal experience had taught her that after every period of slow hard climb, there was a brief plateau of glory, followed by a swift downward plunge.

Certainly in that year of 1952-3, she had leaped like a top-performing thoroughbred over ever-higher hurdles on to more gratifying triumphs. Her painting of Alamo commander Travis, hanging in the Alamo and visited by hundreds daily, marked her as the only woman artist with a painting there. Observing its impact, reporters and news photographers had begun posing visiting celebrities in front of it or placing a commemorative wreath beneath it.

Hardly a block away, the enlarged Joske's of Texas was finished and awaiting its inauguration. If San Antonio had bragged of having "The Largest Store in The Largest State," it was now doubly and more luxuriously so. Zach, Layne and the store planning crew had done a superb job. And almost every major illustration in the promotional campaign bore the Conerly signature. Ruth's illustration showing Joske's peaceful coexistence with St. Joseph's Church had become a Joske's icon featured daily in newspaper ads alongside a picture of the Alamo. Her illustration "From the Panhandle to the Rio Grande," showing a Model-T delivering a package to a cowboy on horseback, had won a national award. Its script, "A charge account makes shopping by mail a breeze!" hinted that Joske's was imitating Sears lucrative catalogue business permitting Sears with fewer stores to harvest larger profits.

That year actress Gloria Swanson had also contacted Ruth. Epitome of the Hollywood glamour queen of the twenties, Gloria had just made a sensational comeback in the movie *Sunset Boulevard*. On winning the Golden Globe and nomination for the Academy Award, Gloria was anxious to put this publicity to more tangible benefit promoting her new line of clothes *Fashions for the Small Woman*.

**Actress Gloria Swanson also contacted Ruth.
After her movie Sunset Boulevard, she was anxious to
use this publicity to promote her new fashion line.**

While posing, Gloria said that before becoming an actress she had wanted to be an artist and sculptor and had studied at the Chicago Art School.

"I gave some classes there in the forties," Ruth said. "Oh, I almost forgot," she added and passed on the message that a leading San Antonio socialite had called wanting to invite Gloria to a dinner with all the city's highlife.

"Ruth, I'm an old woman. If I start accepting invitations from these women with nothing to do but give parties, I'll look terrible the next morning for my show."

Gloria's venture into fashion particularly interested Ann McGrath, Ruth's business manager. For some time Ann had been talking about going into the clothes manufacturing business and her husband Halvor had recently decided to back it financially.

"Ruth, women are on the move today, *working and traveling,*" Ann insisted. "They want casual clothes. Stylish, attractive, but easy to wear, easy to pack. The new synthetics are cheap looking, but there are combination fabrics, wrinkle shedding and more natural looking. Big skirts with tons of fabric and petticoats are not practical for today's woman, or the manufacturer. Halvor has been making numbers and feels we can make a go of this. And we want you in with us. Few people have your knowledge and experience in the fashion world. And those *Visualizer* books of yours are a treasure of what would make a terrific fashion comeback today, the slim classic line of the '30s."

Ruth was convinced Ann's plan was sound thinking. But when she mentioned it to Zach, he issued an ultimatum. Ruth was to release Ann immediately and forget all of this nonsense!

Ruth protested. Ann was an associate whose know-how and insight had greatly improved her economic situation. More important, Ann was a friend whose loyalty and advice she trusted. But confronted by Zach's demand – "It's me or her. Chose!" – Ruth gave in.

On doing a portrait of Ann's husband Halvor for Ann, Ruth insisted on doing Ann's portrait too. She wished them well in their venture, regretting not being able to join them. Something told her that Halvor McGrath Fashions was going to be a fabulous success – like everything Ann did!

Ann
Mrs. Halvor McGrath

But this loss was followed by one more devastating still. Preston's neighbor's son, from Costa Rica, had proposed to Sharon. And Sharon had accepted.

Ruth had nothing against Arthur. A fine young man – Zach frequently invited him over and had even insisted Ruth do a portrait of him – but she never thought Sharon took any serious interest in him. And when Arthur's family asked to have the wedding in Costa Rica and Zach promptly bought plane tickets, Ruth could see the handwriting on the wall. Her daughter, her only child, would be going half way around the world, forever.

Arthur in PMA uniform
Portrait by Conerly

Ruth's daughter Sharon marries in Costa Rica

The wedding was magnificent. But on returning to San Antonio, Ruth was brokenhearted. And finding no one to blame, she blamed Zach. He had favored Arthur over others, all part of a sinister plan to isolate her from everyone she loved. But now he had gone too far, taking away the person she loved most!

Joske's inauguration with its bevy of social events and all the hoopla Texans love, celebrities thronging in, helped to mitigate the pain. But no sooner was that over, another blow hit. The store was done. Zach and the store planners must return to Allied's New York offices!

Ruth did not want to go.

She did not want to leave her home in San Antonio, her brother Preston and especially she did not want to go further away from her daughter in Costa Rica. When Zach announced that he had turned the sale of her home over to a real estate agent, Ruth was horrified. How could he leave the sale of her home with some real estate agent without even consulting her! No agent would keep the house and grounds attended, necessary to get a good price. Her home represented a large part of her equity. And who would see that her furniture and paintings were properly packed and shipped?

But Zach insisted. It was all arranged. She must leave with him now. In the midst of her gloom, there was only one consoling light...

The Art Students League of New York. For years Ruth had yearned to go to this famous art school. There were new ideas and techniques she longed to experiment with. Among the many thrilling new concepts being taught by artist and *modernist instructor extraordinaire* Howard Trafton was the phenomenon of *hot and cold colors*. Trafton, who had quit the commercial art profession in 1936, was known to say, "As a *fine* artist you are a person. As a commercial artist you are merely an instrument."

And why not! Why not become a fine artist, Ruth wondered. *I've worked myself to a bone all these years and can certainly afford it now.* This might well be her long-awaited opportunity to be her own person!

No sooner were they settled in New York's London Terrace Apartments, Ruth enrolled at the Art Students League of New York. Almost immediately she found herself responding to Trafton's guidance and her own creative instincts long submerged, doing art she had long yearned to do, art for the sheer joy of creating. Each day she went out with a new zest and returned with a sense of accomplishment.

One day, while she was busy at work, Trafton paused and addressing the class said, "No artist can say anything worthwhile until he learns his craft first. Even Picasso, the most original artist of our times, began learning to draw as well as the Old Masters." And holding out his hand to Ruth, Trafton said, "And here in this class, I have a student who draws like a dream!"

Ruth floated home. Overwhelmed with happiness, she told Zach. That same evening he demanded she withdraw from her classes.

"But why?" Ruth asked amazed.

"Don't you think I would like to go to art classes too, instead of working like a mule while you live a carefree Bohemian life?"

Crestfallen, Ruth was nevertheless determined to ignore the incident and keep on with her studies. This was a whole new future, an opportunity she had always dreamed of.

But on returning home each evening, seeing Zach's accusing look, the cold silences interspersed with sarcastic comments of how he was working, killing himself, while she was out enjoying herself, she realized that all her happiness was being replaced by a conditioned response of *guilt*. *"Give the gift that lasts... "*

Slowly her illusions faded and after only four months at the League, Ruth sorrowfully withdrew. It was a totally down moment in her life. To further compound her sense of futility, a letter arrived from her brother Preston saying that her home was in shambles, unrecognizable, the yard all grown up in weeds.

"Listen to this!" Ruth exclaimed, showing the letter to Zach. "The place is a mess. Who's going to buy it like that at a decent price! I'm going back and handle the sale myself."

But Zach insisted the contract with the agent would soon expire and to give it a few days.

Two days later Zach announced the agent had sold it. Hearing the price, Ruth became almost physically ill. How could he have accepted such a ridiculous price without even consulting her!

Zach said it had required a quick decision. Well, yes, not wanting her to leave had played a role in giving the green light, but he would make up for the loss in the stock market, if she would sign over the check. There were unusual opportunities in stocks now.

Ruth responded joyfully to the teachings of *modernist instructor extraordinaire* Howard Trafton at the Art Student's League.

"Here in this class I have a student who draws like a dream," Trafton said holding out his hand to Ruth.

Ruth floated home.

Aware that Zach had done well in the stock market, not imaging he would put her money at risk, Ruth signed. But instead of the conservative blue chips Zach always espoused, this time he became more venturous, investing in Alaskan gold. And lost everything.

On telling Ruth, there were tears in his eyes and he seemed so sincerely remorseful she could not find it in her to be angry with him. Later though, on analyzing, it piqued her that his sorrow had not extended to repaying her. But any anger was tempered by the realization that she had lost almost everything she owned and was now totally dependent on him. Not in years could she remember feeling so helpless, downtrodden and poor.

So Ruth did the only thing she knew to do when in crises. Gathering samples of her work, she went job-hunting. Her first stop was at a leading agency where the receptionist phlegmatically told her they didn't need an artist. Ruth smiled and opened her portfolio. The girl promptly called upstairs.

"That's right, she says her name is Ruth Conerly." Seconds later, with a great deal of diffidence, the receptionist asked Ruth to go up. The president wanted to see her.

It was a large office with thick rugs. The president had his back to her when she came in. As his oversized executive chair swiveled slowly around, the man in it began to smile... like a malevolent Cheshire cat observing a mouse.

"Hello, Ruth," he said.

With a sinking heart Ruth recognized the face. It was Harvey. Harvey Hepworth, her agent of twenty years ago. Instantly her last words to him came vividly to mind:

"Harvey, are you sure it's me you're interested in, and not the style of life you'd like to become accustomed to?"

Obviously Harvey had prospered. That or married the owner's daughter. And now as he looked at her, visibly relishing every second, it was obvious he was enjoying his comeuppance to the hilt.

Ruth turned on her heel. She was halfway across the room when he leaped from his chair and ran after her.

"Ruth, Ruth, hold that temper, will you? Please."

Minutes later he was laughing, apologizing, making it clear that whatever differences they might have had years ago, he was delighted to see her and have her with his company. A large-ciphered salary was mentioned and Ruth paused only a few moments before accepting.

She would never work there though. On arriving home, amused and gratified, she told Zach and he forbade her to go back.

"You don't have to go crawling to any upstart who won't respect you. I won't hear of it! You are not to go back there, do you hear me?"

For the life of her, Ruth could not understand Zach. He had made her quit the League complaining that she was enjoying herself while he had to work. Obviously he wanted her to work. He looked hungrily at each check, insisting they must save for retirement. But any success or triumph invariably met with his opposition, the same as any expense on servants, liberating her to work more efficiently. In her most perverse moments, she wondered if he considered her his private property, ever alert lest anything threaten that ownership.

When Ruth's furniture arrived, making it necessary to find a home, other differences between them surfaced. While Ruth considered a proper residence important, Zach insisted on economy and found a "perfectly suitable" place in a New Jersey subdivision. A split-level, it had stairs everywhere, taxing her foot to the limit. When Ruth's carved mahogany dining room set did not arrive, Zach explained that it was too heavy and costly to transport. To replace it, he chose "Swedish simplicity," which Ruth called *varnished plywood*.

Alarmed that her washing machine, dryer and ironing machine were left behind, Ruth insisted they be replaced. But Zach said no. His mother didn't have a washing machine. Ruth could wash smaller things by hand and they would take sheets and towels to the Laundromat.

As Zach's favorite aphorism was "honesty is its own reward," it never occurred to her to ask anyone in his family about his mother not having a washing machine.

Ruth could only reflect that after all these years she was without money of her own, a maid or even a washing machine.

Once again Ruth went job hunting – this time to Metro Associated Services where she had first worked for Dave Shapiro. Still a leader in the advertising world, Metro sold art to a broad range of stores and businesses as well as five thousand newspapers around the world. Dave was still there, and he and his art director, Dorothy Ladore, were happy to welcome Ruth aboard. Metro's biggest clientele, the five thousand newspapers, were heavy buyers of Christmas art and Ruth was soon doing Metro's Christmas illustrations.

Illustration by Ruth Conerly
©**Courtesy METRO CREATIVE GRAPHICS, Inc. New York**

Illustration by Conerly
METRO CREATIVE GRAPHICS, Inc. © New York

Ruth used recollection of daughter for the young mother
METRO CREATIVE GRAPHICS, Inc. © New York

For eight years Ruth worked quietly without fanfare. On
Zach's suggestion, she did Christmas murals for the Lutheran
church they attended and portraits of Zach's family. In 1956,
she went to Costa Rica for the birth of her grandson Arthur
and in 1958, she returned for grandson Sydney. In 1959,
while inaugurating Allied's new Jordon Marsh in Tampa,
hurricane Donna swept in blowing in massive plate glass
walls over their heads. They had just returned to New York
when John Wayne's new movie *The Alamo* was being
premiered in New York. With music by Dimitri Tiomkin and a
budget exceeding that of any film previously made, Wayne
considered it the apex of his career.

Ruth wanted to see it.

On arriving at the theatre, Ruth and Zach were
astounded. There blown up to massive size was Ruth's
painting of Travis.

A large crowd had gathered before the painting and a
group of wide-eyed teen-aged boys gestured wildly as they
exchanged excited remarks.

"See that fellow with the knife!" one exclaimed. "That's
Davy Crockett!"

"No," Ruth corrected. "Davy Crockett was at the South
wall. This is the North wall and that's Travis, the
commander."

The boys turned and stared at the prim lady in her early
fifties. "And how do you know?" one jeered.

"I did the painting," Ruth replied.

A long silence ensued. "Oh, Yeah-h-h."

"That's right," Zach affirmed authoritatively. "That's her
signature down there in the right corner. Conerly."

Necks craned. Silence prevailed. Finally the smallest boy
said, "Gee, you must of been awfully young then."

That night, as Zach told the story to neighbors, Ruth
could not help noticing his pride in that what some once
considered a great artist was now a mere anonymity.

"My own little wife here," Zach said smiling and hugging
her affectionately, "living quietly by my side here in suburbia.
Not needing any fanfare or brass bands."

Sharon

**While in Costa Rica for the birth of her grandson
Ruth did her daughter's portrait.**

XXIV

Return to Texas

In 1962, Allied resolved to build a Joske's of Houston and Ruth was thrilled to learn they were going to Texas. The only thing lacking now was to get Sharon back to Texas.

Incredibly, a window of opportunity opened!

Lizzie's husband Mr. Tate had recently passed away and as he had a previous family, the law required Lizzie to sell their one-thousand-acre ranch to the highest bidder. And the highest bid stood at $50 an acre.

"$50,000 for land worth ten times that!" Lizzie lamented. "Not to mention the original undivided mineral rights. It's a steal!" It did not take long for Ruth to come up with a solution. Zach would buy Lizzie's ranch. Arthur, a rancher, would manage it flying back and forth in his plane. And Sharon would accompany Arthur.

And to Ruth's surprise, Zach agreed – on the condition that Arthur would accept.

On making the long distance call, Ruth's heart was pounding. After hearing the proposal, Sharon was equally excited, thanking Zach profusely for his generous offer. But Arthur refused. He was grateful for their confidence in him, but raising cattle involved close supervision, tax and legal knowledge and running his family ranch in Costa Rica was a full-time job in itself. Ruth's dream collapsed. Her only consolation was that Houston was closer to Costa Rica than New York.

The site chosen for the new Joske's of Houston, Post Oak, had a smattering of houses and small businesses. Realizing that Zach would be retiring soon, Ruth began scouting the area for a home.

One day, seeing a sign announcing *dead-end street* and following its wooded course, she found a FOR SALE sign. The house was in terrible shape with broken windows and a rusted refrigerator in the front yard, but it had an acre of wooded land encircled by a more extensive forest. Zach too was impressed. On asking the owner the reason for so many broken windows, the man explained that whenever a deer would run by, there wasn't time to raise a window. He had to knock the glass out with the rifle butt.

"Of course," Zach agreed.

When Ruth asked if there was a dishwasher in the kitchen, the man pointed to his wife, "Thar she be!"

"Top of the line!" Zach concurred.

It was a mess, but with all that land only minutes from Post Oak, it was a buy. They put in a studio for Ruth with a north light and then argued about everything else. Zach thought slate shingles were fine for the exterior, while Ruth wanted brick. The architect Zach hired suggested brick below and slate shingles above. Ruth cringed. When it was finished, Ruth painted the shingles a ruddy pink to harmonize with the brick, added large pots of red geraniums and as a final touch bought two brass coach lamps for either side of the entrance door. With this final touch, the otherwise lusterless home was magically transformed.

"How much did those lamps cost?" Zach demanded on returning home, and Ruth – unable to lie – told the truth.

"Take them back!" he bellowed. "Immediately!"

"You know why, don't you?" friend Denny Graves, Allied's store decorator, explained. "It wasn't *his* idea."

But Denny told Zach that Ruth had actually made a rare find in those lamps, worth double what she paid. Zach gave in. On one point though, he refused to budge. No washing machine. There was a Laundromat nearby!

As Houston's Joskes progressed, Ruth got busy with the promotional illustrations. Using the theme, "Old in Texas, New in Houston," the series featured an old cowboy and a young one. As with any project for Allied, Zach readily cooperated, posing as the elder cowboy. But Bostonian and store designer, Zach was. Cowboy, he was not. And ultimately Ruth reverted to the real McCoy, Mr. Henry Savage of San Antonio.

That fall when Sharon, Arthur and sons visited, Zach showed them how deer, raccoon, rabbits and foxes would creep out of the woods at night for the food he prepared. Hoping to improve their English vocabulary, he bought a Scrabble set. Sharon was in the kitchen with her mother when she noticed another acquisition.

"Mom, you bought a new set of dishes."

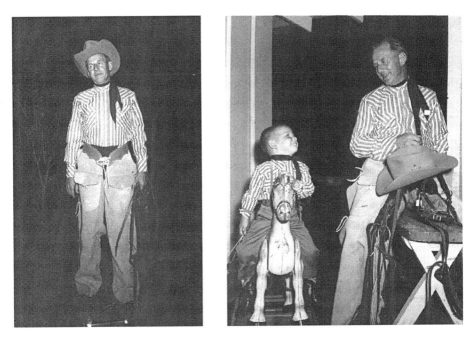

Store designer, Zach was. Cowboy, he was not. But he enjoyed children and was always happy to pose for Allied stores.

New in Houston
Old in Texas

Seventy-five years ago, Alexander Joske opened his little store in San Antonio. This year Joske's of Texas is celebrating its Diamond Jubilee . . . proud of having served Texans for over 75 years. Tomorrow at noon, Joske's of Houston proudly presents a unique store—an exciting new store—dedicated solely to the home . . . eight air-conditioned and completely remodeled

**Ultimately, Ruth reverted to the real McCoy,
Mr. Henry Savage of San Antonio**

Few artists captured the Texas Spirit like Conerly

"Um-hum"

"And the old set?"

"Zach broke a plate."

"That happens. And the others?"

"Well, I broke another."

"Am I missing something here? You two didn't break a whole set of dishes... did you?"

"Yep."

"Why?"

Ruth cleaned off a counter, put away a skillet.

"I'm waiting," Sharon insisted.

"The other night, Ann McGrath called. She and Halvor have made a big success of McGrath Fashions. Ann and Isabel Gerhardt, owner of all those fancy women's stores, wanted me to do some illustrations for them. We were talking when Zach got on the line yelling, 'My wife doesn't need to work! Do you hear me!'

"I was so embarrassed I didn't know what to say. Sometimes I don't know what gets into him. The next day someone at the Alamo called. Some prince or duke was going to put a wreath under my painting of Travis and they wanted me to come to the reception afterwards. I was thrilled, but before I could answer, Zach was on the other line yelling again, 'You can't bother my wife for every Tom, Dick and Harry that goes to the Alamo! Leave her alone, will you!' I was so ashamed I nearly died. On putting down the telephone, I sailed into him! That's when he broke a plate. And I was so mad, I broke another."

"The Lockhorns are alive and well," Sharon chided, imagining her mother capable of defending herself in their little skirmishes. "You *did* call them back and accept, of course?"

"No," Ruth admitted. "I didn't call them back."

"Instead of breaking plates, why didn't you just *go?*"

As the inauguration of Joske's of Houston neared, Layne and Zach pointed out that after fourteen years, Joske's in San Antonio was needful of a facelift. Soon Ruth was busy on those promotional illustrations. Reaching deep into her pioneering roots, she created illustrations portraying the past...

Illustration by Conerly

and a contrasting present...

**Conerly illustration on a Da Vinci scale for the San Antonio
Hemisphere**

**Fashion, always a top-selling commodity,
required glamorous illustrations.**

**From glittering evening gowns
to the composed elegance of the Italian Knit suit**

SIMPLY
BEAUTIFUL..

speranto by Drexel

Exotic furniture designs required artistic detailing

**And what would long be remembered, FANTASYLAND,
a magical series illustrated by Conerly**

There is one in every city, a man considered the epitome of success. And at that time in Houston, Charlie Cohen was that man. Ambitious, hard working and hard playing, Charlie was a man's man, but capable of great charm. He started out in a two-car garage making kitchen cabinetry and quickly expanded into one of the biggest empires in Texas – Triumph Enterprises.

Layne first recognized Charlie's genius for producing the furnishings Allied required for its stores, everything from glass-topped counters to ornate wall festoonery for its French Salon. Soon the orders and contracts tendered were on a scale that would have intimidated a lesser man. But not Charlie.

He expanded on a grand scale, fulfilled every contract and others as large. The much-publicized renovation of Houston's Warwick Hotel was a breathtaking thing for which Charlie stripped down thirteen castles in Europe bringing back paneling, chandeliers and furnishings. Any reporter trying to make his mark hoped for an interview with Charlie and if a Hollywood starlet came to Houston, her agent hoped to get a photograph of her with Charlie.

When Zach mentioned his son-in-law, a cattle rancher, was coming up to the Houston Show, Charlie asked if Arthur might look over a horse he was considering buying. Horse approved, Charlie took Arthur and Sharon on a tour of his company and to his home where he proudly displayed the portraits Ruth had just done of his wife Laverne and three daughters.

"I wanted portraits by an artist who makes people you can recognize," Charlie affirmed, "not some quack doing a bunch of squares and circles where you can't recognize anyone!"

"And since I enjoy painting beautiful people, I accepted," Ruth added.

"But she's still got my portrait to do," Charlie prodded.

Ruth's painting of Charlie had actually developed into two paintings: one as his wife preferred, in formal attire and a background of skyscrapers suggestive of his enterprises, the second, as Charlie wanted, in casual attire with his horse in the background.

Ruth was about to add Charlie's horse when Laverne called. Charlie was dead.

Charles Cohen by Ruth Conerly

Charlie also wanted something smaller, casual, with his horse in the background. Ruth was about to add the horse when...

Incredible as it seemed, it was true. He had gone to Dallas to check on a building planned to be the largest in the city and got a bleeding ulcer. The blood transfusion was contaminated with hepatitis virus.

"Oh, my God," Ruth whispered.

Triumph Enterprises, built on the prestige of a scintillating personality, tumbled. Now more than anything his wife Laverne wanted the portraits Ruth had done of him, and Ruth, understanding the dilemmas of a widow, said not to worry.

Why Zach forbade her to turn over Charlie's paintings, Ruth could not understand. When Laverne offered her Steinway piano, Ruth considered it more than fair exchange!

But Zach forbade it.

"Christine knocked you off her piano stool and Daddy left your player piano in Chicago," Sharon argued. "Give Laverne the paintings and take the piano! Zach can't be that much of an ogre. Stop victimizing yourself!"

But in spite of not *understanding*, Ruth complied.

Over the years Ruth painted many portraits and each bore a story. Ruth's portrait of her nephew Joe was hardly the exception.

Like Ruth, her sister Christine had "only one chick," her beloved Joe. Over the years Christine had kept Ruth posted on Joe's growth in inches and accomplishments. When his scholastic record qualified him for an appointment to West Point, Lizzie's friend Congressman Wright Patman secured the appointment. Joe had just graduated from West Point when the Korean War broke out. As army infantry commander leading 200 men and combat fighter pilot with 100 missions, Joe was described as "where the rubber meets the road in both services." On his return with two Distinguished Service Crosses, Ruth breathed a sigh of relief. Promoted to colonel, Joe was one of the Army men who started the Air Force Academy in Colorado. As a *retread* – colloquialism for Air Force back to Army – he worked with the Joint Staff in the Pentagon. At age forty near retirement, Joe was looking forward to spending more time with his wife Bunny and their three children. He did not have to go to Vietnam. But he felt it his duty.

Christine, almost hysterical, called Ruth and Ruth called Joe, saying she wanted to paint his portrait. It was not entirely a ruse. Joe, in splendid manhood, would make an excellent subject. But Ruth was determined to dissuade him from going to Vietnam.

While posing, Joe explained that his experience in artillery command and air support was sorely needed in Quang Tri. Ruth's hair almost stood on end.

"That's next to the North Vietnam border!"

To that, Joe mentioned the oath he had taken at West Point, "DUTY, HONOR, COUNTRY" and quoted General Robert E. Lee's words to his son, "You cannot do more than your duty; you should never wish to do less."

Ruth then brought up her heavy artillery. She said she had read that sharpshooters were picking off top military personnel and that virtually a whole class of West Point graduates had been killed. She pointed out how his mother was sick with worry, his wife needed a husband and his children needed a father and hadn't he already served his country well?

When Ruth had said everything she could think of, Joe put his hand over hers. "And you're worried too," he said gently. "But don't worry. A soldier gets himself killed because he does some foolish act of heroism and doesn't use his head. I'm too old and experienced for that kind of thing."

As Joe left, Ruth hugged him close.

In a letter from Vietnam, Joe expressed concern about his mother. "Ruth, she's worrying herself sick," Before signing, he quipped, "Remember to buy War Bonds and Support the Boys Overseas," reminiscent of Ruth's WWII illustrations that rallied America to victory.

Nestled close to the northern border of South Vietnam, Khesanh was not considered in danger that January 21, 1969, when North Vietnam forces launched a massive attack. Surviving South Vietnam troops sent an urgent communiqué requesting reinforcements. Communications among army, air force, and Vietnamese with hierarchies of their own, often made coordination difficult. But aware of the urgency, Colonel Joe Seymoe volunteered to lead the relief mission.

As Joe's lead chopper neared Khesanh, an L-19 plane was in the air, obstructing the clearing operation, not responding to calls. Rather than abort the mission, Joe chose an alternate "hot" landing zone, unprepped by fighter-bombers and attack helicopters. Joe's helicopter had just disembarked its troops and was lifting off when an explosive shell hit, propelling it over a hill. The pilot, co-pilot and gunner managed to get out. Joe was alive, they said, but unconscious, pinned by an aluminum bar used to secure stretchers. The pilot claimed he was trying to free Joe when flames ignited the chopper's fuel supply.

On receiving the message that Joe was missing, Lizzie wired grandson David Conerly (Bo), also in Quang Tri. Bo knew Joe was dead but could not officially confirm.

Lizzie wrote Ruth: "Christine is no trouble, but doesn't seem to think for herself. We will see what time will do."

But time brought no consolation for Christine. Heart-sick, Ruth added two medals to Joe's jacket in the painting: the Silver Star and the Purple Heart, awarded posthumously. Packing it carefully, she sent it to Joe's wife and children.

Ruth did not understand the Vietnam War and was saddened that no parades greeted America's returning soldiers, no sympathy for the 58,000 dead. If the news media emerged as a mighty fourth power, it proved itself as divided as the government. For Ruth, the only thing tangible was that Joe would never return.

Combat fighter pilot with 100 missions

West Point Graduate

Lt. Col. Joe Seymoe
Portrait by Conerly

Greek vase, painting by Conerly

XXV

Was I A Good Husband?

Something was wrong with Zach. Never an easy person to live with, by 1970, he had become increasingly difficult, smoking constantly and complaining of a succession of wrongs done to him in the office, people accusing him of errors. Only the feeding of his animals – which attracted neighborhood children to watch as raccoons or an occasional fox crept out of the woods – still amused him. On being offered a retirement settlement, certainly long overdue, instead of being overjoyed, Zach was a man destroyed and embittered. And Ruth began to wonder if he might be seriously ill.

For over a year now, he had complained of a recurring rash, pinkish with scales. A dermatologist had given him every type of salve, ointment and soaks, all to no avail. Finally, at Ruth's insistence, he consulted her doctor, who found that Zach, long-time chain smoker, had lung cancer and lymphoma. The skin problem had been a paraneoplastic syndrome, an outward manifestation of an internal malignancy, now too advanced for any effective treatment.

As his health deteriorated, his temper became more violent and unpredictable, as if to compensate for his dwindling physical strength. Moreover, he refused to let her hire someone to help with his care or the housework, nor permit any visitors, once screaming "kick them out" when friends from the office came to visit. To all of this, Ruth complied, ministering to him with total dedication.

When in his last moments, he turned to her and asked in a tiny, pathetic voice, "Was I a good husband?" Ruth was incapable of lying.

"No, you were *not!*" she replied bitterly.

After Zach's death, Ruth was a shadow of the person she had once been. Far worse than any deteriorated health and appearance, she felt totally incapable of contending with life on her own. For years Zach had made every decision. Locked in his office, he managed their business matters in absolute secrecy, imposing his criteria with dictatorial force in all matters, major and trivial. True, at times Ruth had protested, even broken a few plates, but she had never *acted*. And gradually over the years it had become easier just to let him make all the decisions. So that now, more than any lost physical integrity, Ruth felt herself incapable of making decisions on her own.

Could anything exist of that daredevil spirit of times past? That gutsy little redhead who had marched forth flanked by ancestors, ready to take on the world? Who hitchhiked to New York in mid-depression, arriving with $100 in her pocket? Was it all some far away dream?

At age sixty-four, widowed for a second time, Ruth felt far more helpless than on Ted's death.

Reverend Bob Tucker, pastor of Houston's First Congregational Church, felt the remedy to Ruth's situation was in her art and commissioned portraits of himself and wife Maggi. Bob and Maggi had lived many years in Turkey and shared Ruth's profound interest in ancient cultures. On learning that Maggi played the Turkish national instrument, the saz, Ruth perceived an inner romanticism beyond Maggi's businesslike aspect and posed her playing it.

"Seeing that painting, I fell in love with Maggie all over again," Bob declared and gave a party to premier his new paintings.

When Ruth began examining Zach's bank statements, the pages revealed she was far from poor. Recalling the loss of her home and the many checks turned over to Zach, she felt that justice had at last been served.

She was about to haul the clothes to the Laundromat as she had done all these years, when suddenly she put the basket down – and went out and bought a washing machine. And a dryer.

Then she got a maid. Curiously Alva was from Ruth's hometown of Marshall.

Freed from household chores, she contacted Metro in New York. Dave Shapiro had passed away, but his nephew Andrew Shapiro, now at the helm of the company, was delighted to have her back. They were already working on their 1973 Christmas catalogue.

Soon Ruth's Christmas art was circling the globe again. And a news article called her MRS. CHRISTMAS!

Margaret Newfield Tucker by Ruth Conerly

Illustration by Ruth Conerly
Courtesy METRO CREATIVE GRAPHICS, Inc. © New York

Illustration by Ruth Conerly
Courtesy METRO CREATIVE GRAPHICS, Inc. © New York

Illustration by Ruth Conerly
METRO CREATIVE GRAPHICS, Inc. © New York

Seeing the checks coming in, Ruth dared to consider another long denied dream – a swimming pool. When her doctor said a heated pool with Jacuzzi would help the circulation in her leg and its cost and maintenance would be a tax deduction, she did it!

Exercise brought a significant improvement to her foot and to her figure. Observing the difference, she went out and bought herself some new clothes. Then, something Zach would never have allowed, she had a face-lift! Animated by the change, she gave a party and invited the whole neighborhood. People danced, swam, one played the ukulele, another the banjo. Grandson Arthur now at Texas A&M came and did an act with top hat and cane, "New York, New York," sharply remindful of Ted.

By the end of the year, the neighborhood parties had become a tradition, much like having Ruth do everyone's portraits.

By now, Ruth had done hundreds of portraits, an interestingly diverse group of people of every walk of life. Capturing a likeness was not difficult for Ruth. She did it with exceptional ease, showing an uncanny insight as to personality. Paradoxically, she found that the quicker the work was done, the more accurate and vibrant the likeness. Her painting of grandsons, Arthur and Sydney, completed in an afternoon, were typical of her swift work. "They wouldn't sit still much longer," she said. "About par for children!" Important with children, Ruth told clients, was to paint them *separately*, to avoid quarrels later on concerning who would get the painting. Especially with adults, Ruth felt the portrait must reflect the interests of that person. When architect Walter Dusan said he loved sailing, she went sailing with him. The resulting painting amid surging waves was original and dramatic.

Aside from portraits, there were paintings of every genre: book covers, children's stories, a constant outflow of creativeness. After a visit to Costa Rica, she wrote an adventure tale for her grandsons, illustrated with crocodiles, boas, birds and animals of Costa Rica.

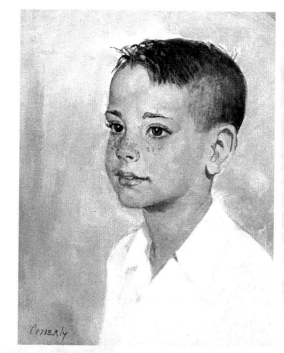

Arthur Wolf

**The portraits
of her
grandsons,
completed
in an afternoon,
were typical of
her swift work.**

**"They wouldn't sit
still any longer,
about par for children"**

Sydney Wolf

Ruth wrote an adventure tale for grandson Arthur illustrated with crocodiles, boas, birds and animals of Costa Rica.

Martha Jane Conerly, Ruth's niece

Cynthia Weaver

Cynthia's cat

Katrina and Sydney McFaden

Stacie Camille Coe   **Paula Kaye Coe**

The Cadenhead
Family of
Houston

Sandra, Ben and
daughters
Mindy and
Jennifer

by Conerly

Mrs. Kay Ford

by Conerly

Guiseppina Greco

Mrs. Arthur Wolf
(grandson's wife)

by Conerly

Arthur Wolf
(grandson)

by Conerly

Evangelina Fournier

Mrs. Victor Wolf
(son-in-law's mother)

by
Conerly

Dinzel Graves
(Denny)

with mother
Odessa May
(center)

and sister
Shirley Ann

by Conerly

Ruth could never think of Zach with benevolence. Perhaps friend Denny, who knew them both, explained it well:

> *"As close as Zach and I were, I always resented Zach's attitude toward Ruth and felt he was jealous of her abilities. She was a great artist and did just unbelievable things. She had an energy that no one I ever knew had, always ready to create something. After Zach died, she and I became very close friends. I felt she was experiencing a new freedom she didn't have with Zach.*
>
> *He was always pulling her down. He would have liked to be like her, do some of the things she did. She simply had no limits with line, space and color. I've never seen anything like it and I've been associated with artists all my life.*
>
> *Layne would tell Zach, 'you're a blankity-blankity for doing that and saying that to Ruth and you know it, so why do you do it?' I believe if things had worked out between Layne and Ruth, they would have made a pair that would have been unbelievable. Layne was not a jealous person. He would have promoted Ruth.. Both Layne and Helene had tremendous creativity. Helene was often upset with Zach. I once heard her tell Layne, 'I won't go any place with Zach – such a pill, always onto Ruth about something.'*
>
> *I felt sorry for Zach. There was no reason for him to be so envious, but he just couldn't take being second fiddle to someone more talented than he was. She had a terrible time with him. But she worked around it beautifully. There were times when she would just tell him she had enough. He'd pout like crazy, but he'd quiet down."*

Sharon found it difficult to think of Zach as such an ogre. True, compared to Ruth's former life with servants and a fine home, things had changed over the years. But wasn't Ruth to blame, turning everything she had over to Zach? Wouldn't their interests have been better served if she had just knocked another tooth out, instead of always giving in and lamenting her misfortune? But more than anything Zach's death left Sharon with serious doubts concerning doctors. And in March, 1973, she called Ruth to announce a decision.

"Mom, I'm going to study medicine!"

"Wonderful!" Ruth exclaimed. "When will you be coming back to Texas?"

"Not Texas, Mom. I've enrolled at the University of Costa Rica."

"Oh," Ruth replied. "Well, that's nice."

In spite of having her hopes dashed, Ruth was proud. And that December, while visiting Sharon, Ruth was delighted seeing Sharon's excitement on finding her mother's Christmas art filling Costa Rica's major newspapers: LA NACION, La PRENSA LIBRE and LA REPUBLICA. Not only were the newspapers filled, but Ruth's Christmas art was on their front pages.

Ruth's Christmas art had a magic all its own
Courtesy METRO CREATIVE GRAPHICS, Inc. © New York

"Why don't I call their editorial offices and tell them that the artist of their front pages, Ruth Conerly, is here visiting in Costa Rica for the Christmas holidays!" Sharon exclaimed.

Ruth shrugged. "Fine by me."

"La artista aqui en Costa Rica?" a dubious voice questioned.

Minutes later, they called back. They had confirmed the story and wanted to know if they might interview her for a story. Thus on December 26, Ruth appeared on La Prensa Libre's front page.

During the interview the editor, a good-looking man in his forties, showed great interest in her career and life. He said he was an amateur artist but greatly enjoyed painting Costa Rica's scenery.

"I don't suppose you might accompany me to paint one day?"

"Why, yes, I might," Ruth replied.

But she was surprised when he called.

"Did you see yourself in today's paper?"

"I could hardly miss it."

"Would you consider going out painting with me? And having lunch somewhere?"

"Yes, I'd like that. Just a minute though." Unsure as to where they were going, she asked son-in-law Arthur to talk to him. And Arthur, not understanding his role in all this, asked the inconceivable question, "What are your intentions?"

Sharon stared aghast. Then seeing Arthur frown, say a brief closing and hang up, she perceived a disaster.

"He wanted to take Mother painting, not get married!"

"I only asked him where he intended taking her."

"Your words were, 'What are your intentions?'"

Ruth burst out laughing. "And what did he say?"

"He said his intentions were serious!" Arthur replied still frowning and obviously imagining him a fortune hunter.

Ruth laughed it off, although she wished she had just accepted. Luckily, there were plenty of things going on. Fiesta week had begun and Ruth quickly learned how a front page news story could exalt a person's status as a visiting VIP. At one party, there was a rodeo, polo games and orchestra for dancing. At another, a coffee farmer asked Ruth to accompany him to Europe where they would visit art museums, while a rancher rushing to bring her a drink, fell head-on into a trashcan drum.

On a visit to Arthur's family ranch Ruth rode horseback among saibo, Guanacaste and Pochote trees, marveling at monkeys, iguanas, and an occasional boa constrictor and doing dozens of pictures of the scenery. On offering to do a painting of Arthur's family home at Chomes, Arthur promptly loaded her and her painting paraphernalia on a pick-up, depositing her under a grove of trees.

The result was splendid!

Chomes, Arthur's family farm by Ruth Conerly

Arthur at Chomes by Ruth Conerly

On her return to the States, Ruth drove up to Clarksville to visit her mother, Lizzie...

Lizzie
Elizabeth Davis Conerly Tate
1878-1975

Lizzie had just closed her Bible and was leaning back in her chair with an expression as though looking through the haze of nearly a century into some infinite horizon. Ignoring Lizzie's protests that she was much too old at ninety-six and not dressed properly, Ruth set to work.

It was a spur-of-the-moment thing, completed in an afternoon, but destined to be one of Ruth's finest paintings, winning first place in both painting and portraiture at the Houston Art League. Audrey Black, owner of Clarksville's Red River National bank, (still never robbed again) insisted on putting it on display at the bank – "Ruth, Lizzie goes way back as one of Clarksville's most prominent citizens," and Ben Black, editor of the Clarksville Times, published an article on Lizzie. Not long after, Lizzie passed away.

In spite of her sadness, while driving back to Houston after the funeral, Ruth felt curiously at peace with the little town of Clarksville, that whatever iniquities she had imagined it guilty of, all was past and atoned for.

Gallery of Clarkville Portraits by Conerly

Abbie Lynn Black   Amanda Jane Black   Dr. Melvin Marx

Audrey M. Black   Mr. Jack Davis   Mr. Pat Beetle

Bryon Black   Abbie's cat

Illustration by Ruth Conerly
Courtesy of METRO CREATIVE GRAPHICS, Inc. ©
New York

XXVI

Trip to Europe

Electronic minds! Personal computers for everyday use! Pretty soon, people will be traveling in space, Ruth thought while incorporating these innovations into her 1982 holiday art for Metro. How true her father's predictions about the wonders this century would bring! She was busy at work with her characteristic "Let's juice this up!" enthusiasm, when the phone rang.

"Mom!" Sharon's voice called out. "Guess what? I'm going to Europe!"

"That's nice," Ruth managed. When Sharon traveled, it was always to Texas to visit her. The same as when Sharon graduated from medical school, Ruth was there in the audience beside Arthur.

"Arthur has finally decided to go to Europe."

"No, Arthur only likes Texas. I'm going alone on a two week tour. Italy, France and England!"

"You can't go to Europe alone. It's not proper!"

"Mother, I'm forty-four with grown children, a medical doctor. Besides you went to Europe when you were twenty-four without Daddy. And fell in love with a French count!"

"Well, if Arthur won't go, I'll just have to go with you."

"You're serious? Europe with my own expert in art and history? What more could a girl want! Except to get stalled in an elevator with Robert Redford."

They met in New York, toured the city and flew to Italy. Ruth marveled at Pompeii, buried under a hail of fire, ash and pumice stone from Mount Vesuvius. After Pompeii, they wound their way to the coast, took a barge to the Blue Grotto and saw Naples by sunset. In Florence, paradise of art and architecture, they visited the Galeria Dell'Accademia, admiring Michelangelo's David. In Etruria, Ruth pointed out that ancient Etruscan art showed men and women enjoying life together and holding hands, evidence that in this ancient culture, women shared a place of respect. In Rome, they visited the Coliseum where Ruth conjured up scenes of pageantry, gladiators in mortal combat and lions devouring early Christians. At the Vatican they saw Michelangelo's "La

Pieta" and the frescoes in the Sistine Chapel. As they crossed St. Peter's square, Pope John Paul drove by waving.

In Paris at the Louvre, Ruth said she never thought the Mona Lisa was all that remarkable and at Versailles she found the Hall of Mirrors "much smaller than I remembered," but the French Revolution, the death of Louis XVI and Marie Antoinette fueled a rich outflow of stories.

"They said that Marie Antoinette's hair turned completely white in those weeks awaiting the guillotine," Ruth whispered with visible emotion. Marie Vigee-Lebrun, renowned portrait painter and close friend of Marie Antoinette and dozens more were resurrected and poignantly put to death.

From Paris, they flew to London and the pageantry of English history. At Heathrow Airport, rushing to keep up with their tour guide, Ruth fell, her head hitting the floor with a sickening thud. Seeing her mother crumpled and still, Sharon was horrified. Within seconds, an English policeman carried her to the infirmary. He was cradling her hand in his and gently calling her name when the haze lifted and Ruth focused in on him.

"I died and went to heaven?" she whispered. Instantly there was laughter and that evening dining out, Ruth was totally recuperated.

"That's the prettiest little redhead I've ever seen," a voice from the next table exclaimed. The two men were both staring directly at Ruth.

"Who came along to protect *who*?" Sharon demanded with mock indignation.

The next day, they visited the Tower and Ruth marveled at all the executions and pathos. The two little princes murdered by their uncle, Anne Boleyn, Mary Queen of Scots, the sixteen-year-old Lady Jane Grey and the seventy-year-old Countess of Salisbury, chased and hacked to death, were all imaginatively resuscitated and put to death anew. Villains, heroes and ghosts of the past were Ruth's wellspring and no tragedy escaped her. At Stratford-on-Avon, Ruth pointed out that Shakespeare was a genius in creating characters and plots, but a practical man, more concerned with making a living and filling the theatre than pleasing critics. "One must always make a living," Ruth stressed.

Each day, they visited more museums and castles, filling more bags with books and each night Ruth would read aloud, choosing the most horrific, tear-jerking accounts.

One night on finding a résumé on George III, Ruth shouted triumphantly.

"Our ancestor! America's last king." Says here he was really quite popular with the English people at a time when the French Revolution was toppling royal heads. He loved to read and had a huge library, basis of the British Library! Says his success as a monarch was impaired by a mysterious disease that brought on periods of apparent derangement. He would say he'd rather die than go mad."

Ruth's face clouded momentarily. "Daddy used to say exactly the same thing when he was having those terrible attacks and doctors didn't know what was wrong."

She scanned the page. "No mention of George's marriage to Hannah Lightfoot. Strange, you never hear anything about her. I do hope we're not illegitimate."

Ruth looked over to where Sharon lay. "Wouldn't it be fun to look into this sometime?"

"Um-hum," Sharon agreed sleepily.

"I'm definitely going to look into this one day," she declared. Then setting the book aside, she turned over and was soon asleep.

Hope your New Year is fit for
a king and rich with happiness and success.

Illustration by Ruth Conerly
METRO CREATIVE GRAPHICS, Inc.© New York

Ruth Conerly, Self-Portrait

Waler Dusan and son Mac, by Ruth Conerly

Lt. Col. Joseph Seymore,
by Ruth Conerly

Nude,
by Ruth Conerly

Nude,
by Ruth Conerly

Col. William B. Travis, by Ruth Conerly

Lizzie, Ruth's Mother,
by Ruth Conerly

Mrs. Ann McGrath,
by Ruth Conerly

The text on the illustration reads:

The
n Antonio
Story

Sam & Bess
Woolford

The San Antonio Story by Sam and Bess Woodford,
by Ruth Conerly

Noah's Ark,
by Ruth Conerly

World of Papagallo,
by Ruth Conerly

Christmas is coming and Santa's all tuned and READY!

He has a medley of presents that are sure to please everyone from toddlers to grandparents. Jump on the exciting Christmas bandwagon — there's a whole jolly holiday preview going on right now inside these pages!

METRO CREATIVE GRAPHICS, Inc. ©,
by Ruth Conerly

METRO CREATIVE GRAPHICS, Inc. © New York,
by Ruth Conerly

METRO CREATIVE GRAPHICS, Inc. © New York,
by Ruth Conerly

METRO CREATIVE GRAPHICS, Inc. © New York,
by Ruth Conerly

Chomes, by Ruth Conerly

XXVII

New Horizons, Haunting Words

By 1988, nearing her eightieth birthday, Ruth was slowing down. No longer could she work long hours, competing in the rapid-paced field, where photography and graphic arts had virtually replaced commercial art.

Worse, her savings that only a few years ago had allowed her to live well no longer produced enough to cover the rising cost of living. Her stockbroker, a Southern gentleman in the midst of restoring his family plantation in Georgia, frequently pressed her to convert her remaining CDs to stocks *for higher returns,* while close friend Kay Ford warned: "That's junk stock he's peddling, Ruth. Aside from a lucrative commission, he gets a kickback on that stuff. I quit him two years ago, and you should too!"

But Ruth enjoyed his calls, always sprinkled with Civil War history and details about his plantation's ongoing restoration. If just before hanging up, he would suggest she sell still another block of stock to buy something "more promising," she could not bring herself to think he did not have her best interests at heart.

When the stock market plunged in 1988, Ruth said, "It'll bounce back. People who rush to sell are the losers." It was sage advice, had her portfolio not been replaced by stock that failed to rebound.

Only one of Ruth's assets had increased in value. Her home. Over the years bulldozers had toppled the surrounding forest, ushering in two-storied mansions on a minimum of land, bought by couples eager to live in one of Houston's best school districts. But school taxes had become enormous. And with thousands on welfare, it was no longer possible to find anyone to cut the lawn or do repairs at a reasonable price.

On finding her last red fox on the side of the road with swerving wheel marks indicating someone had purposefully run him down, Ruth sorrowfully carried him home and buried him in the back yard. Clearly the animals, trees and she were losing the battle to urban sprawl and could not long survive there.

On trying to economize doing her own yard work, her leg gave way. One fall had left her inert in the back yard for hours. Cutting back on the electrical bill brought more disastrous results: one night a burglar forced the front door with a crowbar. The intruder was barely inside though when Ruth's enormous cat, Muffin, leaped on him. Awakened by the noise, worthy of a late-night horror movie, Ruth grabbed her father's Colt 22 and ran to the rescue of her beloved Muffin. The burglar was gone and Muffin was sitting on the blood-streaked rug in front of the demolished door, licking a paw.

Ruth was convinced Muffin was the bravest of cats, but on Sharon's next visit, a neighbor drew her aside.

"Ruth simply cannot live by herself anymore. You have to do something!"

The final blow came when the Spring Valley Police Department sent a card informing Ruth that on October 27, her eightieth birthday, they could no longer renew her Texas driver's license. Over the years, Ruth had survived a stroke, an operation for an obstructed femoral artery and surgery for breast cancer, but she could still drive.

"I may not be able to walk very well," she would extol like a battle cry over adversity, "but I can sure drive like hell!" which, in all respect to the truth, was an accurate description of her present driving skills.

"Why don't you and Arthur come up *here* and live with me?" Ruth suggested. "Or we could move to East Texas. Arthur could buy a farm. You could work as a doctor. Little towns always need doctors."

But Arthur could not leave the family farm in Costa Rica.

A retirement home was their next consideration. One highly recommended place had an impressive building and bragged of innumerable services and activities. But on peeping into the *activity* rooms, there were only grossly fat employees drinking coffee, turning annoyed faces. In another home where people slumped in wheelchairs looked drugged, a sales representative explained the system. The rooms were for sale, but on the death of the owner, the property reverted to the establishment.

"Ideal situation for an Alfred Hitchcock movie!" Ruth declared getting into the car.

The matter was still unresolved when they learned that Ruth's brother Preston was losing his battle with cancer. Preston had recently written an enthusiastic letter saying he'd come across two books: *The King Who Lost America*, by Alan Lloyd and *George III, the story of a Complex Man* by J.C. Long with information on Hannah Lightfoot.

"The one by Long has a painting of Hannah done by court painter Joshua Reynolds," Preston wrote sending a photocopy of the portrait. "She has a curious resemblance to you, Ruth."

"Reynolds was very selective and money-oriented in his choice of subjects," Ruth wrote back. "He would never have painted any ordinary Quaker girl, unless well paid."

"It said George was always sympathetic to the Quaker persuasion and that as an old man, locked away in Windsor Castle, he would call out, 'Hannah, Hannah.'"

Preston's death left Ruth deeply sad but it precipitated a decision concerning her future. There was only one option really – to sell her home and move to Costa Rica!

One buyer sympathized with Ruth about her trees and animals and said it was important to keep the land out of the hands of developers who would just bulldoze everything down. Ruth was about to accept their offer, although far below the land's value, when she learned that the couple made a living buying property from elderly people, and then turning around and selling it to developers.

"If someone is going to make a profit on my land, it should be the one who has lived here twenty-five years!" Ruth declared.

Sharon flew back and began mowing, clearing away dead wood and washing windows. Soon three developers were competing and a good price was negotiated. As they boarded the taxi to the airport with Muffin in his traveling cage, Ruth looked back to where bulldozers were moving in to topple her house and surrounding trees.

Ruth wanted her own home in Costa Rica. On being shown a condominium overlooking the Country Club, she said, "Don't imagine I'm going to live up in any bird cage in a country with earthquakes!" As more agents appeared, she added more specifications: a wide front porch with columns, big rooms, a fireplace, a Jacuzzi and an atrium would be nice, like in Pompeii.

And new. All her life, she'd lived in someone else's old home. She wanted a new home for once.

One morning their only remaining agent, a quiet, determined man, called and said, "I'd like to take you to see a house, not to buy, just to see."

Driving east to a neighborhood called Lomas de Ayarco, they passed the mansion of Robert Vesco who hurriedly left the United States with two hundred and forty million dollars in Mutual Funds. They turned right at the Russian Embassy, left at the French ambassador's residence and stopped in front of an iron gate that opened to reveal a home with a wide front porch and a row of glistening white columns. They walked through double doors into a glass-domed atrium, splendid as any in Pompeii, where workers were sanding, painting and putting on the final touches.

"This is more like it!" Ruth exclaimed. Then pointing her cane to the center of the atrium, "A perfect place for a statue!" and sweeping her hand to the surrounding area, "Plenty of wall space for paintings."

Just beyond the atrium, she peeped through a wide portal. "A ballroom!" Ruth exclaimed looking in. "What a wonderful place for a party!"

There was an enthusiasm in her voice and lightness in her step. This was the epitome of everything she always planned and sketched, magically come to life. On walking out on the wide, column-lined back porch, Arthur observed the lawns and towering wall beyond.

"That's the Russian Embassy behind that wall," he remarked. "Couldn't ask for better security."

Why don't I just buy it and we can all live here together?" Ruth exclaimed and the agent instantly perked up. "What do you think, Arthur?"

Arthur looked at his watch. "It would take me an hour to pack."

A close friend of Sharon's was horrified. "You'd need three servants to take care of this!" But Maria Elena came on the scene. Maria Elena could cook, clean, wash, and iron – while talking on the telephone all day. Ruth never understood why every meal had to include rice, beans and *platano*, but it was a minor grievance, like wondering why people in Costa Rica always had to speak Spanish.

"This is more like it!" Ruth exclaimed.

DRI

Ruth and hero Muffin

With the handiwork of a local wood finisher, Ruth's furniture came gloriously to life and paintings and statues looked as though they had been selected by *Architectural Digest*. On the wall beyond the Jacuzzi, Ruth painted a huge mural of a rain forest with vines, tropical birds and an alligator.

"Gorgeous!" Sharon exclaimed. "Gee, it's fun to be together again after all these years."

"Sure is," Ruth agreed. "How much time do you think I have left?"

Sharon's smile faded only briefly. "Fifteen years, at least!" she replied. "Remember how long Lizzie lived!"

Ruth enjoyed Costa Rica. On attending the inauguration of a new government building, Arthur's cousin President Rafael Angel Calderon (1990-1994) stopped mid-speech, asking someone to please seat "*dona* Ruth", and at the reception he insisted she sit with him and wife, Gloria. When the head of the American Embassy Cultural Program called to ask if the pianist opening the cultural season might stay at their home, Ruth's approval resulted in tickets to the concert and private after-dinner performances. Responding to Ruth's frequent request, "Let's have a party!" Sharon invited an interesting variety of English-speaking guests.

She only regretted not being able to enjoy her mother more. But a medical career was a demanding master. She loved her work, fitting signs and symptoms into a pattern that might detect some malady or simply calm unfounded fears. But it required attention, an attention often sabotaged by paperwork, traffic jams. One evening, when Sharon returned home looking tired, Ruth sensed something was wrong.

"What's the matter, Hon?"

Sharon smiled, but Ruth would not be put off.

"Oh, a man and his wife came in today. They'd consulted a doctor I greatly respect, but wanted a second opinion. After examining him and finding he needed the operation recommended, I said they could have every confidence in his competence. He was a fine doctor. But instead they insisted I recommend someone else. 'Maybe we shouldn't tell you this,' the man said, 'but when we told him we wanted a second opinion from you, he replied, 'Little Miss Rich Bitch playing at medicine?' Frankly we don't want to go back to him!"

Ruth erupted in laughter. "Sweetie, you've arrived!" she cried out merrily.

And seeing her daughter's puzzled expression, she explained. "Honey, when you start out, everyone is helpful and nice. But when you get good and people start noticing it, things change. I remember how devastated I was on hearing someone had made a cruel remark."

"Makes 'em jealous," Arthur put in and quoted his favorite don Quixote phrase: "Ride on, Sancho! When dogs bark, we're advancing!"

Good humor was promptly restored. But later that evening Ruth put her hand on Sharon's. "Can I ask you a question?"

"Of course."

"What sickness do you think caused my father so such suffering?" Her tone and expression made it clear this was no casual question.

Sharon was at a loss how to make a diagnosis of a man dead for seventy-five years. But seeing her mother's sadness, she made a feeble attempt.

"Do you remember his symptoms?"

"He had these terrible pains."

"Where?"

"All over his abdomen. He'd hold his stomach and cry out with pain. His doctors could never find any cause and began to think he was mad. He was so afraid he might be going mad."

"Can you remember anything else?"

"No, not really. I was only twelve."

"He didn't go to a hospital by any chance? Someplace where there'd be a medical record?"

"Not that I know of. I asked Mother about it several times, but she never wanted to talk about it."

"Mom, I see no way to know what the problem was after all these years, with no record, physical exam or tests." Then seeing her mother's face – a look so pitiful and helpless it wrung her heart – Sharon searched her mind for something consoling and finding nothing, hugged her.

"Don't you think you've grieved long enough over this. It can have no relevance today."

They were words that would come back to haunt her.

Ruth's sketch of her Mysterious Pilot

XXVIII

Enigmatic Encounter

Ruth's letters from Costa Rica held exciting chronicles of her new life, her new friends, but nothing achieved the level of importance or captured her interest as much as her mysterious "pilot" or "captain", as she called him.

Perhaps living in a strange country away from old friends and relatives, Ruth felt a degree of loneliness. Perhaps, as she said, the pilot *did* remind her of her father. But then in every man she ever admired, there had been a seeking for that first love, her father. Whenever she told the story of Gutzon Borglum, whose advice changed the course of her life, she invariably added the telling phrase, "he reminded me of my deceased father."

In spite of the seventy-five years elapsed, it was ever there at the root of all her ambition and struggle to overcome – an unjust, never explained death of the man against whom all other loves fell short.

Concerning her encounter with the pilot, Ruth explained it in a letter to friend and confidant Denny Graves:

"Denny, you mentioned seeing an article about me in the newspaper. The reason I'm asking is this May 27, I was in Paris, Texas, waiting for the shuttle plane to Dallas, when the captain came out of the office and put my bags in this beautiful new white jet. He asked if I was Ruth Conerly, the artist who painted the Death of Travis in the Alamo. I said yes. And all the way to Dallas he asked me about how I knew such and such about Travis or the battle and about my life. When we arrived in Dallas, he personally drove me to the American Airline terminal. When the girl at the desk told me I could wait at gate 12, the captain yelled, "I don't want her waiting down there with all those screwballs for five hours! She's not an ordinary person. She's an eminent artist! I'm putting her in the executive lounge where she can watch television and have something to eat."

Ruth told the story repeatedly. When chic, vivacious Lourdes Miranda, one of Sharon's friends, invited Ruth to lunch and heard the story, she exclaimed, "Fabuloso! And have you found out who he was?"

"No, but I promised him a signed copy of my Alamo painting and feel terrible not being able to do so."

To Sharon's question, "why didn't you ask his name?" Ruth replied, "He kept asking me questions about my life and the painting. Then suddenly he was gone. At moments I felt it was actually my father asking me all those questions – not the face so much as his manner, the dynamic personality." She laughed off-handedly. "Maybe he'll find a way to contact me."

But no message came. On seeing an ad for American Airlines, Ruth wrote to them.

In the following weeks, friends and guests heard the story and exclaimed with delight. But as Ruth continued to repeat it over and over, Sharon began to worry that her mother's fixation on the subject might be a sign of some initial senility. On discovering that Ruth had told their maid Maria Elena the whole story with luxury of detail in Spanish, Sharon discarded the matter of senility and began checking Ruth's blood pressure and heart with more care.

"She's not sick," Maria Elena declared clasping her hand to her heart. "She's in love! All the anguish and excitement of romance is the same at any age!"

This seemed irrational, but when a reply arrived from American Airlines, Ruth's eyes were aglow with anticipation. But the letter was little more than formula, thanking her for her compliments and elaborating on the courtesy of all their pilots. For days, Ruth's heavy-heartedness could be felt like a pall. Then suddenly, she announced she was going to Texas, packed her bags and left.

While visiting her sister Janey, Ruth continued to talk about her pilot, his beautiful white plane carrying her away and how he reminded her of their father, until Janey too became worried.

On calling the Paris-Dallas shuttle and finding they had ceased servicing the area, Ruth made a sketch of the pilot from memory to show people at the Dallas terminal. Surely someone there would recognize him.

Shortly before her departure, a poem appeared in the Dear Abby Column of the Paris News. Deeply moved, Ruth cut it out and then copied it in her booklet next to her illustration of the pilot.

I HAD A FATHER WHO TALKED WITH ME

I had a father who talked with me,
Allowed me the right to disagree,
To question – and always answered me
As well as he could – and truthfully
He talked of adventures; and the horrors of war;
Of life, its meaning; what love was for;
How each would always need to strive
To improve the world, to keep it alive.
Stressed the duty we owe one another
To be aware each man is a brother.
Words for laughter he also spoke
A silly song or a happy joke.
Time runs along, some say I'm wise
That I look at life with seeing eyes.
My heart is happy, my mind is free,
I had a father who talked with me.
By Hilda Bigalow ©

On leaving for the airport, Ruth had her notepad with the pilot's sketch. But in the rush at the Dallas airport the notepad was left in the car's trunk, and Janey, fearing something might befall Ruth on such a bizarre errand, told the wheelchair attendant to take care Ruth did not wander off.

Frustrated in every attempt to find her pilot, Ruth was visibly downcast on her return to Costa Rica. Not until December did her mood lighten.

"Let's have a Christmas party!" she exclaimed. "Invite all our friends!" After reviewing menu and decorations, she set to work at her art-board on a *special surprise.*

A Santa with twinkling eyes and a *Merry Christmas* written across the lower corner.

That night, resplendent in long skirt and sparkling top, Ruth greeted the fifty some guests. As caterers plied through the crowd with drinks and hors d'oeuvres, a pianist enhanced the festive mood. People examined Ruth's Christmas art out on display and queued up for a tour of her paintings and sculptures, edging closer to hear her stories. Not until 2:00 a.m., after the last guest departed, did Ruth go off to sleep.

It was her last party, her last Santa.

Merry Christmas! —Conerly

Ruth's last Santa

On January 3, 1994, Ruth was at her art board hoping to finish the portrait of her great grandchild, the blue-eyed Nicole. Putting down her paintbrush Ruth rubbed her right hand. "A bit of arthritis," she said to Maria Elena.

That night Ruth retired early.

"I brought you a glass of wine," Sharon said peeping into her room

"No, Hon... Thank you."

"You have several letters."

"Leave them on my dresser. I'll read them tomorrow."

"There's a big envelope from the Alamo."

A flicker of interest. "Read it to me."

"It's from a Mrs. Dorothy Black. She says her desk is across from your painting of Travis and so many people ask about the painting, she wondered if you might tell them about the painting's creation and yourself. She sent a videotape and cassette in the envelope."

"We'll see," Ruth said vaguely. Suddenly she opened her eyes. "Maybe they'll put the tape on television and my pilot will see it and write me."

They were her last words. Early the next morning she suffered a massive stroke. Four months later, on May 27, 1994, Ruth Conerly passed away.

Did her mother hear her words, spoken in those last seconds, "Mom, you were a wonderful mother. The best! Mom..."

During the funeral services, a beam of sunlight from high in the church fell directly on the silver white casket, lending it an idyllic luminance while a humming bird hovered over the flowers and the priest waxed eloquent in his praise of Ruth's Christmas art: "An artist capable of depicting the Virgin Mary and Christ Child with such reality will surely be seated beside Jesus this very day."

Ruth would love it, Sharon thought. But it brought no comfort.

So many things they had planned to do after all those years apart. At least Ruth was always a call, a letter away, always with that incredible optimism, energy and sense of purpose in life. And now nothing...

Searching For Ruth

XXIX

Journey into Two Legacies

Sharon went back to work. But somehow, the medical practice that had always been a source of pride had lost its luster. The "Hey mom, look at me" fun of life was gone. Life itself seemed pointless.

Absently, she opened the envelope a patient had left on her desk. A note of sympathy, it made an impossible suggestion, and yet there was something compelling, unsettling in its message.

"Sharon, you have such a legacy, so many rich memories about your mother. Why not write these memories down. Use photographs, your mother's paintings and illustrations, newspaper stories. Social history is one of the most exciting sources of our identity and women's history has been sadly neglected. Your mother is alive in so many ways. She is a part of history. Give her the place she deserves." Ilse Leitinger

Sharon realized her mother's art – covering a half a century of advertising history – was a legacy worthy of preserving. But recalling the milieu of tattered newspapers and illustrations filling closets all over the house she was overwhelmed at the thought of putting form to it. And write her mother's life? How? How could a medical doctor explain the creativity of an artist like Ruth Conerly? Impossible to fit all that fight, zest and passion into any orderly narrative form! Worse, before, she could ask, "Mom, how did such and such happen?" and the answer was there.

But Ruth was gone now. And, try as she may, Sharon could not even remember the story Ruth so often told about Gutzon Borglum, who had changed the course of her life or the one about her father fighting off Pancho Villa. Stories she thought she knew by heart.

Wandering into her mother's room, she looked at the antique bed Ruth so loved with its pillows and Southern belle doll, her dressing table, and the sense of loneliness and helplessness was so painfully sharp it almost took her breath away.

"I couldn't do it if I wanted to, Mom," she whispered. "I can't even remember that story about Borglum or your father fighting off Pancho Villa."

Standing there, weighted down by a sense of futility, her eye fell on a little table next to the dresser. On top, lay a stack of papers. Almost idly she picked up a page and was surprised noting that it was in her mother's handwriting.

The title said: The Day I Met Gutzon Borglum.

Stunned, she began reading. Tears rolled down her checks as she read the familiar story, each word like Ruth so often told it. Suddenly she was gripped by the peculiar sensation that Ruth was there in the room beside her.

Looking down at the table again, she saw it held still another group of smaller blue pages, these too in her mother's handwriting. The first page entitled *Recollections about my Father* began with the story of Pancho Villa.

She stood riveted, emotions running rampant. Where did these pages come from? Could they have been here all along? Yes, of course, mere coincidence. Still, the sense of disbelief was overwhelming. That these very stories would appear at this precise moment was incredible.

She looked about uneasily. "Mom, what are you up to?" And a voice from within – like an echo from the past – answered, "You can do it. Just get started. I'll help you."

The next day, restored to comfortable rationality, Sharon marked the incident off as coincidence. Her mother had written those stories before her stroke and left them there. The voice was merely a reflex thought, effect of subconscious memories. Nevertheless, while sending out notes to family and friends she mentioned she was considering writing something about her mother and asked for anecdotes. In her reply to the letter from the Alamo, she told them of Ruth's death and enclosed a short biography. Then on impulse she sent a letter to Marshall Field's in Chicago, Metro of New York and several companies for whom Ruth had done work. Perhaps someone might still be out there who remembered her. Maybe some of Ruth's artwork might still be stored away in an old art morgue somewhere.

A month later, Sharon went to Texas. While visiting her aunt Janey, she found Ruth's sketch of the pilot and the poem, *I Had a Father Who Talked to Me* copied on a next page and they speculated at Ruth's strange fixation on that enigmatic pilot. Thinking it a bit ridiculous, Sharon called The Paris News and a reporter, fascinated by the story, wrote an article: *Mystery: Unknown Pilot Leaves an Impression.*

In Marshall, Texas, Sharon found Ruth's statue, *The Passing Herd* in the top floor museum of the courthouse. No one knew anything about it, but a secretary on hearing about its youthful sculptor called the newspaper that published a full-page article on the life and career of Marshall's long-forgotten sculptor.

While visiting Ted's brother Christian, a professor of Latin and ancient Greek in Austin, she listened to his stories about "going out to that tumble down old mansion in Long Island."

"Remember, I made tapes of Ruth, her memories of New York." he reminded her.

"You're right! Those tapes are probably at home!" Sharon exclaimed.

While visiting her father's sister in Temple, Zelda whispered, "See that old lady over there in a wheel chair. She was a girlfriend of Ted's, but she had a stroke last year and was left paralyzed and speechless."

Touched, Sharon went over and gently put her hand on hers. "I'm Ted's daughter," she said and was amazed when the silver-haired old lady looked up, her blue eyes instantly alert.

"Ted?" she responded. "I was his girlfriend. Get me a pen to write him a note."

Overwhelmed by this pathetic plea, Sharon wanted desperately to lie, say he would love that. But to leave her waiting for a letter that could never come?

"Daddy passed away many years ago," she finally replied and watched as the white-haired lady slumped back in her chair, not to speak again.

Perhaps Maria Elena had been right about Ruth, Sharon reflected. Age might dim the senses, but never the heart's yearning for love.

Before visiting her father's grave, Sharon bought baby roses, reminiscent of the night she was born when he, Ira

Gershwin and the doctor went out on the town, coming into Ruth's room arms full of baby roses.

"Mother always said you were a lot of fun," she whispered laying the roses on his grave.

In San Antonio, she visited the Alamo. Standing before Ruth's painting of Travis, she recalled the comment Ruth so loved, "By God, this is a painting by a *man* who knew war!"

Alamo library director, Cathy Herpich, urged her to write Ruth's biography. Opening a drawer she took out a photograph.

"I came across this the other day. Lots of people are posed by your mother's painting, but I thought you might find this one interesting. It's a photograph of Prince Charles taken on his visit here in 1977."

HRH Prince Charles observing Conerly's painting of Travis with C. Stanley Banks, lawyer and historian and Lila Cockrell, then San Antonio mayor. Photographer: Joe Elicson

"Coincidence your giving me this," Sharon commented. "By old family tradition Ruth was descended from the marriage of George III and a Quaker girl, Hannah Lightfoot. Mom was always saying she wanted to check into that."

In Houston, Ruth's friend Denny Graves shared a wealth of information concerning Ruth's career and troubles with Zach. "Did she ever find that pilot?" he questioned. "I have her letter telling me all about it."

"No... she never found him. Mind giving me a copy of it?"

"Not at all. I keep everything of Ruth's. She was an incredible artist, you know. See that painting over the piano? She put it there herself, said 'don't touch it, it's still wet!' She painted it in just a few hours for my birthday, a little girl in a meadow picking flowers. It's my greatest treasure."

A Girl in the Meadow
Painting by Conerly, Courtesy of Denny Graves

Oh, I have something else from Ruth. A fern in my greenhouse that came from a palace in France. She said it was given to her by one of the nobility.

"The French count."

"That's right! When I asked if I might have a cutting, she told me it was from someone she cared for very much."

"She didn't tell you his name?

"I think so, but I don't remember."

After photographing Ruth's paintings at Denny's, Sharon visited Ruth's friend Kay Ford, who told stories Ruth had confided to her. After photographing Kay's paintings, Sharon drove to Burkhart Road where Ruth's neighbors brought out their paintings to be photographed. Reviewing the resulting photographs, she was pleased. The lens for flat surfaces and techniques the camera shop owner advised had produced good results. Taking multiple shots of each painting helped.

But that night on going to bed, Sharon's thoughts turned to the photograph of Prince Charles looking up at her mother's painting of Travis. Recalling how Ruth was always saying she wanted to look into the matter of Hannah and that Preston had mentioned finding a portrait of her by court painter Joshua Reynolds, Ruth's favorite maxim "look it up!" clicked in.

"OK," she whispered into her pillow. "I'll go down to the library tomorrow and see what I can find."

There was nothing on Hannah. Her portrait was not even listed in any of the various books on Joshua Reynolds's work. There was a book on George III though. "KING GEORGE III, A Biography on America's Last Monarch" by John Brooke. She took it down and started reading the chapters about his youth when the romance supposedly occurred. No where was there any mention of Hannah. Thinking it unlikely to find anything, she nevertheless turned to the back index. And there it was!

Hardly more than a paragraph, it said that no British King had provoked so many legends as George III, but the most ridiculous was his alleged marriage to Hannah Lightfoot, a Quaker girl. It briefly mentioned two versions saying that both were totally false and there was no evidence the King so much as heard of Hannah. A final line explained that royalty was particularly prone to such fables, invented by people anxious to believe that they were descended from royalty.

Why should her cheeks be burning? Wasn't that what she always suspected? No wonder Ruth could never find anything about Hannah in any book. Clearly the family tradition was some ridiculous fable. She was putting the book back on the shelf when suddenly it slipped from her hand, falling open to a page entitled Foreword by H.R.H. Prince of Wales.

Sharon looked again. She had gone to the library because of a photograph of Charles looking at her mother's Alamo painting and here was a foreword written by him? She sat back down.

A creditable piece of writing, Prince Charles said that if Americans remembered anything about King George III it was that he was the mad, tyrant king against whom the American colonies had fought, but that he was actually well loved in England and it was now known that he had not been mad at all but suffered from a painful illness, a rare metabolic imbalance that...

"We're closing now," a voice whispered. "The last bell rang some time ago."

Disappointed at having to give up the book, Sharon jotted down the title, author and publisher.

On her return to Costa Rica, ticking off all she had learned, the task ahead seemed somehow less overwhelming. She was filing away her mother's letter, the one Denny had given her about the pilot, when she noticed the first line.

"On May 27..."

It was a date now deeply engraved on her mind. On that date Ruth died. Meaning her encounter with the pilot had occurred exactly one year previous. The coincidence had an unsettling effect. More unsettling still, she was certain she had heard that date before in relation to something Ruth considered important.

Then it struck. Hurrying to the library she looked for Ruth's old family book, *SOURCE RECORDS from Pike County, Mississippi*. And there on page 53 she found the familiar passage:

On the 27th of May, 1759 he (George III) was married to Hannah Lightfoot. They had a son, Buxton Lawn..

Once again the sensation that Ruth was there enveloped her, strong as on the day she had found those stories. But again on analyzing, logic prevailed. Her mother's fixation on that pilot was a silly thing of no importance. The family tradition of descending from George III was obviously a mistake or hoax of some prankish ancestor. The triad of May 27 dates – meeting the pilot, Ruth's death, and the Hannah-George marriage – mere coincidence. Brushing it all aside, she filed the letter away.

A few days later, however, her cousin David (Bo) Conerly called. Bo, now an electronics expert for NASA, had been in Vietnam when their cousin Joe died.

All was well, Bo assured. He had just found something he thought might interest her.

"I was cleaning out an old armoire that belonged to our grandmother Lizzie and I found two letters behind an inside panel. They're Grandfather's, written just before he killed himself."

For long seconds, Sharon was incapable of speaking. "After seventy–five years these letters just appear out of the woodwork?" she finally managed. "What do they say, Bo?"

"Mostly he's talking about that illness of his." Then lowering his voice, "You knew he was crazy?"

"Mother never thought so."

"He writes up the side of the page."

"I do the same when short of paper. Does he say anything about his sickness? Mother always wondered about that."

"Yes, he's talking about that."

"What does he say?"

"I'll send them to you."

"Send me photocopies, Bo. Don't risk the originals."

A week later, the letters arrived. Heart pounding, Sharon touched the envelope almost reverently. Like a precious gift out of the past, the coincidence of these letters appearing now after three-quarters of a century verged on surrealistic. Frayed and yellowed, with large brown stains, they were obviously the originals and she shuddered to think they might have been lost in the mail.

A quick perusal revealed that in, effect, her grandfather was explaining his illness. Recalling her mother's questions about what had caused his illness and her own inability to answer, Sharon could not help feel a surge of guilt, and wonder too that these letters should come to her hands by blind chance alone.

As with a patient before her explaining his symptoms, she focused in on what he was saying. His main concern was abdominal pain: "My liver and stomach hurt all the time." Another phrase, "I bring up pure yellow gall" was the discreet way then to describe violent vomiting to the point of bile, while "My liver won't act" was the polite form of describing constipation in those days.

"Food has to be softened to pass through" meant he was having difficulty swallowing, *dysphagia* in medical terminology. "No medicine does me any good," together with the fact that not even an operation had revealed the cause: "no appendicitis, gall stones, cirrhosis or cancer" was significant information of an undeterminable cause. He named other symptoms too, unrelated to the gastro-intestinal tract: headaches, insomnia and leg pains – "nor does any doctor seem to know what the matter is." Two sentences, "I do not want to go off and be shut up to suffer" and "My mind would not cause me to bring up pure yellow gall" confirmed what Ruth had always said – that doctors found his many symptoms totally bizarre and thought him deranged.

While reading the letters, she marveled at the clarity and preciseness of his descriptions. True, such a variety of symptoms affecting so many diverse organ areas was indeed bizarre and might conceivably perplex doctors trained to look for a single illness. Admittedly, a doctor might suspect hypochondria or some psychological disorder – unless someone considered the possibility that a single metabolic disorder might be at the root of it all, causing manifestations in many organ areas.

And suddenly an idea flashed to mind. What was the name of that illness? Some one-in-a-million thing that medical students delight in and doctors of long experience glare them down, saying, "For God's sake, when you hear stampeding hoofs, don't think of zebras!"

In her library of medical books, she fingered through a shelf, choosing "Reilly's Practical Strategies." In the chapter dedicated to abdominal pain she found a table titled, "Clues to Uncommon Causes of Recurrent Abdominal Pain." And heading the list was the *zebra* she was looking for.

Acute Intermittent Porphyria.

A rare inherited malady, it jumped to number one suspect when the pain was severe but the physical examination revealed nothing wrong. Decidedly the case here, she granted. "Harrison's Principles of Internal Medicine" gave more explicit details. The underlying cause was an inherited genetic disorder causing an excess of porphyrins, the molecule that gave color to the blood. Among porphyria's many symptoms, abdominal pain was the most manifest, described as the most severe known... *as though the whole intestine was at war with itself.* Accompanied by vomiting and constipation, it could simulate an acute abdomen, requiring surgery. The excess of porphyrins also caused a variety of neurological alterations like headache, insomnia, pain in the limbs, difficulty in swallowing – *dysphagia.* The person could become agitated, excited and even be considered *mentally unstable.* Finding nothing on physical examination, doctors often considered the patient deranged or even "mad." The diagnosis, it said, required *a high degree of suspicion* – meaning doctors never thought of it.

It read like a blue print of what her grandfather was describing.

Other medical books offered further details. First described in 1930, no doctor could have suspected it in 1920 when Preston died. Only one thing seemed to oppose the diagnosis – its being inherited as a dominant trait. That meant at least two of Preston's five children should have had the same symptoms. And to Sharon's knowledge, none had. But another sentence explained otherwise. *Incomplete expression.* Acute intermittent porphyria had the unique peculiarity among genetic diseases that only one in ten of those carrying the mutation ever manifested its symptoms – meaning it could slip down generations unnoticed, striking again when all memory of it was gone. Judging from Lizzie's refusing to ever talk about it, families might well erase it from memory.

In all this, three statements gave her particular unrest:

1) Previous knowledge of its existence is a lifesaving key;

2) Attacks can be avoided or effectively treated, if recognized;

3) Evades diagnosis by the best clinicians, unless previously suspected.

Never recognized, but essential to recognize. *Sinister little thing,* she reflected.

But in spite of this overwhelming evidence, doubt prevailed. To make a retrospective diagnosis on the basis of two letters was tempting, but hardly conclusive!

That Fall, when Arthur suggested going to the Dallas Fair, Sharon immediately agreed.

"While up in that area, could we drive to Marshall? I don't know why, but I keep wondering if there might be some clue of something about Granddaddy's death still up there, in an old newspaper maybe."

It was only a hunch, but armed with the date of her grandfather's death, September 24, 1920, they went through the microfilmed newspapers in the Marshall library. And there it was!

DEATHS
Preston Conerly

Mr. Preston Conerly died some time during last night, from the effects of a wound self-inflicted with a small piece of wire in the side of his neck. A time back, Mr. Conerly's health failed and he became extremely despondent. He underwent a major operation here, and later went to (name of hospital) where he received but little encouragement. He returned, but never, day or night, got his mind off his affliction and in the course of time he became so engrossed with his condition that all else was a blank. His mother kept him at home until authorities and doctors said it was not best and he was taken to the jail pending a vacancy at Terrell asylum.

"In a jail cell alone, with no one believing him," Sharon whispered. "What he must have suffered! No wonder Lizzie never wanted to talk about it. I'm glad Mother never knew of this. It would have broken her heart."

"Sometimes it's best not to know things," Arthur replied.

"But look here! It mentions the name of the hospital he went to. One of the most prestigious in the United States. Do you think they might still have his record?" And like a gambler on a role, she dared to hope.

In her letter to the hospital, Sharon explained her suspicions of an inherited malady unknown at that time and asked if her grandfather's medical file might still be there. Ten days later, a form letter arrived requesting the patient's full name, birth date, name of spouse. She quickly sent the information.

Recalling the book in the Houston Library with the foreword by Prince Charles, was it her imagination or did Charles say something about a *metabolic* disorder in regards to George III?

She ordered the book through an out-of-print book agency and as soon as it arrived, searched for the part about King George's illness. A rare metabolic imbalance, it said, which gave physical symptoms consisting of severe abdominal pain, leg pain and mental anguish. And that present-day doctors with psychiatric training studying the available evidence had come to the conclusion that George III had suffered porphyria.

George III suffered from porphyria? The same inherited malady she suspected in her grandfather?

Another sentence proved more thought-provoking. That although not totally satisfied with this diagnosis, Prince Charles was convinced that George had suffered a *physical* illness, not a mental one, and that the stigma of madness attached to the poor king had persisted far too long.

"How Mom would have loved that!" Sharon exclaimed, recalling how Ruth always thought her father had suffered a physical illness and not any madness. On reading those lines, Sharon could not help being touched by Charles's defense of the old king, obviously a favorite ancestor. Chagrined too on realizing that while George III's porphyria might be considered a thing of historical relevance, no one remembered her grandfather's tragic death. Or cared.

Clearly in England, literature concentrated on the privileged while other families must keep their own histories alive and do their own investigating.

Recalling those three May 27 dates – her mother's death, meeting that pilot so remindful of her father and the George-Hannah marriage, Sharon wondered if it might be indicating that George and Hannah's marriage and the death of Ruth's father were intrinsically connected? Although she realized it was all mere coincidence, she decided to go down to the medical library and see if there might be an article on those studies Charles mentioned.

"Would this be what you're looking for?" Ana, the librarian questioned. "Vignette of medical history: Porphyria in Royalty by Joseph M. Miller, M.D."

"You're an angel!" Sharon exclaimed. "Can you give me a printout?"

The article, based on studies by two doctors, Macalpine and Hunter, gave an overview of George III's illness and persons in the royal houses of Stuart, Hanover, and Prussia afflicted by porphyria, and how it had altered the course of English history. Going back to Mary Queen of Scots down to George III's granddaughter Charlotte, heir apparent who died while giving birth, porphyria was considered the cause for Queen Victoria being left sole heir to the English throne. But the article's source studies by doctors Macalpine and Hunter, published in the British Medical Journal, were not available.

How she wished her mother, far more adept in history, were here. Conscious of her lack of knowledge in this realm, Sharon made inquiries. Everyone said that if it had to do with British history, Albert Williams "Bert" was Costa Rica's foremost expert. Businessman, writer, brother-in-law to the QE II's first captain and agent of British Intelligence in Central America during World War II, Bert's credentials read like a fictional James Bond. Sharon doubted Bert would remember her from the Noel Coward play he directed her in at the National Theatre years ago. She was wrong.

"My Blithe Spirit!" Bert exclaimed joyously. "How could I forget you!"

Now in his eighties, Bert still retained the air of elegance she recalled. With a mind agile, complex and extensive as his collection of books and source information, Bert clamped onto the subject like a bulldog. It was obvious he delighted in anything having to do with royalty. It became equally apparent that Bert considered the most unimaginable methods, like word patterns, syntax and parapsychology of prime importance in tracking a subject.

"Take the words porphyria, porphyrin, porphyry," he cited. "All coming from a common root. Porphyry refers to a rock with a purple hue. Are you acquainted with ancient Byzantine history?"

"Mother was, Phoenician, Greek, Ottoman, you name it," Sharon replied, hoping not to seem discourteous, but not really seeing the point.

"Patience, my dear." Then after a lengthy digression on how everything had meaning, he went back to Byzantine history. "In ancient times there was a room in the Byzantine palace gardens lined with porphyry stone where the empress gave birth to the new emperor, thereby perpetuating the sense of awe and being *born to the purple*." After explaining that most people were incapable of grasping anything abstract or at variance with the logical and pragmatic, Bert made a surprising statement. "I suspect that your mother, an artist, had great sensitivity for what I'm describing. You, who showed talent as an actress, probably have an inclination, but have let scientific logic override it. Take those three May 27 dates you mentioned. You sense they have meaning, but choose to consider it mere coincidence. There are no coincidences, my dear. Striking parallels of two or more events happening in unison are never merely by chance."

Returning to the subject of porphyria, he showed an instant grasp of the subject. "An illness due to an excess of porphyrins, a molecule which gives the blood its color. Perfectly logical," he deduced. "Bloody Royals are a bunch of blue bloods after all!"

A few days later, Bert sent her a packet with two magazine articles. One from a recent Time magazine was about a new movie just out, "The Madness of King George." Time Magazine was calling it a hit with talk of an Oscar for the leading actor. The second article, "When Your Doctors Don't Know", gave examples of disastrous medical misdiagnoses. One in particular cited the case of a woman and her twenty-year pilgrimage to doctors who considered her a mental basket case. Finally near death, she was barely saved by a doctor who diagnosed porphyria. The woman, Desiree Lyon, had founded the American Porphyria Foundation.

"Contact her!" Bert ordered.

A phone call revealed the foundation's office in Houston was open and functioning. On a next trip, Sharon invited Desirée Lyon to lunch. Attractive, personable, highly knowledgeable in her subject, Desirée showed deep interest in Sharon's story concerning her grandfather's death and the revelations concerning George III and urged her to contact others in the various lines of descent. In the meantime she would keep an eye out for any incoming information from her worldwide contacts.

"Things will start happening now," Bert assured on Sharon's return. And not long after, Desirée forwarded a letter from Australia.

"It's talking about some article that came out in a newspaper somewhere concerning George III and Hannah Lightfoot," Sharon reported to Bert. "But it doesn't say what or when."

"Get on Internet," Bert replied.

"Internet?"

"Internet has everything."

Surprised that the imaginative Bert would suggest something so cursory, Sharon nevertheless enlisted the help of an Internet expert to make a search. And was astonished on viewing the results: U.P.I – Domestic News – Europe July 18, 1995.

"BBC reporters opened a royal can of worms when they sifted through the royal archives with permission of Queen Elizabeth II for information for an upcoming documentary about "mad" King George III. They found a certificate of marriage for the king to English Quaker Hannah Lightfoot that took place when he was Prince of Wales. This validated the long-rumored secret marriage of George and Hannah and would make their son the rightful heir to the throne, according to royal genealogy expert Richard Mineards. He said King Edward VII, was aware of the situation and tried to destroy all records... but the royal archive is enormous and obviously he didn't get them all."

"It says the marriage certificate was dated May 27, 1759," Sharon reported to Bert. "The same date as in our old family book. And that the reason subsequent regents were so determined to wipe out all evidence of the marriage is that George never divorced Hannah. That would make his marriage to Queen Charlotte, from which the present monarchy descends, bigamous and illegal.

"A bunch of bloody bastards!" Bert declared gleefully. "They've been sweeping dirt under the rug for so long, the bulge just won't stay down."

"No wonder Mother could never find anything in any official book. The trouble is all this makes it highly unlikely I could get any help from them in researching this porphyria thing."

Bert grew silent. "True," he agreed gravely. "Just the same, you must write to Prince Charles. A proper letter would be answered, especially one with a collection of Costa Rica's new postage stamps on ecology!" he added.

They composed a letter. No answer came.

More discouraging still, months had elapsed since she had requested her grandfather's medical records. After sending the information the hospital requested, an answer came saying no information could be released without authorization from the surviving spouse, parent or estate representative. In a next letter, they acknowledged the impossibility of this in a person dead for 75 years, but then asked for death records of everyone in the patient's descent. A tremendous task, this requisite was finally satisfied.

But instead of sending the medical record, the hospital sent copies of fourteen brief letters, replies to letters her grandfather had obviously sent them.

Puzzled that after fulfilling every requisite, the promised record was not sent, Sharon again explained her suspicion of an inherited illness and the importance of having these records to substantiate or discard that suspicion. To this, a hematologist replied that no diagnosis of porphyria was made at that time and he could find no indication of porphyria in the record.

It was tacit admission the medical record existed. Then why wouldn't they send a copy?

Making a supreme effort to be courteous and business like, she enumerated the symptoms her grandfather listed in his last two letters and asked for basics of any physical exam: blood pressure, pulse, urinalysis.

The reply was brief, "Records at that time were not as complete as at the present and not a lot was analyzed."

He had analyzed the diagnosis of another doctor without having even the basic elements of a physical examination? What in hell was going on?

"Just send what you have," she wrote back. "And send me his letters. The hospital sent me 14 letters, copies of their replies to him. There could be important information in his letters." In closing, she assured him the hospital could not be blamed for not recognizing a malady unknown at that time and included a letter waiving all legal claims on any material sent.

No reply came. Realizing over eight months had gone by in these entanglements, she phoned the doctor. The secretary, obviously embarrassed, said he had refused to take her call and suggested Sharon try their legal department.

Convinced of the hopelessness of the cause, she was resigned to defeat when an incredible coincidence occurred. A colleague called saying the Costa Rican Medical Association was sponsoring a series of conferences with guest speakers from a hospital in the United States. Would she help them out with translations? It was the hospital with her grandfather's record.

Amazed, Sharon called the U.S. hospital, asking to talk to their legal department. She mentioned that she had just been contacted to help with the conferences their hospital was coordinating in Costa Rica to attract patients from Latin America, and she wondered if some further consideration might be given to the matter of her grandfather's medical record.

An hour later, a return call offered a gracious apology. The case had been reviewed and the complete file was being sent DHL, free of charge.

The medical record was indeed brief, one page with the diagnosis, "*hypochondriac, nervous wreck.*" But her grandfather's seventy-six letters, cards and telegrams, also sent, contained a detailed description of his ailment. No longer did she harbor any doubt as to the diagnosis. But since the doctor at that time attributed his symptoms to psychogenic causes, she decided to seek the opinion of a present-day expert in psychiatry.

Dr. Alvaro Gallegos, a world-class specialist with publications in international journals, friend and former professor, kindly agreed to read the letters. He was curious about the reason for her interest in the case, but Sharon begged his forbearance, explaining she felt it important not to predispose him.

The next day, Dr. Gallegos called back. He had read the letters and found no sign of any mental disorder. "In all his letters, this man is explaining *physical* pain in a very rational and consistent way." Then after a moment's hesitation, "I do see something though. I don't know if you've ever heard of it – it's a very uncommon medical disorder. In all my years of practice I've come across only two cases. But after reading these letters, the only thing that would explain all of his symptoms is porphyria – acute intermittent porphyria."

"Would you put that in a letter for me?"

"Of course."

Sharon had almost given up hope of hearing from any company for whom her mother had done art when in August of 1995, Holly Tatson, an executive at Marshall Field's in Chicago, faxed saying that she had found eight Conerly originals on World War II in their top floor art morgue. Sharon could barely believe it. Over a year had gone by since she had sent out those letters.

"I'll be right up!" she faxed back and booked a flight for Chicago. On Sharon's arrival, Holly had still another surprise – a bound volume, "A Store Goes to War," holding fifteen reproductions of Conerly art documenting major battles of World War II. The bound volume also contained a letter to Mr. Field describing the art as "the very best of the whole campaign."

Leafing through its pages, she felt herself being whisked back a half century to a time brought suddenly to life in her mother's illustrations. Holly then took her to meet their buyer in the book department who said, "We'll have a book-signing party with all your mom's wonderful illustrations in the background!"

After an evening out with Holly at one of Chicago's liveliest restaurants, Sharon was drifting off to sleep when the matter of those medical articles on George III came to mind. Houston's medical library did not carry the British Medical Journal. Might Chicago's medical library have it?

"Eureka!" she whispered on finding both articles by psychiatrists Ida Macalpine and Richard Hunter. *The Insanity of King George III: a Classic Case of Porphyria*, published in January 1966, was a remarkable example of retrospective diagnosis with symptoms that read like a blueprint of her grandfather's illness. The second study, *Porphyria in the Royal Houses of Stuart, Hanover, and Prussia*, published two years later, went through 400 years and 13 generations of porphyria in the royal family, producing two cases of modern-day descendents with symptoms.

After making photocopies, Sharon checked her watch, wondering if the Oak Park apartment building where they lived in 1941, might still exist. Armed with only a first grade report card with the name of the school she had attended and a vague childhood memory of the direction from there, she set out arriving at the school just as they were closing. The principal, in the midst of reprimanding a remorseful-looking little black boy, glared at her with annoyance. But on hearing her story and seeing the ancient report card, she shooed the child off. It was almost four o'clock by the time Sharon could break away. Exploring the streets from there, she repeatedly passed a building, vaguely familiar but far smaller than she recalled. But she had been small then. Things seemed *big* to a child.

On knocking at the apartment door, a small black face peered timidly out, eyes widening in surprise.

"You're the lady that saved my ass," the boy said smiling broadly and Sharon instantly realized it was the child in the principal's office. Throwing open the door, he invited her in. Immediately memories came flooding back.

"There was a radiator behind that piece of furniture," she pointed out in the dining room.

"There still is," the boy replied.

"I used to run up the back stairs, put my mittens and socks on top waiting impatiently for them to dry."

"I'se do the same," the little boy said softly.

And suddenly, Sharon remembered Alma, wondering if that story her mother wrote might be filed away someplace...

On returning home and taking inventory, Sharon realized that her quest for her mother's work had actually become a journey into *two* legacies – one for her mother's art and a second for the illness that had caused her grandfather's death. Hardly did she suspect it was yet to lead her across continents and back into time enlisting the enthusiasm of persons with expertise in a variety of fields.

Mary Yonker, a former patient retired in England, considered the mystery of Hannah and son Buxton Lawn a fascinating enigma. With the diligence of Angela Lansbury in "Murder She Wrote," Mary tracked down the baptismal records of six of Buxton's children. On one he was identified as an *excise man,* a collector of taxes. But Buxton's own baptismal record could not be found.

Another person greatly intrigued was Dr. Geoffrey Dean, famous for his discovery of variegate porphyria in a Dutch family of South Africa. He sent her his book, "The Porphyrias," signing it, "For a descendant of George III with a fascinating story." But in a letter Dean questioned, "Might your grandfather's porphyria have come down from another ancestor?" He felt it important she trace down Buxton's descent forming a genetic tree, as he had done in South Africa.

"I've got more than I can handle with Mother's story," Sharon protested. "What you suggest would mean going back two centuries, eight generations. Names change, people move. And different from variegate porphyria, in acute intermittent porphyria only one in ten carrying the mutant gene manifest symptoms! How does one track that?"

"Difficult," Dean granted. "Variegate's skin lesions made detection far easier and the Dutch system of names in South Africa helped in tracing people. Nevertheless, you should try!"

He reminded her of Bert and she made a mental note not to be lured off course.

In January of 1996, Mary Yonker sent an urgent fax. She had seen a TV show, Schofield's Quest, all about George III and Hannah. "A woman called Sheila Mitchell, considered England's major expert on Hannah, was on it!" Mary suggested Sharon contact Sheila.

"Do it!" Bert insisted.

To Sharon's amazement, Sheila Mitchell replied with a lengthy letter. "I have no family connection with Hannah," she explained. "Only a strong and urgent desire to discover what happened to her, when and how she died and where she is buried." Sheila said many people thought they were descended from George-Hannah children; currently she had a list of hundreds, descending from some fifty supposed George-Hannah children, all with varying qualifications. A trial in 1866, the Lavinia Ryves affair, made the marriage a much-commented thing. "Another thing worth knowing," Sheila pointed out, "in the eighteen hundreds some well-meaning woman at the Thomas Coram Foundling Home, apparently began telling the orphans they weren't really orphans, but little princes and princesses, children of George and Hannah, hardly realizing that her well-meant attempt to boost their self-esteem would muddy up historical waters considerably."

As a final touché, Sheila said that in all her twenty-five years of researching Hannah, she had never heard the name of Buxton Lawn mentioned!

On making inquiries at the Thomas Coram Foundling Home and finding no record of Buxton Lawn, Sheila tried to locate a baptism registration. None appeared.

It was then that Dr. Geoffrey Dean proved himself an inveterate investigator. "I have moved one step further in regard to your ancestor, Buxton Lawn," Dean faxed. "The Archivist in Norfolk has found his Baptism Registration. Buxton was baptized the son of John and Mary Lawn on February 10, 1759. As you know, Hannah Lightfoot's marriage to George III was on May 27, 1759."

"Mother was always afraid Buxton might be illegitimate," Sharon confessed to Bert.

"The underlying reason for many a respectable marriage," Bert observed.

But Dean made another suggestion, that Buxton might have been the *legitimate* son of John and Mary Lawn, as his baptismal record testified.

"Or a royal infant farmed out," Bert countered.

"It was common practice to farm out inconvenient children," Sheila asserted and suggested Sharon order two books, "The Lovely Quaker" by John Lindsey and "The Fair Quaker" by Mary Pendered, which explained most of the known facts concerning Hannah and George.

The two books gave similar stories, that Hannah, a Quaker born in 1730, disappeared in 1753 and that George III, then Prince of Wales, abducted her, supposedly married her and had children by her. Queen Charlotte was said to have become so worried that her marriage to George might be bigamous and her children illegitimate that she arranged for a second marriage ceremony at a court function – presumably after Hannah's death.

After George III's death in 1820, letters published in newspapers gave varying stories. Then in 1866 – when the supposed marriage document was produced in a court of law – a new wave of scandal ignited. Called to testify, leading handwriting experts of the day considered the document and its signatures authentic. But the court declared it forged and impounded it in the royal archives for one hundred years.

"Mom would love this!" Sharon commented to Bert.

"And who says she's not telling you?" Bert replied.

A few days later, Sheila faxed an urgent message:

"Sharon, I have so much here on file. It was quite a coincidence really. I was looking for something else and the name Buxton Lawn literally leaped out of the page at me..."

The letter Sheila found, written twenty years previous, was from a Mrs. Shearer, widow of a descendent of Buxton Lawn. While researching her husband's family, Mrs. Shearer had discovered that Buxton Lawn had written a book on the Corn Laws. "And in it he talks about his *father*," Mrs. Shearer wrote.

"Get that book!" Bert demanded.

All attempts to contact Mrs. Shearer failed – she had long since passed away – but her message set wheels in motion and a copy of Buxton's book was found in the library of London (founded with the books of George III's own personal library). Buxton's book, two editions actually – one published in 1800, the second in 1801 – revealed Buxton Lawn to be well-educated, well-informed on political and economical matters of the day, particularly the Corn trade. (Corn at that time meaning grains, an issue of great political relevance) But in both books, Buxton Lawn pointedly stated that his father was a *tenant farmer in Norfolk.*

If any vestige of credibility concerning Buxton's royal lineage remained, Sheila faxed that she had found an old news announcement that at the time he was writing his book, Buxton Lawn was being sought on charges of bankruptcy!

"Case ended!" Sharon declared to Bert matter-of-factly. "In bankruptcy, a wanted man, and by his own admission, a tenant farmer's son! End of story!"

"To have said otherwise would have meant the tower!" Bert declared. "This man's life and that of his family is on the line. Note on the title page of both Buxton's books he says he is living in Bath in the home of the Duke of York, as baker. Focus in. Bath is a place of fashion with gossip rampant, where mothers take their daughters to find a likely match. And everyone knows who's who. 1800 is a time of crises in England. George is ill and his eldest son is trying to take the throne. Don't you find it curious that at precisely that time Buxton would be sought, a wanted man? And stranger still that this *wanted man* would be living with the Duke and Duchess of York, George III's favorite son, and writing a book on the Corn Laws? I suggest Buxton is pointedly referring to his *father* as being a Norfolk tenant farmer, *true in the adopted sense*, for a purpose – to expiate Buxton from treason, execution, and free the crown of any embarrassing danger as to the succession."

Curiously, Sheila, far from discouraged, was showing a heightened interest in Buxton's books, namely the parts where Buxton described the frequent visitors to his father's home. One of these persons was no other than Sir William Wyndham, aide-de-camp to George III's brother, the Duke of Cumberland. Wyndham's wife, formerly the mistress of George II, held a position at Court.

"The trusted tenant of someone so close to court would have been the ideal place for a royal foundling," Sheila pointed out, adding there was once a painting of the Duke of Cumberland waving goodbye to Hannah.

"A painting of Hannah visiting the Duke of Cumberland, lord of Norfolk, where this little boy Buxton is?" Bert questioned slyly. "Interesting. Ask Sheila where the painting is." But Sheila reported that the painting had unfortunately disappeared following a fire in 1896. Gone, like so many things relating to Hannah, including a trunk with marriage records thrown into the Thames.

In spite of Sheila's first inauspicious fax, Buxton Lawn was becoming a source of compelling interest. So much that Sharon decided to reexamine those books on Hannah that Sheila had recommended. Perhaps under the light of what they now knew, she might find something significant.

And to her amazement, there it was! Published in Notes and Queries in July 1853, the letter was considered the most authentic of any information relating to Hannah:

"I have heard my mother speak of Hannah Lightfoot. Her family belonged to the religious community called Friends, or Quakers. My mother was born in 1757, and died in 1836. The aunt of Hannah, Eleanor Lightfoot, was next door neighbour to my grandfather, who lived in Sir William Warren's Square, Wapping. The family were from Yorkshire, and the family of Hannah was a shoemaker's and kept a shop near Execution Dock in the same district. He (Hannah's father) had a brother who was a linendraper, living in the neighbourhood of St. James's at the west end of the town, and Hannah was frequently his visitor; and here it was she became acquainted with the great man of the day. She was missing and advertised for by her friends; and after some time had elapsed they obtained some information as to her retreat, stating that she was well provided for, and her condition became known to them. She had a son who was a corn merchant, but from some circumstances became deranged in his intellect, and it is said, committed suicide... All this I heard my mother tell when I was a young lad... T.M.C."

Sharon read the sentence again: "Hannah had a son *who was a corn merchant*." Buxton's books on the Corn Laws clearly bespoke a person of authority in the corn trade and the following words, *but from some circumstances he became deranged in his intellect and committed suicide* were a chilling reminder of her grandfather, suggestive that Buxton Lawn not only transmitted the porphyria mutation but manifested its symptoms.

It suggested, moreover, that others in Buxton's descent had suffered porphyria and even now someone might be visiting doctors, being called hypochondriac or mad like her grandfather.

Recalling Dr. Geoffrey Dean's insistence she trace Buxton's descent, she examined Ruth's book *Source Records of Pike County*. It traced the family's descent for six generations giving numerous last name linkages, but only up to 1920. An improbable errand, she resolved to try. A friend living in Louisiana supplied a list of names and addresses and Sharon sent out letters asking, "Are you descended from Buxton Lawn?"

She never thought that newspaper article about Ruth's pilot would meet with success. Apparently though, Ruth's sketch of him had created an expanding circle of curiosity extending to the Dallas airport. The pilot turned out to be Joseph Rose, Chief Pilot of Lone Star Airlines, who had recently appeared on the cover of PROFESSIONAL PILOTS. Curiously, he vividly recalled the incident. Some ten persons who had helped in the search were present for their reunion. And as Joe and Sharon posed in front of the white jet that Ruth had so accurately described, a beam of sunlight ripped through the clouds directly on the plane, a brand new Dornier DO-328.

"The reason I remember the incident so well," Joe said, "is because it happened on May 27th, an anniversary my wife and I always celebrate. The year before on May 27th, we celebrated by going to the Alamo."

On December 1, 1996, Sharon received a fax from Andrew Shapiro, president of Metro Creative Graphics of New York, saying that while cleaning out old files he had come across duplicates of several books with her mother's Christmas art. Would she like them? That same day a letter from Continental Airlines came, saying that if she traveled to New York before the year ended – it lacked only 22 days – she would attain *elite* status. Doubling her air mileage, meaning virtually a free trip.

"I know what you're going to say," Sharon commented to Bert. "It's a sign I must go to New York."

"Go!" Bert ordered.

"But in December all the hotels are full."

"Something will appear."

And confirming Bert's prediction, Zach's niece, Dr. Loraine Bloomquist knew of a hotel. They had a single vacancy.

"I'll meet you there and we'll take in some shows," Lorraine volunteered.

Andrew Shapiro, at the helm of Metro, was a tall, nice-looking man, surprisingly young. Grateful for this find of art and remembering her letter, Sharon thanked him effusively for the books with Ruth's Christmas art. He wished her luck on her project, then almost offhandedly asked, "Have you seen Dorothy Ladore yet?"

"Ladore? Mom's art director? Alive and well, here in New York?"

"Very much so," he said dialing a number.

Sharon and Dorothy met at a restaurant not far from Metro and were soon talking animatedly.

"This book you're planning," Dorothy said. "More than Ruth's art, you must tell about her humanity!"

"Yes, but *you* must tell me what she was like *professionally*. That's a facet I never knew. Meeting you is an incredible find."

Dorothy needed little prodding. "Ruth put vitality, action and anatomical know-how in all her work. Never shuddered at deadlines, never allowed anything to interfere with her work. The toughest assignment couldn't faze her. She'd simply fire up fresh enthusiasm and get on with the job! The moment she grasped a project there'd be strong strokes of the pencil and before my eyes a sketch would come to life! Then she'd murmur, 'Let's juice it up!' And do just that!

Overwhelmed with this barrage of vivid description, Sharon scrambled in her purse for paper and pencil and began taking notes, racing to keep up with the fast clip of Dorothy's words.

"During my only involuntary absence, a hospital stay, Ruth worked up layouts for all the fashion pages of that month. Dozens of figures had to be composed in appropriate layouts for the artists-in-waiting assigned to do finishes. I learned upon my return that the artists all agreed that Ruth's layout figures were virtually perfect, leaving little for them to draw! My top fashion artist was totally awed by the techniques on Ruth's layout roughs and raved about Ruth's ability to draw fashion figures without seeing them modeled."

"And the Christmas work," Sharon prodded.

"The Christmas greeting service, which I handled, always needed new variations of the holiday theme – Nativity scenes, shepherds, stable scenes, wise men, angels, carolers, Santas, choirs, children, family groupings, winter landscapes. My plans inevitably included features for Ruth. I knew the results would be inspired and classic, right on target. I always felt a rush of pleasure when I saw them."

"In the work sphere, was she difficult to work with?   A diva attitude?"

"I managed and directed dozens of artists, many of whom had big egos. Ruth was neither egotistical nor haughty. She never exhibited temperament. She was rather reserved, pensive, didn't mingle freely or talk much. Occasionally when we had time, we'd share confidences and she'd open up. I've found there is a special inner intelligence inherent in those with unique gifts. Call it a touch of genius, Ruth was one of the elite, a veritable rarity. We had a long-term meeting of the minds that fostered a strong relationship, the likes of which rarely occurs in the hectic world of advertising and publishing. It contributed to the integrity and the quality of the METRO family of publications and METRO'S success as *numero uno* in the field of providers of advertising services to thousands of newspapers worldwide."

"And Dave Shapiro? What was he like?"

Dorothy smiled and a soft nostalgia was detectable. "A very attractive man, meticulous, a bit theatrical, always wonderfully dressed with custom suits and haberdashery.

"Write that down now!" Lorraine cried out on hearing Sharon's report. "If not, you'll forget! Then send her what you wrote to proof. No liberties should be taken in quoting!"

They talked late into the night. Sharon admitted to being confused about Zach. "We always got along fine... after almost killing each other that first year. But interviewing people close to Mom, I'm finding she had a deep resentment towards Zach, seemingly justified. What was your opinion of Zach?"

"Uncle Zach was a wonderful person as an uncle. But that doesn't mean anything. You have to put him the way Ruth saw him. Remember some men are two people. I had a friend married to a preacher, nicest guy you can imagine, a monster at home. His favorite song was 'I did it my way!'"

After a lengthy laugh, Sharon asked another question. "There's something I've always been curious about. Did Zach's mother – your grandmother – have a washing machine?"

Lorraine looked puzzled. "Of course, she had a washing machine. Always the latest model. Why do you ask?"

And when Sharon told the story of Ruth's years without a washing machine, Lorraine shook her head.

"Undoubtedly, some men do not make the most ideal husbands."

In April of 1997, Sharon's cousin Fields Smith called. Owner of a shipping supply company in San Francisco, he and his wife Manolita were experienced travelers and a fun couple. Fields said they were going to Turkey, Greece and the Greek Islands. Would she and Arthur like to accompany them? Arthur instantly approved and Sharon, recalling Ruth's love of Greek and Turkish history, quickly agreed.

Traveling to the Cradle of Civilization fulfilled her every expectation. Seeing the ruins of Ephesus defied all imagination, although the many statues with faces and genitals bludgeoned off by the crusaders brought to mind her mother's sadness over the mutilation of these irreplaceable treasures.

"Nothing worse than ignorance and religious fanaticism," Ruth would say vehemently.

In Greece they climbed to Delphi, site of the oracle of Apollo, god of light, poetry and prophecy, where in ancient times a priestess told travelers the will of the heavens. And standing there amidst the awe-inspiring scenery of Greece, Sharon asked her question:

"Will this search for Mother's life and art and this family mystery be successful... or prove some futile odyssey?"

Moments later, their tourist guide nudged her back to reality, saying the answer given by the gods was inevitably the same to all:

"The truth lies in your own heart."

Back in Costa Rica, a message was hanging from the fax machine. Dr. Geoffrey Dean, world recognized expert in variegate porphyria, said two genetic scientists in London had been authorized to exhume two princesses in the Hanover line and do DNA studies to determine porphyria and identify the mutation. Could she exhume her grandfather for them? They would be contacting her.

A few days later, a fax from the scientists repeated the request. Could she exhume her grandfather and send a bone to them in London?

"With respect to the testing of your grandfather's specimen, we would be interested to see if we can find any correlation with the DNA we are currently sampling from European Royal family members. We are currently examining DNA extracted from the bones of two princesses whom we believe suffered with either acute intermittent porphyria (AIP) or the variegate porphyria (VP) and would be able to examine his DNA for similar polymorphisms and/or mutations. If similar sequences exist, it would suggest that he was related. The presence of a mutation would also be conclusive proof he did indeed suffer with porphyria."

In spite of overwhelming doubts, Sharon found it difficult to repress her excitement. Identifying the mutation was a painstaking process, comparable to searching a whole library for one misspelled word, made far more tedious on old bones with fractured DNA. And yet, if the miracle did happen, and they were able to identify the mutation, an inexpensive laboratory test could determine who in the family was still at risk. A lifesaving tool that would permit treatment for those at risk and free the unaffected *and their descendents* from all future worry. A person not carrying the mutation could not pass it on to any descendant!

It was such an incredible breakthrough, she hated to harbor doubts. But surely the scientists must realize that porphyria was a unique genetic illness, wherein each family had a distinguishing mutation, *virtually a family marker.*

Proof of a marriage so long denied. After all the records thrown into the Thames, documents "sanitized" and confiscated?

"It would indicate an admirable change and opening," Sharon commented to Bert.

"Do you know where your grandfather's grave is?"

"Yes."

"Well, find out if you'll be allowed to exhume him. If so, ask the scientists what they'll need as a sample and how they advise it be transported. Get all your groundwork first."

But on consulting Dr. Minor Vargas, a leading pathologist in Costa Rica, Sharon learned it was improbable anything would be found in the grave.

"In a royal crypt yes, but not in an ordinary grave, seventy-five years old. Only in rare cases exhumers are stunned on finding a perfectly preserved body, but it is a rare phenomenon. Moreso to find any soft tissue like spleen or ganglia, material suitable for such studies. After seventy-seven years, if there are any bones, they will probably be totally calcified, so friable they'll crumble on manipulating or even touching them, difficult for extracting medulla with lymphocytes for DNA.

They're asking for bone. Osteocytes are less ideal to determine a genetic alteration than lymphopoietic tissue, but there is a small possibility that a bone quite dry, might contain something of medulla in a scraping. They are talking about several grams. If you find a femur, cut a piece six or seven centimeters and put it in a container. They say freeze it. I don't know how important freezing would be for remains buried seventy-seven years. It suggests the supposition that a bone suddenly exposed to light, air or bacteria could deteriorate in a few hours. I would certainly comply with what they request though. Should there be any danger of rain, delay exhuming for another day."

Finalizing, Dr. Vargas emphasized that the chance of finding anything was highly unlikely.

To this, the London scientists replied:

> "*Our experience of recovering samples from graves is that the bones are generally well preserved, but this is a reflection of the high standard given to Royal grave sites where the remains are buried in crypts.*"

But they were anxious she should do it:

> "*Sending the material to us should not be too problematic.*"

Dr. Geoffrey Dean joined in with another note:

> "*If you can send some of your grandfather's bone, Dr. Warren should be able to answer your two questions:*
> 1. *Whether your grandfather had porphyria <u>and</u>*
> 2. *Whether he was descended from George III.*"

But the problems loomed enormous. During a second consultation with Dr. Vargas, he said the sample could be held up for days in transport or in some custom warehouse.

"Dry ice lasts hours, but not days, and only a few hours when exposed to air. With good insulating material, packed in Styrofoam, sent DHL, it might make it within two days, if there is no delay."

To this, Bert was adamant. "Take it to England yourself! Natural good sense. Have you called the American and British embassies concerning regulations?"

Both the British and American consuls considered it a highly unusual case but advised obtaining an affidavit from the funeral home doing the exhumation giving data about the deceased and saying the remains were free of dangerous substances which could harm human life or environment.

The drive to Marshall that September morning along winding country roads brought poignant memories of Ruth's love for East

Texas. After settling in at the hotel and contacting the persons in charge of the exhuming, she drove to the cemetery.

She felt guilty disturbing the sanctity of her grandfather's grave, regardless of the reason. Before people bludgeoned into his grave the following day, she wanted to spend a few quiet moments at the gravesite. But once in the cemetery, the grave eluded her. More unsettling, it was growing dark and there was something disquieting about being alone in a graveyard at nightfall. Again and again, she went over the area where he was supposedly buried. Finally, as darkness was closing in, she cried out, "Grandfather, where are you?"

And suddenly there it was! Almost in front of her, the marble glistened in the twilight and the name THOMAS PRESTON CONERLY stood out with imposing clarity.

Drawing closer, she set the flowers on the grave and knelt beside it. Soon she found herself explaining who she was, how her mother had loved him very much.

"Mother always remembered your words, 'My little girl is going to be a great artist someday.' And just like you said, she *did* become a great artist." Sharon explained how she was his grandchild, a doctor, and had read his last letters and been deeply moved. How she believed his illness was due to acute intermittent porphyria, an inherited illness, not known in his time. And that some scientists in England thought it might have something to do with his being descended from George III, as the old family tradition said. These scientists had asked her to exhume him to do the studies.

"In England, people make much ado with anything having to do with royalty and I'm grateful for any help, of course, but the important thing is to identify the mutation and prevent others in Buxton's descent from suffering the way you did. It was a terrible thing. I wish I could have helped you. But perhaps between the two of us, we can help others."

The following morning men would come, she explained. Hopefully there might be something still there of him, a piece of bone with a bit of marrow...

The sound of crickets and the flickering of fireflies in the darkness brought a comforting feeling, as though he were actually there beside her listening, as she explained a procedure trying to ease away doubts or fears.

The next morning as she drove up, two men were already there – one laying out equipment, another positioning a large backhoe. On her signal, the work began.

They had barely dug down a few inches when they hit cement, what proved to be the vaulted ceiling of a massive underground crypt. The amount of concrete, over two feet in thickness, made the operator elect to go down parallel to the structure and attempt to enter through the side. For hours he worked. The adjacent tunnel completed, it was decided that before going in under the massive ceiling, precaution dictated propping it up. As they waited for more equipment to be brought in, the mortician examined Sharon's file with photographs of Ruth and her father. Then picking up the portrait of Hannah in the file, he set it beside a photograph of Ruth.

"Have you ever noticed the similarity between your mother and Hannah Lightfoot?" he questioned.

"There is a similarity," Sharon agreed.

"More than that. As a mortician I do a lot of facial reconstruction and if given either of these photos as a basis I'd say they're the same person, only in a different epoch in different dress."

The backhoe operator had stopped working and was signaling. He had penetrated the lateral wall and the props were now in place. Peering into the vault, she could see a redwood casket. Within that were strong bones, remarkably well preserved.

Seeing her grandfather in that underground crypt she was seized by a wrenching heartache at the pathos of his untimely death. A man, still vigorous and young with so much enthusiasm for life should not have died that way.

Looking up, she recognized the owner of the funeral home, a tall, elderly man, who had shown great interest in the case. He was standing beside the pathologist and both seemed visibly impressed by the enormous crypt and its content.

"Never seen anything like this up here in East Texas," the backhoe operator declared. "Every bit like one of those tombs for royalty."

Clearly Othermama had built a tomb worthy of a prince for her beloved son Pressie.

In a letter to her aunt Jane, Sharon described the ensuing events in London:

"*The trip to London went smoothly. Decided to go business class to ensure Grandfather's femur would be safe all the way. In London went directly to University College London where Dr. Marten Warren and Professor David Hunt were waiting. I never imagined their study had such far-reaching implications. Dr. Warren is surprisingly young. Both have significant credentials and articles on their work in scientific publications. Professor Hunt discovered the mutation of Daltonism (color blindness) by extracting DNA from the 200-year-old preserved eyes of John Dalton, an incredible story published in SCIENCE. Warren and Hunt have combined talents to prove Dr. Macalpine's hypothesis of Porphyria in the royal families of Europe by DNA testing – a milestone in molecular genetics. When I walked into their office, a picture of Porphobilinogen Deaminase – the enzyme responsible for porphyria – was circling about on a computer screen. The image, in brilliant color and third dimension with full anatomical detail, brought to mind Mother's talent in drawing a figure from any prospective out of her head. It gave me a sobering jolt realizing that a mutation in this molecule was responsible for so much tragedy in our family.*
Warren and Hunt had just returned from Germany where they had exhumed Princess Charlotte, sister of Germany's last Kaiser, Wilhelm II, granddaughter of Queen Victoria. On studying her letters to her doctor, they felt they were highly suggestive of porphyria. They were most anxious to know all about Grandfather, his symptoms and the family tradition of descent from George III. We talked all morning, had lunch in a restaurant with old English atmosphere and after that they took me on a tour of their installations and equipment, and their people explained what part of the process they were involved in. Fascinating what can be done today.
On my second day in England, I went to Knole House at Sevenoaks, where the painting of Hannah is.

Home of the Earls and Dukes of Dorsett, it's an impressive place containing a large collection of portraits, including the coronation painting of George III. The Hannah painting is in the Reynolds room with other paintings by court painter Joshua Reynolds. There was no explanation about it though.

On Saturday morning I met Sheila Mitchell, who has studied Hannah for over twenty years and came in from Swindon with her husband James. It was wonderful to be able to meet her after all our correspondence. We talked for hours. On seeing prints of Mother's art, she was visibly impressed and said, 'Sharon, I know the research for this royal connection and its medical implications are compelling, but don't let this trivialize your mother's story. Her art and life are far too important and inspiring and must be your major focus.' I always felt that was true.

Meantime Sheila's husband, James, a Scot and a military man, had became engrossed in the chapter on the Alamo. He said he had always wanted to go there and would definitely go now.

My hotel on Bayswater faced Kensington Park, where Princess Diane lived; there were still flowers all over. Sheila said a news article mentioned Diane was investigating Hannah, England's lost queen shortly before her death."

On her return from England, Sharon found that her search for descendents of Buxton Lawn brought only one answer. But it proved a veritable jackpot. She immediately called the writer and after a lengthy long-distance conversation booked a flight for New Orleans.

Mrs. Buxton Lawn Layton II, a delightful person with the poise of a Southern belle, lived in a large home filled with antiques, paintings and portraits. The widow of a descendant of Buxton Lawn through son Robert (who changed his name to Layton), their line had established the Southern Bank, the only bank in the South to survive the Civil War. To Sharon's delight, Mrs. Layton had an enormous cache of family memorabilia, including a book published in 1875, with the birth, marriage and death dates of everyone descended from

Buxton Lawn. Dr. Layton, the author, a grandson of Buxton Lawn, recalled how on a trip to England in 1820, he had met his grandfather, "a fine-looking old gentleman, dressed in uniform and living in an elegant home with servants and carriage."

Dr. Layton's papers included a document in which his aunt Mary, Buxton's daughter, testified that Buxton, her father, was the son of George III and Hannah Lightfoot.

Although there was no evidence that Robert's line had transmitted porphyria, research brought to light other unexplained deaths in the line of Buxton Lawn's daughter Ann. The line from which Ruth descended.

A year before Ruth's father's death in 1920, his first cousin, John Lampkin, had died after suffering attacks of unexplainable abdominal pain. Similarly John's son, Robert, developed the same unexplained symptoms. Hospitalized for six months, he was found dead in his hospital bed in 1962. On requesting his medical records, Sharon was told that all copies had disappeared. Not even the microfilms could be found. In spite of a seeming total block, a family member discovered a copy of his file in pathology – documenting a tragic course, multiple operations, with no one suspecting an underlying genetic cause.

A nephew of Robert would follow. After a lengthy internment, enduring similar unexplainable symptoms and multiple exploratory operations, he died in 1993. His record could not be obtained.

Each incoming case brought stories of families ripped apart by controversy, resentments and guilt. Had their loved one gone mad, as doctor's hinted? Sharon was consoled she had complied with the scientist's request to exhume her grandfather. Identifying the mutation would permit testing her two sons. It all lent a pressing urgency to the work being done in England.

But as weeks stretched into months with only an occasional message mentioning continued difficulties, Sharon's hopes floundered. Reading the first lines of a brief discouraging message, she was resigned to the hopelessness of it all, when a last paragraph held her transfixed:

"During the extraction, Anna, the technician working on the samples, noticed a range of peculiar coloured compounds. These could be porphyrins, which may be associated with porphyria. The next time we do the extract we will analyze these materials a little more closely."

"Porphyrins!" Sharon faxed back, barely able to contain her enthusiasm. "You realize how important this find is! Porphyrins are produced in large quantities during an attack of porphyria. Grandfather was having severe attacks shortly before his death."

Certain this would give impetus to their search for the mutation, Sharon anxiously awaited their answer.

But no word came.

A message finally came saying they were discontinuing their work on her grandfather's sample. Their funding from Wellcome Trust had given out.

"Wellcome?" Sharon faxed back. "That's a royal trust."

Bewildered, heart-broken, she could not believe it was all ended. After complying with everything they asked, and now at the most propitious moment they were quitting? Was it financing? Might she help?

Not long after, Sheila wrote that their book, "Purple Secret," was already published and sent a copy. Well written and documented, full of detailed material on royalty, porphyria and the two exhumed princesses, it contained a gracious mention in acknowledgments to her. But no mention of any study on her grandfather. One chapter referred briefly to alternate lines, mainly concubines, quickly dismissed.

Sharon called Bert, but he did not seem surprised.

"In England," he explained, "people have been breathing through the noses of royalty for so many years they don't know anything else exists. Any mention of royalty wields tremendous interest. It sells books, it influences appointments, it can move mountains, but it's not something you can ever understand or count on. Royal trusts have a lot of money to back scientific research. Apparently someone in the royal family became interested in investigating porphyria, *their* porphyria. Who knows who or why they became interested in your grandfather. Or why they dropped it like a hot potato. One can never tell... or be too judgmental."

"But just at the most promising moment! To be left with no mutation, no hope to learn the truth!" Sharon wailed.

"You must satisfy yourself as to what *you believe* the truth is."

"Bert, I went to the ruins of Delphi where a guide said the priestess told everyone, *look to your own heart.* And you tell me the same?"

"Sharon, Sharon," Bert reproved gently. "People are obsessed with finding the *treasure*. It's not the treasure. It's the search, the *quest*. I once became obsessed with the tales of Morgan's treasure buried on Coco's Island. I dug all over the damn Coco's Island, spent a fortune. Yes, I was disappointed. Bloody disappointed. But it wasn't a failure. It's the adventure, what Homer described in his Odyssey."

"Mother would have loved that."

"Of course she would. Look, you went searching for a mother you thought you knew, yet never really knew. And found much of her still alive. That's the real treasure."

Pondering on Bert's words, she realized they held an element of wisdom. She had gone on a quest across continents and back into time. Maybe – like in those childhood mystery and pirate hunts her mother would invent, Ruth had lured her on this adventure.

Admittedly, she had found a healing, and some knowledge others might build on.

And a grandfather, she never knew, but who once said:

"My little girl's going to become a great artist one day" and *"Illustrations stir people's imagination, make them want to read books,"* and *"This century is going to bring unimaginable things."*

He was right, on all three counts.

Her grandfather also whispered to her, "Keep another piece of bone set aside, just in case..."

EPILOGUE

Ruth Conerly never learned the cause of her father's death. Her daughter, a medical doctor, considered it an unsolvable mystery of no practical relevance, any more than the family's supposed descent from "mad" King George III. But on searching for Ruth's art in old art morgues, interviewing people who knew her, she began to suspect it might have life-threatening importance.

More formidable than the centuries-old cover-up of a marriage between a prince and a Quaker girl was a more ominous foe: the determination of modern-day hospitals to bury past errors, even at the cost of present lives.

As evidence accumulated indicating that Ruth's father had suffered *Acute Intermittent Porphyria*, the same rare, inherited malady attributed to George III, research revealed that others in the family had died suffering the same symptoms. And in each case, doctors had thought the patient "mad", while families were left torn and destitute. In each, no one suspected an underlying genetic cause, susceptible to treatment.

Ruth was right to question her father's death and her daughter was wrong thinking it of no importance. Perhaps in some mysterious way Ruth helped her to see this. At least many descendants in the line of 'The Corn Merchant" Buxton Lawn (1759-1825), whose children Robert, Mary, Eliza and Ann came to Louisiana in the early 1800s, are now alerted and the family mutation might one day be identified. Hopefully, this book will alert doctors that beyond a difficult case there could be *a genetic cause*, susceptible to life-saving treatment. But it requires examining medical records of persons who died under unclear circumstances. Denying these records to doctors and families who suspect a genetic illness is to thwart the very essence of medicine.

The quest for Ruth's art and life and the cause of her father's death was a remarkable adventure. All those who so generously helped, at times disagreeing among themselves, were nevertheless unanimously in agreement on one point... the most incredible story was that of Ruth Conerly, **A GIRL FROM TEXAS**.

Ruth Conerly
An Extraordinary Artist

List of Art & Photographs

Color Inserts

A GIRL FROM TEXAS

S.E. Wolf, M.D.

Soft cover pre-publication limited edition $19.95
Plus shipping and 8% sales tax in Texas

FOR ORDERING CONTACT:

Antigua Odisea Publishing

E-mail: antiguaodisea@msn.com